THE CHANGE RIDERS

The Addison-Wesley Middle Manager Series
Consulting editor, W. Warner Burke

The Change Riders, Gary D. Kissler

GARY D. KISSLER, Andersen Consulting

THE CHANGE RIDERS
MANAGING THE POWER OF CHANGE

ADDISON-WESLEY PUBLISHING COMPANY, INC.
Reading, Massachusetts • Menlo Park, California • New York
Don Mills, Ontario • Wokingham, England • Amsterdam • Bonn • Paris
Milan • Madrid • Sydney • Singapore • Tokyo • Taipei • Mexico City

The publisher offers discounts on this book when ordered in quantity for special sales. For more information please contact:

>Corporate & Professional Publishing Group
>Addison-Wesley Publishing Company
>One Jacob Way
>Reading, Massachusetts 01867

Library of Congress Cataloging-in-Publication Data

Kissler, Gary D.
>The change riders : managing the power of change / Gary D. Kissler.
>>p.   cm. — (The Addison-Wesley middle manager series)
>Includes index.
>ISBN 0-201-56340-1 (alk. paper)
>1. Organizational change. 2. Management.   I. Title. II. Series.
HD58.8.K55   1991
658.4′06—dc20   91-17751
>>>>>>>>>>>>>>>CIP

Cover design by Hannus Design Associates
Text design by Kenneth J. Wilson
Set in 10 point Palatino by Total Concept Associates, Brattleboro, Vermont

Text printed on recycled and acid-free paper.
2 3 4 5 6 7 8 9 10- MA -95949392
Second Printing, June 1992

To Jake and his vision . . .

CONTENTS

FOREWORD

In addition to wandering through a good wine shop reading label after label in search of a fine chardonney, one of my favorite activities is bookstore browsing. When I get to the business and management section, however, my browsing pleasure often turns into despair. The books are either "This is how I did it and therefore you should" or one anecdote piled on top of yet another example of excellent vs. bad practice. The lessons to be learned from such books are usually trite and void of any evidence based on relevant data, much less linked to sound, appropriate theory.

And while I am at it, another beef of mine is the distinction between the so-called "real world" and other presumably "unreal" worlds, usually targeted as the academic one. I live and operate in both the business and academic worlds. Both are quite real to me. Different, to be sure, but real, nevertheless. Yes, there is theory and there is practice; sometimes they match, sometimes they do not. I tire and am quite intolerant of those who come from either extreme. What is important, certainly for me, is the bridge between the two; or, if no bridge exists, to begin the process of constructing one.

The objective of this Addison-Wesley series of books for managers is to build bridges between what we know to be sound and therefore what can be depended on in practice. For example, if you want ownership by your associates of a decision with subsequent implementation, then the more you involve them the greater the likelihood of commitment. You can count on it. This principle of behavior is grounded in research, theory, and in a myriad of people's experiences. Our intent in this series of books is to provide example after example of these linkages. Our intent is *not* to provide fluff, the latest rage in management, or overly academic or overly "practical" books.

The author of the book you are now holding has been there. He kept notes, at least mental ones, about what he observed and experienced there, reflected on these observations and experiences, and gradually began to see linkages to theory, models, and research (especially in the final chapter). Moreover, his linkages are invaluable in helping us to sort myth from reality, especially with respect to the effects of change on people in organizations and even more particularly with respect to the effects of downsizing (a euphemism for permanent layoffs).

Thus, this book sets the example of the kinds of books we will be publishing in this series, books that are practical and grounded in knowledge that one can trust, that are readable rather than obscure, and books that one will want to refer to more than once.

W. Warner Burke
Pelham, New York

PREFACE

About ten years ago I found myself trying to sort out the linkages between the behavioral sciences and the practice of what had come to be called human resource management (HRM). During this time the business community began to witness some very distressing events. Organizations were losing their stability, and the cause didn't seem to be a lack of either financial or technical capacity. Rather, it seemed to be related to the inattention to human assets.

I was spending a disproportionate amount of time trying to distinguish strategic from tactical/administrative HRM and sorting through the "hard" versus "soft" debates among various behavioral science practitioners. Still, the cataclysmic events of the 1980s kept intervening in these debates and forced me to confront something that had become painfully apparent. Managers caught up in this tumult had been educated, recruited, trained, developed, rewarded, and positioned to manage fairly static business environments—a condition that was fast fading from existence. In the face of the turbulence around them, many sought the refuge of their earlier decision models and paradigms, only to find them useless sources of guidance under these new conditions. New thinking was needed, and opportunities for input were opened up.

At first I was pleased to see that many behavioral science practitioners had figured out how to blend quantitative and qualitative approaches when working with organizations. Also, I was pleased to see that strategic HRM players had finally made it to the decision-influencing stage at better run organizations. But something still was missing; all this was skirting around an even bigger issue. The impact on businesses grew in intensity, and the world began witnessing events few would have dared to predict only a few years earlier. Giant firms toppled because of their inability to bend and adjust themselves in the face of change. Millions of people found themselves without work, and the jobs went in search of cheap foreign labor. Those who sought refuge through technical solutions found themselves in a neutron bomb scenario where technical devices and internal logic hummed along uselessly because the people—in a state of change shock—had psychologically, if not physically, left the scene. And on and on and on. . . .

In the midst of all this, I myself was caught up in a major organization change as both an observer and participant in a downsizing process. I set out to catalogue the experiences of managers who were held accountable for managing both the day-to-day business as well as the change impact. This opened my eyes to what had yet to become obvious. Managers were having to learn a totally new discipline: managing the impact of change. It was not being taught in schools and probably couldn't be anyway. The lessons were being handed out in a harsh, ruthless, and explosive manner. Somehow a confluence of forces had emerged to confront assumptions that had gone unchallenged for longer than most managers could remember. The market-place, capital markets, customer demands, advanced technology, and societal mores had all shifted in largely unpredictable and apparently uncontrollable ways. The chaos around managers made it seem pointless to do much other than head for the bunkers and wait out the storm. Not a particularly creative—or effective—approach, unfortunately.

Managers, often out of desperation, turned to sources whose "fuzzy" ideas or stereotyped roles had rendered them inaudible to managerial ears in the past. More fads began to surface. Lots of quick fixes. Random shots in the dark. The HRM approach seemed to be useful, but even here there were too few people who could look beyond their function to appreciate an even greater drama unfolding. The time had come to step away from any single discipline or function and ask some hard and often embarrassing questions about things that had not been discussable in the past: what the vision of the business is, who the stakeholders were, how one could empower a work force and simultaneously transform managers into leaders and failing orga-nizations into successful ones. The time had come to drop back and reexam-ine some of the basic impediments that kept getting in the way.

Why were so many people ducking the issue of how complex the problems were? Why couldn't managers better articulate the interrelationships among key aspects of their organizations that, once changed, began to change others in unanticipated—and often destructive—ways? Books that began to emerge with "excellence" in their titles further goaded people into asking themselves what they should be doing differently. But these books were rarely prescrip-tive, except in broad terms.

Returning to my roots, I began to think about parallel situations in which people had to confront superior forces and find ways to position themselves to take advantage of the situation without being overcome by the event itself. This was different from claiming to be a "change master" because it openly admitted that change *cannot* be mastered, no more than one can master the tide or the wind. Rather, it faced the challenge of managing within change.

Examples from my past that came to mind were rodeo events during which the brute strength and fury of untamed horses were pitted against the abilities of riders. Riders respect the superior strength and unpredictability of horses and approach them with a mixture of wariness, timing, and courage. The objective is not to master the animal so much as it is to exploit the horse's strength to achieve the rider's goal. Riders know from experience that such relationships are difficult to achieve and can never be taken for granted. For just as the horse can benefit the rider, it can as easily become an instrument of his destruction. As I reflected upon the examples of success and defeat I have witnessed in the arena, it struck me that today's organizations are having to confront change in a similar way.

The title of this book, *The Change Riders*, describes the leaders and managers in today's organizations who recognize that their challenge is to position themselves and their organizations to take advantage of change. Their arenas also offer unpredictable outcomes, and the hazards go beyond a single individual's exposure. Instead, we are witnessing whole organizations, economic sectors, and societies "putting it on the line" during such times. The opportunity to be part of a major change allowed me to capture information and insights that have formed a rich case history. To put it into perspective, I needed to paint a broader picture of change impact and insert parts of the case to underscore this message. My intent was to write a book to pass on what I have found to be helpful to Change Riders who have faced the challenge. Some have fared well; others not. The lessons to be learned from both are contained in this book.

Therefore, the purpose of the book can be divided into three major objectives. The first was to provide real examples with the kind of detail not readily available, the kind of information that draws the reader into organizational depths often reserved for inside participants. Next, I wanted to offer lessons and guidance for Change Riders, the leaders and managers who need to develop their skills in this new discipline: managing within change. Finally, I intended to provide literary and philosophical infrastructure so as to draw on what I regard as a wealth of excellent thinking and experience that has preceded this work. This last objective should provide some future avenues for readers to follow beyond this book.

AN OVERVIEW OF CONTENT

The chapters are presented in a sequence that makes sense to me. I would recommend that Chapter 1 be read first to gain some reasonable backdrop for the others and that Chapters 8 and 9 be read as a set because both deal with the actual measurement of change impact. Other chapters offer insights that can be taken in any order that meets individual needs. Here is a brief overview of the chapter contents:

Chapter 1 examines a broad array of emerging social, political, marketplace, and organizational issues. The breadth and depth of change surrounding these issues help set the stage for subsequent discussions of the challenges leaders and managers face in terms of change impact.

Chapter 2 examines the management of communication and planning as well as the benefits from handling information in open and productive settings. In an opposite direction, it reviews some myths that are often cited as justification for withholding information, thus leading to impediments in gaining organizational support for change.

Chapter 3 looks at how work management paradigms are shifting in today's changing environments. Some historic precedents are offered to explain how we got here and how the future may actually be merely catching up with what has already occurred in the minds of others. The role of leader/manager is explored so as to outline a working definition of leadership. Some major paradoxes facing the leader/manager are examined, and an answer to the question, "What's in it for me?" is offered.

Chapter 4 offers insights into the motives and practices behind offering safety nets to people facing the impact of change in organizations. Some major dilemmas reviewed are related to balancing cost and benefits, exchanging accumulated loyalty and goodwill for a delayed sense of security, and the potential impact of a demographic shift that could find organizations rehiring the armies of employees-cum-mercenaries they helped to create through restructuring, downsizing, and early retirements.

Chapter 5 takes a micro view of the impact of change on the health of those in its path. A review of related literature highlights linkages between change and pathology. Some learnings from a case example are offered. The unique impact change can have on managers is explored, and an overview of issues to address to minimize negative outcomes is provided.

Chapter 6 discusses issues related to the management of human assets and offers a model to guide such decisions. Specific tools and techniques are reviewed that support this model. Several myths surrounding the management of human assets are exposed, and a discussion of the need for upper-level operating managers to take a more active role in this area is presented.

Chapter 7 shows how profitability has managed to mask poor management practices and how this often comes to light during times of change. Alternative approaches are examined that cast "effective management" in broader terms. Employee involvement, often a major part of the definition, is examined in terms of its robustness during the turbulence of change. This strength, ironically, can threaten the status quo, including the justification for certain staff functions. How their counterattacks manifest themselves is discussed.

Chapter 8 offers a rare look at the hypothetical and actual impact of change on both productivity and product quality within an organization. Its dual focus on both closing locations and those designated to remain open allows a comparison of these two conditions. This hard information is held up for examination and helps identify how such variables can be affected by large-scale change decisions.

Chapter 9 goes beyond the hard data presented in Chapter 8 and examines the impact of change on the actual management practices behind them. Major issues surrounding the adjustments made by management are reviewed, showing which ones were more successful than others and why.

Chapter 10 looks at forces that support the status quo, to the point of driving an organization out of existence "by the book." The need to reexamine unquestioned assumptions is discussed. To help guide thinking on how an environment must be prepared for change, some major lessons learned by an organization that was fairly successful in managing the impact of change are cited.

Chapter 11 is a mixture of whimsy and more than enough reality thrown in to make it worthwhile. It draws attention to the crazy things that can and do happen during a period of change. Twisted logic, zealots, and organizational liposuction are but a few of the areas covered for both amusement and amazement. . . .

Chapter 12 puts into perspective the idea that managing the impact of change successfully requires at the outset the right tools: blueprints and roadmaps. The blueprints are models showing major organizational components to be considered during the period of change. Roadmaps are frameworks that help chart a path to minimize the change turbulence. Some examples of organizational models are reviewed to provide material that can be used by leaders and managers. Methodologies that can help plan for the arrival of change are discussed.

AN ECLECTIC FROM WYOMING

People often wonder why anyone would go to the trouble of putting all this kind of stuff in writing. It takes an incredibly long time and, if you are like me, no one comes up and says, "Why don't you take some months off and write?" There must be something that drives people to do this. George Orwell, in his essay "Why I Write," claims that writers, if candid, will admit that they are motivated by the need to show off and by the habit of noticing unpleasant facts. He's probably right, so I'll plead guilty to the first charge and confess further that I have been frustrated with how poorly organizations have handled change. The advice they have been getting has bothered me as well. Too many "experts" have never actually had to confront these issues themselves and so are directing the battle from both a psychological and an experiential disadvantage.

I'm just an eclectic from Wyoming, although my wife says I may be confusing eclecticism with having a short attention span. Nevertheless, this whole book unabashedly draws from a wide variety of sources ranging from the erudite to the mundane. Often I find that literary insights are often pale reflections of my own previous "unsophisticated" experiences. For example, my father owned an appliance business and taught me things about customer service that I would later find written up in *Harvard Business Review* articles and contemporary management books. In addition, I had lots of jobs while growing up and it exposed me to how people think about work—insights I rediscovered in several best-sellers. In sum, I have come to a point where I feel comfortable talking about the impact of change and how Change Riders can prepare themselves for it.

Finally, on the subject of "talking to," I want to reserve the right to violate a principle hammered on incessantly by my graduate professors. As they took great pains in pointing out, technical writing should not be "conversational." I always had a problem with that, because I have enjoyed writing as a form of conversation with readers, and this book will be no exception. For those who disdain the use of such an approach, I can recommend several excellent sources that are marvelously successful in creating great distance between the writer and the reader. My hope is that you and I will join together on the pages to follow and that you'll allow me the freedom to step away from the formal reporting role on occasion to provide some personal reflections on what I think is going on as well. In short, think of this book as a conversation between one Change Rider and another.

Gary D. Kissler
London, England
January 1, 1991

ACKNOWLEDGMENTS

I suppose it would be easier to list a bibliography and assume readers understand these are the sources from which the underpinnings of this work emerge. Easier—but it would certainly leave out a lot of other influences. To sort some of this out, I will try to do justice to the small army of people who have had incalculable influence on both my thinking and my behavior as they relate to this work.

Some early influence came from people who showed excellent examples of how to lead and manage. These include Nick Hartsook, Harry Redd, Laurie Broedling, R. Peter Mercer, Alan Eckert, Marty Dorio, John Gardner, Tony Lefkowicz, Bob Nardelli, Mike Butler, Bill Watson, Bruce DeVore, Fred Grunewald, Barry Fader, and Paula McCarty. They represent several types of businesses, private and public sectors, and a wide geographic spread as well. What they share in common, however, is an undeniable influence over my appreciation of the influence of outstanding leader/managers.

Over the years I have had the good fortune to work with and learn from people I regard as "thought leaders." These include Warren Bennis, Peter Block, Warner Burke, Stan Davis, Jay Galbraith, Ralph Kilmann, Robert Laud, Ed Lawler, Noel Tichy, Bill Pasmore, Tom Peters, Mike Schuster, and Dick Walton. Others I have come to know through their work, and they are included in both the chapter notes and the bibliography. Taken together, they have offered me tremendously valuable points of view that have shaped my thinking over the years.

In my current position I have had the good fortune to work with business consultants who focus on the impact of change on people and their organizations. Within the Change Management Services (CMS) arena are several of my partners who have played key roles in shaping the U.S. practice: Bill Bramer, Jim Caldwell, Tony Clancy, Bob Hunter, Dick Johnson, Don Kabat, Carla Paonessa, and Chuck Winslow. Jane Hemstritch and Willie Cheng have nurtured CMS through trying times in "Australasia." Finally, my European partners, Arnaud Andre, David Clinton, Massimo Merlino, Hasko Neumann, Terry Neill, and Keith Ruddle, deserve credit for creating an exciting pan-European practice.

Some pieces of work are so long in their development that early significant contributors are often overlooked. This is certainly the case in Chapter

12, where the Andersen Consulting Change Management Services methodology are shown. Two pioneers were Susan Bachman and Jeff Cartwright, and they deserve credit for producing an early version that, to a great extent, has survived many subsequent modifications. The principal architect was Bob Laud. I commend him for his patience, attention to critical detail, and insistence that the final product reflect the level of quality a world-class consulting organization should offer its clients.

There are literally hundreds of people who were gracious enough to give me some of their time as I gathered the detailed information that has served as the book's predominant case example. Respect for the anonymity of their organization prevents me from listing them here, but their input as either participants or co-investigators was invaluable. Related to this group are two people who showed a level of professionalism that stood out in times of great organizational turmoil: Jane Russell and Debora Humphreys.

The next group consists of people I may have already mentioned, but I include them a second time because they are a life force around me that has bound friendship and expertise in ways I cannot even begin to explain. Much gratitude to: Barry Fader, Warren Wilhelm, Harry Redd, S. J. Pettengill, Bruce DeVore, H. E. Dunsmore, C. W. Dreese, and Bob Laud. They have challenged me and offered several "tsk-tsk" commentaries over the years in order to keep me from becoming too comfortable in one spot.

Although they are rarely found within formal acknowledgments like these, I feel compelled to mention the truly marginal leaders and managers I have had the opportunity to observe and to work for over the years. They, sometimes more than any other source, have etched into my memory literally hundreds of things that I advise people never to do. To paraphrase a quote I heard some time ago, "Good managers come and go, but a bad manager can last you a lifetime." At long last I have put their incompetence to good use—as bad examples.

Finally, as you might expect, there are those people who know what you look like without your "uniform" on—your family. My parents are the kind of people who have always encouraged me not to become too enamored with my accomplishments because "we all stand on the shoulders of giants." And after all is said and done, there is Jan. As a spouse, she has put up with all my foibles, possibly for the same reason people go to zoos. To these people, I suspect there is practically nothing I could say or do at this point to surprise them.

Chapter 1

WISDOM ≠ Σ[FACTS]

. . . and you know something's happening, but you don't know what it is, do you, Mr. Jones?
—Bob Dylan

Everybody gets so much information all day long that they lose their common sense.
—Gertrude Stein

The sum of the facts may have little if anything to do with the wisdom needed by managers as they face a world of global transitions, turbulent domestic issues, and a major shift in how people will have to perform if their organizations are to survive and compete in the future. Some of this is understandable because those caught up in the turbulence personify the old one-liner, "When you are up to your ass in alligators, you don't have time to drain the swamp." Unfortunately, using expediency as an excuse for taking the time to recognize patterns of significant change occurring becomes a dangerous strategy. Let us look more closely, therefore, at the "facts."

Within a five-year period, 1979–1983, 11.5 million American workers lost their jobs because of organizational restructuring, plant closings, or related activity.[1] Bill Fredericks lost his job at a small manufacturing plant in a rural part of Ohio in 1983. At age 47, he had spent 24 years working at that location, as had his father and several other relatives before him. He surveyed the aftermath and summed up his frustrations, "It's hard being 18 again."

Bill's managers found themselves facing a situation none had believed possible. A huge corporation they had viewed as "family" had not only forsaken its children but had asked these managers to face the impact of this change with no warning or preparation. It was a scene that would be repeated again and again as companies confronted a bewildering economic landscape filled with strange and threatening scenes. At first, the most anyone seemed capable of doing was to observe and report on "facts."

The U.S. economy had fallen into a deep recession by 1981–1982. The inflation rate had peaked at 13.5 percent by 1980 and fell to 6.2 percent by the

1

end of 1982. On the other hand, the unemployment rate in 1981 stood at 8.6 percent but had risen rapidly to 10.8 percent by the end of 1982. The major economic issues involved the recession, world debt, major wage concessions obtained from large U.S. unions, and the decline of the American steel industry. The auto industry was laying off thousands of workers, and a similar ripple effect was felt among suppliers to this industry.[2]

The cost of borrowing—"renting money"—had risen to the point that businesses were folding at an alarming rate, housing was no longer affordable for the majority of first-time buyers, and the specter of a whole generation living below the standards of their parents began to take shape. An amazing reversal in consumer thinking was in the making as well.

THE ECHO OF LAUGHTER

In the 1950s the butt of much American humor was the simple label "Made in Japan." A comedian could get a lot of mileage out of telling the audience that you could tell a Japanese camera because it went "crick." The laughter soon died as it became clear that this small island nation had become a serious economic competitor—based largely on the quality of its offerings. By the 1970s Japanese cameras compared favorably with historic models like Rollei and Leica. This achievement was soon followed by an avalanche of consumer goods.

In upstate New York, a major manufacturer of television sets closed its facility because its return on sales had dropped below 6 percent. As it was closing its doors, a Japanese firm opened a television plant nearby. Its focus was on longer term market share versus short-term profits, and now it was positioned to accomplish both by way of U.S. default. The U.S. industrial base was eroding at an accelerating pace, and thousands of U.S. jobs were being exported in search of cheaper labor.

Managers and workers watched their equipment and processes dismantled and shipped to foreign countries where products could be made by people working for a fraction of U.S. labor rates. A whole new vocabulary emerged. People talked of *maquiladora* operations in Mexico, economic dislocation, and the redundancy of the work force. Earlier, the Japanese had found it necessary to buy technological innovation from abroad and introduce it into their businesses. Now, in an ironic twist, U.S. firms were bringing their innovation with them and allowing host countries access to it in exchange for access to less expensive employees. Too late, many recognized the danger of this strategy. Less developed countries were learning how to turn this newfound technology to their own advantage, and Americans began finding imported goods being sold alongside domestic items—only at less cost and with no discernible difference in quality. This was possible, in no small part, because of a Faustian exchange of technology for short-term profitability. For years, many U.S. firms had not only played a "Fortress America" game but had also stubbornly refused to believe that foreign competitors could breach their economic equivalent of the Maginot line: their cherished distribution networks. In fact, few took seriously the notion that goods could even reach U.S. shores because of prohibitive transportation costs. All in all, several major errors in judgment were made that ultimately delayed a meaningful U.S. response to global competition.

Since many U.S. businesses believed they could not afford to send their goods abroad and still make the level of profits deemed necessary at home, it was easy to assume that the same would be true for foreign competitors. One American manager in a lighting business found this whole argument ludicrous and responded, "Hell, they could load up every Toyota sent here with lightbulbs and the whole transportation issue would be over!" The people who were lining up for those Toyotas formed another major shift in thinking about the relationship between cost and quality.

CONSUMERS: THE QUIET REVOLUTION

The preferences of consumers were grossly misunderstood. By the mid-1970s, the majority of cars being driven in the state of California were of Japanese origin. U.S. automakers dismissed this phenomenon, despite California's long-standing reputation as a bellwether state. In a classic push-versus-pull approach to marketing, huge, expensive, inefficient vehicles of lesser quality continued to be offered. Meanwhile, Honda dealers were able to get away with adding "special preparation charges" over and above sticker prices and still have people willing to be put on long waiting lists for their cars. Paying above sticker price? For all the fuss over "sticker shock" due to increased auto prices, too little has been made of this dramatic mind shift and subsequent consumer behavior. The quest for quality and efficiency was made manifest at that moment.

By far the most egregious assumption made was in regard to market share and customer loyalty; both were assumed to be owned, when in fact they had only been "rented."[3] The nationalistic slogans, bumper stickers, advertising campaigns, and so on caused many to espouse solidarity on macroeconomic issues. Of course, many of these same people would drive home in their Nissans, rewind their Matshushita video recorders, and watch the network news on their Sony TVs—possibly hearing an anchorman explain how the United States was being transformed from a creditor to debtor nation in record time.

The cycle was becoming well established. The United States, driven largely by consumer preferences, bought more goods than it sold abroad, resulting in a massive trade deficit. Meanwhile, the government was continuing to spend more money than it was collecting in revenues and therefore was forced to borrow ever larger amounts from foreign lenders in search of higher rates of return. Japan was subsidizing U.S. deficit spending. Before long, a "reform" was on its way in the form of tax law changes. Long-term capital gains taxes increased, discouraging investment. The law also encouraged consumers to save even less than before, thus continuing to borrow heavily to support long-held habits of consuming beyond their immediate means. The federal government was playing Polonius to the consumer Laertes, and the son wasn't buying the advice.

THE THIRD-WAVE UNDERTOW

People can show a stubborn pragmatic streak when it comes to economic issues. Too many trips to the auto repair shop, too many examples of built-in obsolescence, and ultimately too little value for the dollar had finally created a consumer-led revolt with an unlikely banner at its head: "Made in Japan." However, the turbulence of the marketplace was being matched by several demographic and societal shifts that also seemed to catch businesses off guard. Again, businesses continued to operate against several questionable assumptions:

- Entry-level employees are readily available.

- The incoming work force's skill levels are sufficient to meet job demands.

- People's job expectations are about the same as always.

THE PIG IN THE PYTHON

"The pig in the python." Baby boomers. Whatever the label, they may not vote as a bloc or have easily discernible consumer preferences or social consciences, but their numbers and the trend in these numbers cannot be mistaken. The last of the bunch has already entered the work force, and the picture from now on gets pretty bleak insofar as entry-level hiring is concerned. In 1979 nearly 26 million people aged 16 through 24 were available for hire. By the year 2000, that number will be closer to 22 million and dropping. What's worse, the growth of available jobs will outpace available job holders during this period. As this demographic freight train is heading down the tracks, many businesses are "encouraging" older workers to retire early—short-term cost reduction again the major driver.[4]

Not only are the absolute numbers changing, so are the characteristics of this group. Forty-seven percent of the 1985 work force were U.S.-born white males, a group predicted to be only 15% of the year 2000 work force. Immigrants, minorities, women, and senior citizens will have to be assimilated into organizations to meet future demands. At least one forecaster describes the future "typical" employee as follows:

- A 34-year-old baby boomer, has two children and a working spouse.

- Plans to work past retirement—doesn't trust the Social Security system.

- Doesn't belong to a union and wouldn't consider joining one.

- Willing to accept a certain amount of risk in exchange for the possibility of being rewarded for superior performance.

- Increasingly likely to have some sort of flexible work schedule—or would prefer one.

- Increasingly, that "average worker" is a woman.[5]

DUMBING IT DOWN

The amount and quality of skills possessed by the incoming work force continues to be part of a national debate. As a society, the United States already faces competition from the Japanese in the area of literacy; their rate is over 95 percent, compared with only 80 percent in the United States.[6] A much bigger issue, however, is not often discussed—the ability to think! Future jobs will require people to develop and use diagnostic skills. In the working world of the future, automating will give way to "informating," a quantum jump in availability of information that opens up new possibilities for people to make contributions—and creates major transition challenges requiring revised management roles and responsibilities.[7]

Improving our educational output—regardless of the process or source—

forces us to contend with another variable. Detroit automakers are not only behind in product quality—they are forced to aim at a moving target as their foreign competitors continue to improve quality as well. Likewise, the improvements in education face the daunting prospect that the demands of the workplace, driven to a great extent by the influx of sophisticated technology, will ultimately outpace the overwhelming majority of workers. In only a handful of years, 95 percent of employees will be unable to master jobs requiring skills beyond a high school education.

In the 1940s, foremen on production lines had a significantly greater degree of power and autonomy than their counterparts do today. They often wore white shirts and ties, were addressed as "sir," and were deemed intellectually prepared for this demanding role because they had a high school diploma. Today, by contrast, nearly all production workers have a high school education; a large number have attained college degrees.

There is another and more troubling side to this. The diminishing number of white males in the entry-level labor pool is coupled with increased awareness of the educational limitations found among minority candidates. Nynex recently had to screen 60,000 job candidates, a substantial number of whom were minority-group members, to fill 3,000 positions. The dropout rate among blacks and Hispanics is substantially larger than for whites. Managers therefore face a work force with attitudes ranging from indifference to impatience. In short, society has delivered the results of its institutions to the doors of organizations and has said, in effect, "Good luck."

DO YOU HAVE CHANGE FOR A PICKLE?

The future is being played out in thousands of fast-food establishments. Managers responsible for finding, motivating, and retaining employees in these businesses have more than their share of "war stories." Because the employee literacy rate was low, cash register keys were changed so that the names of food were replaced with pictures. At least one major fast-food corporation is testing a further step—the equivalent of an Automated Teller Machine that will bring the customer closer to the griddle. In the meantime, the turnover rate among the younger employees is in the three-digit range and managers walk on eggshells because, in a seller's market, even minor criticism can have disastrous results. One manager said, "If you try to point out areas for improvement, they just walk out! Down the street they go and have another job in an hour—for more money. How in the world am I supposed to deal with that?"

DISPOSABLE VALUES

You can read it in the graffiti and on the bumper stickers: "He who dies with the most toys wins." "When the going gets tough, the tough go shopping." "Inaction speaks louder than words." This is a consumer society on the move, and people's choices clearly reflect a major shift in values. People own machines to watch TV for them, answer the phone for them, run their houses for them. They don't hesitate to check themselves for pregnancy, colon cancer, hypertension, and—perhaps soon—AIDS. They have fueled the fastest growing category of publications, do-it-yourself literature, and they buy a larger percentage of available hand tools than do craftsmen. Clearly we see a pattern of behavior that underscores a drive to take increased control over one's life—including one's work life.[8]

A WORLD GONE MAD

Such a shift in direction is not without recognizable cause. For one thing, a major principle of trust had been breached. For many people, there simply was no choice. They had grown up believing in the implicit wisdom of large institutions, trusting those in power to make just decisions that would be in their best interests. In their innocence, they felt secure and did not consider it necessary to involve themselves in seemingly abstract debates over domestic or foreign policy. Then the letters began to arrive in mailboxes.

> Mike Beck could be seen beneath the transparent plastic cover of his coffin. His military uniform somehow made him seem small. For his friends and classmates, this funeral in a relatively small Wyoming community in the spring of 1966 shattered their childhood illusions of safety and invulnerability. For as much as they grieved for their fallen contemporary, their unspoken fears were clearly focused on their own mortality. "If they could do that to Mike, they could do it to me." This terrifying revelation was taking place throughout the nation and events to follow would soon convince them that the world had indeed gone mad.

The common denominator was a bullet. The names and their causes differed as much as did their tactics: Malcolm X, George Lincoln Rockwell, Martin Luther King, Robert Kennedy—all torn from the scene by violence. The trusted institutions were viewed as faltering. How could they let this happen? Who is in charge here?! J. Edgar Hoover's fanaticism and abuse of power was exposed. The Central Intelligence Agency was found to have overstepped its charter. The so-called Pentagon papers made public documents giving evidence of infighting among military and civilian leaders. The result often surfaced in the form of lies trumpeted as facts to justify the continued war effort in Vietnam and to cover up embarrassing facts, such as the full impact of the Tet offensive in 1968.

Meanwhile, the economy was straining to fight a domestic war on poverty and a foreign war against communism. The inevitable tax increases struck many as more evidence that we were out of control. The downfall of a vice-president because of questionable pre-election business activities and the resignation of a president because of the Watergate scandal shredded what little credibility government officials had left in the minds of millions of citizens. Coupled with racial tensions and war-induced cynicism, the last helicopter lifting off from the roof of the U.S. ambassador's compound in Saigon symbolized not only a lost war, but also the loss of the trust and innocence of a generation of Americans entering the work force. This impact was felt immediately by their managers.

"Man, I spent two tours in 'Nam, saw more death than anyone should ever have to see, and this turkey comes up to me and says, 'You gotta have my permission to leave the production line' and I said, 'Bullshit'."

"I was a man in Vietnam, but they wanted me to be a little boy when I went back to school—no way—I split."

Disturbing research findings point out that disillusionment had taken its toll on those who would stand to inherit the leadership of business in the future. The results found that a sizable number did not respect their leaders and preferred not to become leaders themselves. Who was there to emulate? When U.S. citizens were taken hostage by a foreign government in Teheran, we were powerless to help them. In just a handful of years we would learn that a deal was made to trade sophisticated weapons with this same government for the release of a different set of hostages. Someone summed it all up by saying, "No matter how cynical you are, you just can't keep up."

Medical science was making breakthroughs that underscored how quickly technology could outstrip humanity's ability to absorb it and adjust its social mores and credos. Test-tube babies. Biological engineering. Surrogate mothers. The same country that produced the defoliant Agent Orange was now accused of creating another, known as "acid rain," and its fluorocarbons were punching a hole in the world's ozone layer. By the time Three Mile Island and the Russian equivalent, Chernobyl, hit the newspapers, citizens became convinced that environmental incompetence transcended ideology. It is no coincidence that all of this, plus Wall Street scandals, has been followed by a surge of interest in courses on ethics. Not content to wait were those within the business community who grew impatient and disgusted with the myopia above them.

INSURGENTS IN THE BOARDROOM

In the business setting, an interesting sign of hope is appearing. The next generation of leaders and managers appears to have some different views of how to handle their business and its assets. One key difference is that they are far more willing to consider collaborative approaches to making decisions. Also, they are more aware of the limitations of the work force in the face of technological change in the work setting. They will therefore go to greater lengths to create joint proposals with the government in order to focus on longer term market objectives. They will also accept more responsibility for improving the quality of U.S. education. This is particularly encouraging as the full impact of economic dislocation becomes known. One study found that 59 percent of 512 companies surveyed between 1982 and 1985 conducted big layoffs or plant closings. Yet only 11 percent offered retraining. The new wave of business leaders appears ready to address this issue more directly.[9] Willfully or not, these people are preparing themselves to take on a far more global set of challenges.

WHAT'S HAPPENING AROUND THE GLOBE THESE DAYS?

Much of what has been discussed dovetails with the idea of "megatrends" identified by John Naisbitt. Of these, I would like to focus on one that acknowledges the existence of a global economy. In the early 1980s, there was a newspaper photo showing United Auto Workers union members taking sledgehammers to a Toyota in a display of anger and frustration over the threat of foreign imports—Japanese automobiles. In the late 1980s, there was another photo in the news. This time it was Japanese farmers pounding away at an American car in a display of anger and frustration over the threat of foreign imports—American agricultural products. These two events show graphically how rapidly the world economy is shifting.

The UAW is working with Toyota and General Motors to produce higher quality, lower cost automobiles. The Japanese are peering nervously over their shoulders at their own "Japan" in the form of consumer goods imported

Table 1.1   Percentage of Japanese Market Won by Foreign Products

Category	1980	1986	1987
Hot-rolled sheet steel	2.1%	23.9%	31.0%
Milling machines	15.4	20.1	41.9
Calculators	12.9	44.7	49.0
Black-and-white TVs	1.5	14.3	54.4
Radio-cassette players	4.6	15.3	47.5
35mm cameras	7.7	19.4	46.6
Outer garments	20.8	34.8	46.3

from the Far East. Consider the figures in Table 1.1, from the Japanese Ministry of International Trade and Industry.

These are startling numbers.[10] For most U.S. consumers, the 35mm camera was their first encounter with an imported Japanese item that was the exception to the rule of shoddy knock-offs by that country. To discover that nearly half of Japan's cameras are imported surely stands as mute testimony to the impermanent nature of global marketshare. However, the Far East is not the only emerging major economic force today.

FORTRESS EUROPE

For decades it was almost a truism that Europe was destined to exist as a set of economic feudal states, jealously guarding their borders, markets, languages, exchange rates, and exposure to any external influence that might effect significant change.[11] Charles De Gaulle once observed about France, "Who can be expected to govern a country with 512 types of cheese?" This less than charitable remark might have applied throughout most of Europe. Travelers who have encountered long lines at the frontiers and unpredictable experiences surrounding currency exchanges have witnessed this firsthand. Given all this historic baggage, who would have expected something as dramatic as the declaration by the 12-member European Community: In 1992, all economic boundaries are to be eliminated! There is talk of a common currency, no checkpoints at borders, and the potential for increased European trade barriers. Assuming these nations could join as planned, they would present a formidable trading block. Together they represent 320 million consumers and exceed the gross domestic product of either the United States or Japan. The implication for non-European players is clear: Get in before it's too late. One need only look at the strategy of Japanese manufacturers in the United States to anticipate the moves to come. Foreign operations will need to move quickly to establish jointly owned and operated business ventures that can be woven into the 1992 fabric. All of this suggests that, despite lingering nationalistic debates, Europe intends to become a much stronger economic competitor in the 1990s and beyond.

Within a span of months, we have recently witnessed an extraordinary series of events within central Europe. The collective spirit of freedom has smashed its fist through walls, dispatched dictators, and released millions of silenced voices for the first time in decades. While these surface events have had undeniable emotional impact, the true turbulence is just behind the roar. Now there comes the time for dealing with change on a scale unimagined by nearly everyone. Social upheaval has also brought about the opportunity to shape the future, and the marketplace has already begun to make its move. Pepsi was filming commercials as the Berlin Wall was being broken through, and planeloads of entrepreneurs have already arrived to help discover how to blend capitalist and socialist economies. What they are already discovering is that the linkage between social, political, and commercial changes must be both acknowledged and managed if any are to achieve significant progress. The impatience of the crowd is more than understandable, and this is no time for trial and error—the change riders will receive no second-place ribbons in this arena.

THE 51st STATE

A recent set of agreements between the United States and Canada, the so-called free-trade issue, further points to the need for more cooperation among strong trading partners. In Canada, the United States has long been regarded as a strong—perhaps too strong—trading partner. For many Canadians, this has masked the reality of a global market beyond these two players, a market whose influence greatly exceeds the free-trade issues that resulted in such heated debates. For Canada, the real issue beneath this agreement is the recognition of the global market and its threat to North American economic stability. One Canadian told this story during the debates to point out the shortsightedness of the free-trade opponents:

> Two backpackers were in the Canadian Rockies and had retired for the night. Around 2:00 A.M. a loud noise awoke them, and one peered out and was stunned to find a huge bear by the tent. The first guy immediately began putting on his

jogging shoes, and the second one told him that it was impossible for him to outrun a bear, even in running shoes. The first one replied, "I don't have to outrun the bear—just you."

This apocryphal tale bears [no pun intended] an unfortunate resemblance to the logic displayed with increasing frequency by nations trying desperately to make amends for years of business practices that paid scant attention to the gathering economic storm.

In his book *Future Perfect*, Stanley Davis says that "the meaning of market 'place' is shifting away from the physical space of industrial economies toward less-fixed locations in the space of the new economy."[12] Daniel Bell recently provided an example of this in a speech to a group of multinational chief information officers. He told of how the Rotterdam spot market for oil no longer exists as a "location." Instead, it has become an electronic market, with companies tied into a network of buyers and sellers, resulting in ships criss-crossing the globe, moving excess crude oil to multiple ports in response to electronically transmitted demand. In fact, the advent of technology challenges the Western concept of time, space, and mass—all encapsulated in nineteenth-century machine logic, a challenge that—unfortunately—has yet to be viewed as more of an opportunity than a threat by many.

SUSHI: DEBATE DE BAIT

In a final look at the global situation, it is worth revisiting Japan. No phenomenon has been so poorly understood by outsiders as has the rapid success of the Japanese. From cameras to consumer electronics to cars to computer chips to whatever comes next, Japanese successes have received truncated, shortsighted, and culturally biased assessments throughout the 1980s. Here are a few of the assumptions that Western business leaders have expressed:

- The Japanese management style is largely responsible for Japan's success and cannot be imported.

- The Japanese government plays a strongly influential role in shoring up its country's competitive advantages.

- Japanese firms are reckless in their pursuit of growth and are not profitable.

- The Japanese may be able to copy ideas and exploit their advantages in the area of manufacturing, but their culture prevents them from being innovative and creative.

In their book, *Kaisha: The Japanese Corporation*, James Abegglen and George Stalk address these and other misperceptions of the Japanese.[13] They down–play the notion of Japanese management style as the sole reason for the advances seen by outsiders, while still crediting it for helping Japan's work force to accept technological change more readily. The Japanese government is described as being similar to others in at least one regard: It can prevent great harm but cannot do great good. It is dissimilar in its willingness to work with businesses to help them make financial transitions out of unproductive markets and into those with more promise, but this facilitating role is far weaker than its characterization by Western observers. Japan's profitability, as measured by Western standards (e.g., return on sales), is lower than that of the average U.S. firm. However, when profitability is assessed against the after-tax return on shareholder investment, the situation is reversed. Finally, Japanese spending on research and development is substantially larger than is found among its Western counterparts, and the number of patents being awarded to Japanese firms suggests that this approach is paying off.

Japan is not immune to competition and cannot suspend the realities of economic life. Its sources of advantage have shifted over the years, from low wages to high-volume output, to focused production processes, and now to the embracing of technology to allow for higher degrees of market flexibility. *Kaisha* points out that Japan's next moves can be predicted. The criteria are as follows:

- The product is already produced in large volumes in Japan.

- Japanese demand for the product is stagnant or declining.

- The Japanese have a factor cost advantage.

- The Japanese have a labor productivity advantage.

Variations on these themes may serve as good predictors of broader global competition as well. Having looked at the competitive issues outside the United States, it is important to keep in mind the key domestic issues that must also be addressed.

KEY ECONOMIC INFRASTRUCTURE ISSUES IN THE UNITED STATES

Not since the Great Depression have average citizens shown so much interest in information about the economic health of the United States. Further, it is noteworthy that best-sellers have included numerous books about businesses and the people running them. Why all the interest? A short list of punchy titles gives a clue:

American goods shunned abroad despite plunging dollar.

Children's economic future threatened by unbalanced budget.

Decaying roads, bridges, and sewers pose safety threat.

Public education system produces societal incompetents.

Tax laws punish investing in the future.

Middle managers, an endangered species, fight change to the death.

Technophobes resist "automated intrusion" —boast of computer illiteracy.

Clearly, the array of domestic issues have the potential to dilute any effort the nation makes at shoring up its worldwide competitive stance. As this positioning has taken place, its effects have not gone unnoticed by people in the work setting.

VOICES FROM THE VARIABLE-COST TRENCHES

In today's business climate, it is common to find some variation on the phrase "People are our most valuable asset" strewn throughout recruiting brochures, annual reports, internal publications, and mass-produced videotapes used for various promotional purposes. Many of these same businesses will deplete these assets at the first sign of economic distress—done generally through layoffs, plant closings, forced early retirements, and the like. Put differently, the business decisions appear to treat people as variable costs instead of fixed costs associated with appreciating assets. The following quotes were taken from a study of a major plant closing effort by a Fortune 50 company I'll call Glacier, Inc.[14] Most of the people losing their jobs were long-service employees who had never faced forced unemployment before:

I think a law should be passed so that plants can't move without taking their employees with them. The company doesn't realize how it ruins people's lives at the cost of *profits*.

I'm sick and tired of hearing [people not being laid off] saying how good they think we have it, the newspaper making it sound so good about severance pay, and the company finding so many jobs for us. I have almost 12 years here and down the *shitter*. I hope the remaining locations fall on their faces.

Yes, I need a job. I know better than anything how to work. I just need someone who will hire me and let me prove my worth.

Close the plant and get it over with. People are going nuts waiting now that the company has turned its back on us. It's time to turn mine on the company.

The money offered for retraining is not enough to retrain most people in the skilled trades.

One thing this closing has opened my eyes to is, education. I never figured I would need to go for more schooling at my age (47), but I am going to protect my future a little more by going to college, if I can get the right hours.

After spending so many years with the company, it is very hard to adjust to such a blow.

I have not told the kids. They will learn soon enough that the company's only concern is with *larger* profit and no concern for those people who made the product in the first place.

This is the worst problem I can think of, short of death.

These are the voices of the future, not the past. Their sons and daughters have taken on lessons vicariously that will serve to reshape their relationships with organizations for years to come. This will pose a significant challenge to managers who expect unquestioned compliance from those they view as lucky to have a job.

ORGANIZATIONAL MERCENARIES

Some have spoken about a decrease in organizational loyalty. A loss of loyalty is likely to track with a loss of faith in a company's willingness to provide sustained employment. An example of this erosion of confidence is shown in employee responses to a survey item regarding job security within Glacier, Inc. (Figure 1.1). It is clear that a substantial shift in views has taken place over the survey period. More recent information suggests that these figures are somewhat on the conservative side within this business. A senior vice-president was shown these and other figures outlining a major decline in perceived employment security and responded, "So what?" It is a good question, one whose answer will prove to be one of the more major challenges for managers throughout the 1990s. These figures are part of a mosaic forming the image of employee as mercenary. For organizations who depended

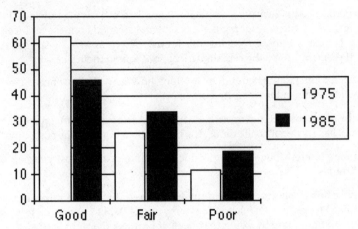

Figure 1.1   How Do You Rate This Company as Providing Job Security for People like Yourself?

on a commitment based on intangible forms of reward, the future holds a rude jolt. The executive raising the question was used to counting on people to give extra effort naturally because of their historic belief in the company—a form of trading on the logo. As this loyalty erodes, organizations will find themselves facing a work force whose loyalties are tied to more tangible rewards than the good will and sense of belonging that once served as a rallying point for so many.

Questions about "portable pensions" and "equity positions" and challenges to policies and practices developed in a time when people planned for long periods of single-employer commitment are beginning to be raised more frequently. History will record the 1980s as a time when organizations forfeited a historic source of strength in exchange for a reduction in costs. The hollow phrase, "People are our most valuable asset," will come back to haunt the business environment because it has become clear to millions of workers that their organizations are unwilling to make bilateral commitment to employment. Jack Welch, chief executive officer of GE, is quoted in the *Wall Street Journal* as saying, "Loyalty to a company, it's nonsense." Subsequent problems with its myriad of "General Eclectic" businesses, such as Kidder Peabody, and the loss of key talent from some of its core businesses (e.g., plastics), suggest that Mr. Welch's message has not been lost on those who have chosen—to use another GE phrase—to "flourish elsewhere."[15] Were it not for large organizations like IBM and Delta Airlines, with their proven employment commitment policies, it might be argued that massive dislocation of employees is the only viable option left to an organization facing a turbulent marketplace.

Given the demographic shifts occurring, the push for early retirements and the wholesale exiting of so much "corporate memory" and organizational continuity strikes me as another of those actions that will be judged harshly in retrospect. It is not at all difficult to envision these same businesses begging many, if not most, of these same people to return to fill the vacancies exceeding job candidates in the near future. The managers who inherit such a work force, already experienced in being "downsized," will need to manage in a far different manner than before. Those who want a preview should just revisit the plight of the managers of the fast-food franchise outlets.

DILEMMAS FACING MANAGERS

Each fall, the *Peanuts* cartoon strip displays another in its long series of confrontations between Charlie Brown, Lucy, and—of course—the football. For those who don't follow the series, each year Lucy beckons Charlie to run and kick the football she is holding. And each year, despite his past experiences and misgivings about Lucy's reassurances, he goes for it. As always, she jerks the football away just as Charlie is about kick it. The result—Charlie lying flat on his back—is now legend, and he is given to musing in this position about life and its inevitable outcomes, regardless of one's illusions.

There are some less amusing parallels between Charlie and many managers who are facing career path mirages, being blamed for playing by the old rules and winning, having to do even more with even less, and now being asked to manage the consequences of change—over which they feel little, if any, control.

As managers face up to these dilemmas, they are finding a number of oftentimes disturbing events and trends occurring on the job—some so dramatic as to change forever the role of their position. Here are just a few of these changes:

- A reduction in the number of layers within an organization, coupled with training for production workers in group-oriented problem solving, has resulted in fewer managers, broader spans of control, and a need for managers to play more of what Peter Drucker describes as an orchestration role.[16]

- Reward systems are being revised to reflect one's acquired skill and knowledge versus one's position or seniority. This change is coupled with the advent of evaluation methods that focus on group accomplishments and with the use of other methods allowing the group to evaluate the leadership they are receiving.[17]

- The growing acceptance of factory automation is moving the production environment closer to what some term a "lights-out" factory where few, if any, people are required to touch the production flow. Just as Just-in-Time inventory systems have been used to identify weaknesses in the production process, Computer-Integrated Manufacturing points out where humans do and do not add value in the overall manufacturing setting.[18]

- People working in entry-level jobs have as many years of education as managers did in the 1940s, coupled with exposure to multiple forms of media pitches. They bring high—and perhaps unrealistic—expectations of what a job will be able to offer them. Managers find many of these expectations a direct challenge to their authority.

- The needed competencies for successful managers now include skills that many view with alarm: negotiating skills, group-oriented motivation techniques, innovative job design options, and impression management.

SUMMARY

This chapter looks at a broad array of world events that form a collage of "facts" which often become confused with wisdom. Beneath this barrage of information are managers struggling to support the status quo. Despite their exposure to these "facts," there have been major changes that have gone on largely unnoticed by the business community, or at least have not been considered important enough to alter strategic plans—until recently.

Subsequent chapters will explore the changes faced by managers. To help in this quest, a number of references will be made to major organizational events that have occurred—acquisitions, mergers, downsizing, and the plant closings at Glacier, Inc., to show the impact on managers and others. The intent is to use the information from this chapter as a backdrop to help set the stage for a more in-depth treatment of experiences managers will encounter in today's changing workplace. From this approach will come lessons and guidelines that should help business leaders and managers understand and deal more effectively within the changes surrounding them.

Notes

1. The 11.5 million jobs lost during 1979–1983 were first identified by Paul O. Flaim and Ellen Sehgal in their *Monthly Labor Review* article, "Displaced Workers of 1979–83: How Well Have They Fared?" (June 1985). A January 1989 *Personnel Journal* article by Paul D. Staudohar cites general estimates that put the continuing annual loss of jobs due to closings and cutbacks at about 2 million.

2. For more discussion of the overriding economic issues accompanying the early 1980s, see W. J. Abernathy, K. B. Clark, and A.M. Kantrow, *Industrial Renaissance* (New York: Basic Books, 1983). Another source is a 1983 publication from the Bureau of National Affairs entitled *Layoffs, Plant Closings and Concession Bargaining*.

    For a more detailed analysis of the U.S. auto industry, see B. Yates's book *The Decline and Fall of the American Automobile Industry* (New York: Empire Books, 1983). Phillip Elmer-DeWitt's January 16, 1989, *Time* article, "Battle for the Future," revisits the underlying issues in an updated examination of U.S. internal competition among technology firms and the deleterious effects this has had on U.S. efforts to compete with Japanese advancements in areas such as superconductors, advanced semiconductors, high-definition TV, and biotechnology. The author states: "The danger is that by focusing too much on short-term competitive standings, U.S. industry will spend too little time preparing for the future. The most complex technologies require long-term planning and investments, and payoffs, while potentially enormous, may be long delayed."

3. Few writers and proselytizers will ever match the volume and intensity of Tom Peters. Following his joint authorship with Robert Waterman—*In Search of Excellence* (New York: Harper & Row, 1982)—and Nancy Austin—*A Passion for Excellence* (New York: Random House, 1985)—his work, *Thriving on Chaos* (New York: Knopf, 1987), develops even further the theme that U.S. business continues to confuse product with service, often trying to disguise the former as the latter.

4. The documentation and discussion of the impact of demographic shifts can be further explored in Andrew Nussbaum's *Business Week* (September 19, 1988) article, "Needed: Human Capital"; in Andrew Kupfer's *Fortune* (September 26, 1988) article, "Managing Now for the 1990s"; and Robert W. Goddard's *Personnel Journal* (February 1989) article, "Workforce 2000."

5. A fuller treatment of John Naisbitt's view of future trends and their implications for people and organizations can be found in his book, *Megatrends* (New York: Warner Books, 1982).

6. Aaron Bernstein's *Business Week* (September 19, 1988) article, "Where the Jobs Are Is Where the Skills Aren't," presents a compelling array of examples underscoring the disturbing trend toward underprepared workers headed for jobs demanding even more from people than ever before.

7. The term *informating* was coined by Shoshana Zuboff. Her excellent book, *In the Age of the Smart Machine* (New York: Basic Books, 1988), covers a number of critical areas related to management and the impact of technology.

8. Alvin Toffler's work, *The Third Wave* (New York: Telecom Library, 1980), examines a wide range of societal changes. Toffler's prescience regarding so many things destined to influence society in general makes this a valuable resource.

9. Selwyn Feinstein's October 10, 1988, *Wall Street Journal* column, "Views of Younger Managers Suggest New Way for U.S. Business to Compete," provides interesting insights into the thinking likely to influence U.S. business operations as the next generation of leaders moves into the top positions.

10. The Japanese Ministry of International Trade and Industry figures on the trends on Japanese imports were taken from a *Wall Street Journal* chart published on July 20, 1988.

11. In an Andersen Consulting publication, *Strategic Services Insights* (December 1988), Clifford M. Simms examines a number of issues related to "1992" in an article entitled, "1992: A Brave, New Europe?" In her *Wall Street Journal* columns on February 13 and 21, 1989, Karen Elliott House provides a less than sanguine view of the likelihood of "1992" having the intended impact. The lack of unifying leadership and the millstone of history are but two of the many impediments in the path of progress. Additional material on this topic can be found in Andrew Kupfer's *Fortune* article, "Managing Now for the 1990s" (September 26, 1988) and in a *Wall Street Journal* article entitled, "Fortress Europe 1992? Don't Hold Your Breath," by Victor K. Kiam, CEO of Remington Products (September 11, 1989).

12. Stanley M. Davis, in *Future Perfect* (Reading, MA: Addison-Wesley, 1987), explores a number of fascinating avenues surrounding some stodgy assumptions made by business organizations. The concepts of time, space, and mass are challenged by societal and technical shifts.

13. One of the most insightful treatments of the Japanese "miracle" is found in James Abegglen and George Stalk's book, *Kaisha: The Japanese Corporation* (New York: Basic Books, 1985). Stripped away are the oversimplifications too often used to explain away Japan's powerful challenge in terms like "homogeneous culture" or "compliant government" or "reckless economic and marketing tactics." This comprehensive work shows a much more detailed and awesome network of interwoven forces that both explain and predict Japanese business practices.

14. Much material for this book was taken from an internal study completed for a Fortune 50 company that was downsizing its manufacturing and distribution entities over several years. The identity of the business will be kept confidential, and the pseudonym "Glacier, Inc." will be used throughout the book. The lessons learned, data analyses, and managerial insights will be woven throughout subsequent chapters. The value of the material can be traced to the willingness of this business and its people to offer up candid—if sometimes painful—information about what they were going through.

15. Janet Guyon's 1988 *Wall Street Journal* column, "Combative Chief: GE Chairman Welch, Though Much Praised, Starts to Draw Critics," reviews the actions of GE's

chairman and the result of decisions that have been made since his rise to his current position. In private conversations with current and former GE people, there appears to be a mixture of pride, fear, and contempt that emerges from conversations about Jack Welch. They all agree that he has managed to change the GE culture dramatically, and most believe the overall work environment is more negative as a result. In subsequent *Wall Street Journal* articles (January 27, 1989, and February 3, 1989), more details emerge regarding how GE is managing the turbulence within Kidder Peabody—a business with a culture very different from its own. The defections of top traders and GE's change of leadership and financial inducements to the top players remaining are described in detail as part of a strategy to contain the damage. Richard Pascale provides a useful overview of GE and an insightful comparison between Jack Welch and Ford's president Donald Peterson in his book *Managing on the Edge* (New York: Simon & Schuster, 1990).

16. Richard E. Walton's *Harvard Business Review* article (March–April 1985), "From Control to Commitment in the Workplace," outlines several major differences that separate work environments that rely on a philosophy of controlling people from those that rely on gaining commitment from people. Within this work are several key observations about the changing role of managers. More recently, Peter Drucker's *Harvard Business Review* article (January–February, 1988), "The Coming of the New Organization," goes further by offering the orchestra conductor as a metaphor to present what he sees as an emerging role of leadership in new organizations.

17. For additional material on innovative reward systems and implications for managers, Edward E. Lawler III provides considerable background research and suggestions in his books, *Pay and Organization Development* (Reading, MA: Addison-Wesley, 1981), *High-Involvement Management* (San Francisco: Jossey-Bass, 1986), and *Strategic Pay* (San Francisco: Jossey-Bass, 1990). Ed has also provided numerous insights into the relationship between education levels among employees and their increased expectations of their employers. This relationship, Ed believes, can help explain some of the friction found within many organizations today.

18. Ann Majchrzak's book *The Human Side of Factory Automation* (San Francisco: Jossey-Bass, 1988), reviews numerous issues that businesses often overlook when a major change in technology is introduced into a work setting. She provides valuable observations and suggestions pertaining to the human resource and organizational impact that is likely to occur as a result of poorly planned changes.

Chapter 2

CORPORATE SECRETS: THE ULTIMATE OXYMORON

*They must think we are all idiots. Like we wouldn't **notice** the "For Sale" sign put up in front of our plant?*
    —Plant Manager

In general, the human mind is conservative. Long after an assumption is outmoded, people tend to apply it to novel situations.
    —Daniel J. Isenberg

The restriction of information flow within an organization is an activity that breeds both a siege mind set and a cast of misogynous supporting characters. It underscores a dark vision of the trustworthiness of people and leads to several myths. To gain a deeper appreciation of the impact of change, it is helpful to see how information is treated during times of change within organizations, and with what consequences.

The *Wall Street Journal* has become the de facto employee newsletter for millions of people. This has less to do with journalistic hustle than it does with the simple fact that corporate secrets are notoriously difficult to safeguard in today's tumultuous environment. With the extensive business coverage across all media these days, few have escaped the overriding message: Organizations are having to contend with extraordinarily difficult decisions about how to survive—let alone prosper—in the very near future. One irony, however, is that leaders often become obsessed with an "enemy within" perspective, withholding key information and limiting critical input from the very sources of past success—the people who work there.

In one sense, it is understandable that a conservative approach to communication would emerge. Never before have the challenges been so stark and clearly threatening. Many in the business community are struggling to discover *what* questions to ask, much less decide *who* to seek out for advice and counsel. What kinds of issues cause these otherwise clear-thinking executives to head for the bunker, where they produce "secrets" that become known only to the immediate world?

CHANGE DECISIONS AND THEIR DRIVERS

In today's organizational arenas, domestic and international, there are strong, turbulent, and disturbingly unpredictable forces that bring leaders to make decisions having dramatic implications for their future. The business press is filled with descriptions of mergers, acquisitions, privatization, downsizing, delayering, decentralization, centralization, divestitures, plant closings, geographic reallocation of resources, technological overhauls, and other equally startling moves. A litany of forces or drivers of change are behind these decisions:

COSTS

The costs of doing business parallel an organization's key assets—technical, financial, and human. For example, the computer industry is witnessing amazing changes in the cost and capacity of microchips. The cost and availability of these items have already resulted in major losses because executives were unable to anticipate their market dynamics. Buying too few retards the capacity to generate revenue; buying too many creates an expensive inventory of components that could be rendered practically worthless in the face of a near-term technical breakthrough.

Financial costs have become a critical concern because of the need to focus on an interwoven network of global economies and their impact on decisions on capital improvements, debt-to-equity ratios, and the capacity to balance short-term demands of the financial marketplace with long-term staying power in terms of market share, even if this means lower return on revenue.

The previous chapter highlighted the impact of demographic changes and the lack of qualified people to handle the future demands of their jobs. Related to this are costs associated with third-party stakeholders who are concerned with other human issues such as reduced tax base for schools, hospitals, and physical infrastructure, environmental impact in areas such as air and water contamination, and the sluggish acknowledgment of the need to accommodate major shifts in life-style requiring assistance in areas such as day care for children, care for elderly parents, portable pensions in the face of economic dislocations, and massive retraining to contend with increased job demand that outstrips the knowledge gained prior to employment. A key point for leaders to consider is how the dissemination or restriction of information can affect the overall costs across these three key assets.

MARKET COMPETITION

One executive summed up his business competition with a military analogy:

> I am fighting World War II and the Vietnam War at the same time. On the one hand, my domestic competitors fight by time-honored rules of combat and we know the location of the battlefield. On the other hand, my foreign competitors play by very different rules, and I never know where the battle—or skirmish— will be fought. They require less capital investment, can move more adroitly in the market, and can niche me to death in selected high-margin product areas because they don't plan on offering broad product selection until they establish a beachhead.

The key to much of this is for businesses to take a cold, hard look at themselves and ask: What business am I in? Would I do this again if I had the opportunity? Am I cognizant of other alternatives? For example, a manufacturer of drills may not realize it is really in the business of selling "holes"— customers may not care if these holes are created by steel bits, laser beams, or bioengineered organisms that secrete a substance-dissolving acid.

Although there is evidence to support the claim that businesses who build consensus around an overarching vision or mission are more profitable than those who do not, a great many leaders have yet to tap into this resource.[1] As one executive in a Detroit automobile firm put it: "The trouble is that you have the Japanese executives and the Japanese workers against the American executives—something is missing from this equation!" Managers appear to still have great difficulty handling the input from within their organizations and the potential turbulence that is likely to follow.

MARKET SHARE

This issue may prove to be one of the key pivotal points in the global market. GE's Jack Welch has stated that his organization will be the "number 1 or 2" player in markets in which it competes. However, market share—like employee loyalty—is not something you own. At best, it must be earned, and its temporariness causes some to see it as only able to be "leased." For example, GE has sold off many businesses based, in part, on a rule of thumb that their return on sales (ROS) had fallen below 6 percent. Japanese and European businesses frequently operate with ROS expectations of 4 percent or less. These competitors take a longer term view of market share and will sacrifice profitability to protect it. Recent examples have been the modest increase in the cost of Japanese imports despite the significant drop in the value of the U.S. dollar against the Japanese yen. To compensate, Japanese firms have worked at increasing efficiency and product quality. This market share strategy appears to have worked well—witness the cost of a Honda Accord at approximately $5,000 in 1976 versus $16,000 ten years later. This shift parallels a product-line change that is continuing to aim at the more profitable luxury car market after establishing a customer base well acquainted with the company's dedication to quality, innovation, and dependability.

The fundamental issue facing U.S. businesses in this area is what degree of flexibility they have with regard to the trade-off between market share and short-term profitability. This is sometimes referred to as a "Main Street versus Wall Street" debate because financial analysts continue to promote stocks that pay high quarterly dividends over those that pay little or no dividend but, instead, reinvest for future growth. The U.S. government plays a role here as well because of tax laws that do not reward companies for making longer term capital investments, continued double taxation on corporate profits, and increased capital gains tax rates. This last point is interesting because it seems to operate on an assumption that capital is a stationary target. The logic appears to go something like this: Wealthy people will allow their gains to be taxed at whatever rates the government dictates, without ever considering alternative ways of protecting their money. Of course this is ludicrous, and such a "soak-the-rich" strategy merely serves as an incentive for people to pursue investments that minimize the tax bite and—unfortunately—results in less of their money being used to create jobs.

Market flexibility requires that businesses be able to identify a clear set of widely accepted objectives, continuously communicate them, and reinforce the kind of support needed to reach them. The principal factor in gaining wide support will be the degree to which people feel a sense of ownership and control over both the formulation and the execution of these objectives.

DISASTERS

There is a long list of calamities that can occur within the business world. The collapse of many U.S. savings and loan institutions is a recent example of the crushing effects of financial mismanagement, akin to bankruptcy in nonfinancial entities. But natural disasters like fire, flood, explosions, earthquakes, and tornadoes can cause an abrupt cessation of operations as well. Unfortunately, there is a growing awareness of another form of disaster that is proving to be one of the most insidious: terrorism. Recently the world witnessed the economic reaction to the call for execution of an author whose work was judged to give blasphemous treatment of a major religion. In a matter of days numerous governments had banned the work, and U.S. bookstores had either removed it from their shelves or were "taking precautions." The bombing of civilian aircraft, shopping areas, subway stations, airport terminals, and embassies, along with random shootings of innocent people, is casting a pall over all forms of life and making organizations look for new ways to continue to do business under such conditions.

Too often one discovers either that businesses have not developed contingency plans for disasters or else that such plans as exist have been developed with insufficient input from people close to the day-to-day operation of the business. In this latter case, the plans that result can be tragically narrow and practically useless in the face of disaster. A sad truism appears to be that such plans are always criticized with hindsight by those who could have improved them but were never asked.

LOSS OF BUSINESS

Alvin Toffler's book *The Third Wave* depicts the shift from an agrarian-based economy to an industrial-based economy to a information- and service-based economy as representing three "waves." Toffler describes these waves as overlapping versus being laid out in series. Therefore, at the point of overlap, one can find evidence of thriving segments of one wave coexisting with emerging segments of the other.[2] This overlap can result in some seriocomic events and interpretations of events. In 1900, for example, about 4,000 automobiles were produced. Twice that many people showed up at the New York auto show that year, arriving in horse-drawn buggies and on bicycles—10 million bicycles were in use at that time. The audience found the gasoline automobiles less preferable than those powered by electricity or steam. Buggy-whip manufacturers were probably reassured by the judgment made in the November 10, 1900, edition of *Automobile Topics*: "The horse will continue indispensable for a long time to come."

Technological change has brought about other dramatic shifts in consumer preferences. Examples such as slide rules and mechanical rotary calculators being sidetracked by cheap solar-powered credit-card-sized devices, and message delivery services decimated by facsimile machines come to mind.

Societal standards and mores can have an equally devastating impact. The fashion industry is a prime example of how important it is to time the introduction of items carefully, given the transitory nature of the market and its whims. Of course, legislated impact is another that can have a devastating impact on business. Certified financial planners were doing a land-office business in Individual Retirement Accounts and income tax shelters throughout most of the 1980s until the government removed most of the incentives for this type of activity from individual taxpayers. A dramatic slide in both areas resulted almost immediately.

One point here is worth emphasizing. The distinction between *decline* and *disaster* often gets lost. A loss of business may signal a need to shore up a core product line and exit areas that *are* less profitable or are beyond the organization's ability to manage them profitably. This loss may also be somewhat transitional and cyclical, indicating that changes made need not be viewed as irrevocable—that few are is a point not lost on people who have been through this experience more than once. This point was driven home to a young strategic planner who eschewed contact with the top-level managers at the manufacturing plants because he doubted their quantitative analysis skills. After being persuaded to attend an annual plant manager meeting and listen to them discuss how their businesses could compete more effectively, the planner observed, "These guys are really much sharper than I realized. We use a lot of different terms and I can see that they don't crunch a lot of numbers, but we seem to end up at the same point—they seem to have gotten there a lot faster!" This is just a small example of the schism that can be established on the basis of stereotypes. Naturally, the decisions related to communication and soliciting input track right along with these biases.

I would like to add one more category that doesn't fit as well with the others but seems to be a theme of much business literature. Somehow, amid all this chaos, there are supposed to be those intrepid individuals who might be characterized as ships' captains who steer from atop the crow's nest. Their view of things to come cannot be turned to their advantage unless they can convince the hands below that they aren't hallucinating. The exchange might go something like this:

Captain: Look out for the rocks!

Crew: What rocks?

Captain: Look out for the reef!

Crew: What reef?

These heroic figures I like to call Philosopher Kings because they are often characterized as living in a different cosmic plane, able to remove themselves from, if not actually predict, the Sturm und Drang of the fray, and to make dispassionate, brilliant, and prescient business decisions.

PHILOSOPHER KINGS

A simple-minded definition of a Philosopher King would be a leader who fixes things that ain't broken. This is obviously not a common situation. In fact, a senior executive once told me, "Your vision is never clearer than when you are standing on the gallows." It is easy to develop a jaded perspective when it comes to what ultimately drives business leaders to make direction-changing decisions. Daniel Isenberg, after observing senior managers and their decision-making processes, drew the conclusion quoted at the beginning of this chapter. The point is that some dramatic event or revelation usually seems to be necessary before organizations are able to effect significant change.

The biology class example of the "boiled frog" serves to describe this issue.[3] The frog will adjust its body temperature to that of surrounding water, even to the point of ultimately being boiled to death—provided the change is gradual. Organizations make similar adjustments, until they lose their ability to be adaptive,[4] unless some ruinous event takes place that sweeps away all the pretense and commands the organization's managers to act precipitously to survive.

Given all this, where are the Philosopher Kings? A consultant was describing two organizations that had contacted him for advice. One was headed by a new president who was concerned about the disunity among his key executives. These managers seemed more interested in promoting their individual business unit interests than in looking at the total business from new strategic perspectives. The business was a leader in its market, highly profitable, and suffering from what has been described as "organizational arteriosclerosis"—a hardening of the policies. The other business was in serious financial trouble, facing a window of 12 to 18 months to put its house in order or else go out of business. The entire management team had decided to seek out expert help to reexamine their strategic position and explore any uncovered ground. The consultant said he always preferred the latter group because he knew that they were more interested in the future than in protecting the past. In the first group, he would find himself being asked to present his credentials in order to guarantee his pedigree, as opposed to being judged by his track record. No matter how close his past experiences were to the current one, this group would staunchly defend the uniqueness of their business and would often dismiss his observations as irrelevant.

The Philosopher King scenario is an unlikely one because the person not only must be a visionary, but also must be able to mobilize a critical mass of influential leaders within the organization who will put aside personal short-term goals for the greater good of the total organization. It must be underscored that the prime impediment facing the Philosopher King is the organization's past history—it is a victim of its own success. Under these conditions, the key executives and quite possibly the board of directors as well will view the urgings of the Philosopher King to create a "vision" shared by top management, or to reexamine organizational philosophy, strategy, structure, reward systems, and market presence, as tantamount to heresy and, at minimum, disrespectful of the rich legacy that had preceded this upstart's tenure.

In fairness, a Philosopher King *could* emerge and, given sufficient leverage, begin to effect significant change. But this is not likely to be a short-term move. To accomplish the task, major human resource systems need to be engaged. A fair assessment of the organization's impediments to change must be followed by the selection and grooming of key players who will support the new direction. More important, the players will have to develop an agreed-upon interdependency that is quite out of character for those who take the Lone Ranger organizational approach typical of U.S. firms. The strategic and structural components must be aligned carefully and, finally, the reward system will have to be retrofitted so as to not reward nonsupportive behavior.[5] The numerous strategies to win the hearts and minds of key players and others include training and development experiences, carefully crafted "events" to symbolize a change in upper-level commitment to change, and careful adherence to performance objectives that serve to support the new direction. All this is predicated upon the willingness of the Philosopher King or the ersatz King to involve key players in the development and execution of the business strategy. This appears to be a major hurdle that so far few have been able to clear, mainly because of the restriction of two-way communication at the top levels in the organization.

Of course, there are many other drivers that lead businesses to make decisions, but the list shown is sufficient to underscore the seriousness of the issues that organizational leaders have to face.[6] A natural response might be to invite the input from a broad array of sources, with particular attention to those with inside knowledge of the business, its heritage, and ideas for the future. Unfortunately, quite a different reaction generally occurs. A sort of circle-the-wagons mentality emerges and the quest for *a* decision that meets a minimal versus a maximal set of criteria begins down a narrow and often hidden path.

A discussion of communication is like a discussion of humor. Once you begin to pick it apart, the absence of context undermines insights to be gained from the exercise. To breathe life into our discussion, let us look at the treatment of information in a real-life change impact situation. It will become clear that the dynamics, if anything, have been understated.

A "SECOND WAVE" EXAMPLE

A concrete example of this approach is provided by Glacier, Inc., a large consumer products business faced with the challenge of reducing its manufacturing sites by 25 percent over a three-year period. An overview of Glacier and its need to manage through several forces of change can help set the stage for discussion of how planning reflects an overall management philosophy.

Glacier is among the oldest and most profitable consumer giants in the United States. It has held more than half the domestic consumer market and one third the domestic commercial market for many years. Its domestic product lines are supported by numerous manufacturing locations and several distribution centers throughout the country. In fact, its stature in the marketplace had been so secure that it began to be concerned with aggressive marketing strategies only in the early 1980s.

As Glacier passed into the late 1970s, it became clear that it had too many production facilities that were using an older, relatively slow and costly 1950s technology. Therefore, the major impetus for a facilities reduction plan came from two directions, cost reduction and the need for advanced technology.

The main criterion used for cost reduction was based on cost per unit produced. The business had always been volume-oriented. There had never been a reduction of wages at Glacier's plants, and the older ones were requiring greater levels of investment. The business was viewed as being in a vulnerable cost position versus its competition. The final picture contained these elements:

- Its labor rates were greater than foreign rates by a factor of 10.

- Overhead costs were excessive by internal standards.

- There was a need to eliminate redundant positions and "recrew" to increase hourly productivity by 50 percent.

The need for advanced technology was supported by data obtained from external consultants who examined Glacier's position versus its competition. It was possible to increase production line speed, but only at the expense of efficiencies. An earlier suggestion to introduce continuous operations into Glacier's processes in the 1960s was revisited. By shifting to the use of integrated groups of production equipment, a more productive operation requiring less floor space was created. However, this grouping had a significant cost basis attached to it. From a technology standpoint, the picture was:

- Production equipment had to be developed that produced 8,000 units per hour on a continuous operating schedule.

- A continuous schedule for Glacier's major assembly plants had to be developed.

- The equipment would require fewer people and newer locations to accommodate the different layouts, thus necessitating the rationalization of older plants and the layoff of excess employees.

As the business contemplated these issues, it was facing two reasonably well defined sets of risks if it went forward with such a program: technical risks and human resource risks. The technical risks included the following:

- The reliability of the production electronics needed was questionable.

- The ability to manufacture more complex consumer units on existing equipment was uncertain.

- The plant reduction program would require the movement of nearly 80 percent of its product lines from "closing" to "receiving" locations.

- Much was riding on high-tech promises (e.g., CAD-CAM).

- Cost estimates for introducing new technology were rough at best.

- Excessive delays could damage Glacier's market position. One of its longtime domestic competitors had exited this business because of a poor market position even though its cost position was reasonable.

The human resource risks were:

- The costs associated with a large reduction of people had previously been considered excessive.

- Issues such as preferential hiring, hourly transfer allowances, and continuous assembly operations were not resolved.

- Company-wide product boycotts were considered possible.

- Work stoppage was also considered as a possible result.

- The corporate image of social responsibility could be damaged.

- Political influence by elected officials could work against the business.

- The business might be viewed as greedy.

- There could be an increase in the unionization of Glacier's plants.

Glacier is considered by many to be a cash cow for its parent corporation. Its product lines represent historically strong income-producing sources that, along with a few other corporate segments in a similar market position, allow the corporation to invest in some high-tech and service-oriented ventures it believes represent a more forward-thinking future.

The management philosophy within Glacier had undergone little change over the years and still retained vestiges of decades past when a paternalistic and predictable environment fostered homogeneity, predictable career paths, and—above all—job security for those willing to live by the rules. These rules, largely unwritten, included some of the following elements:

- Open disagreement over business issues was considered improper, impolite, and probably disloyal.[7]

- The financial picture of the enterprise was kept secret from all but a select few managers at the top of the business.

- The organization's hierarchical structure, multiple fiefdoms of power, emphasis on pedigree over track record in its recruiting process, and unwillingness to confront a changing marketplace and shifting societal expectations helped create a formidable challenge to change.

- The often-heard phrase, "If it ain't broke, don't fix it," underscored much of the sentiment at high managerial levels.

- Philosopher Kings need not apply.

As Glacier became increasingly aware of major influences that would ultimately force it to reduce its production facilities drastically and lay off a large number of employees for the first time in its history, another confrontation was also in the wings: confronting its own management style and the impact this would have on both the planning and the execution of this program. Yet, by most standards, this was a very successful business, and it could be argued—indeed, it *was* argued—that such historic success underscored the need to protect the status quo.

AN ANCIENT LEGACY

Such logic was to be expected because it reflected both the current economic hubris and something deeper that formed the basis of Glacier's paternalistic approach to its employees. This we-versus-they attitude has its own roots in antiquity; it can literally be traced back to some of the earliest efforts to harness the efforts of people in collective settings. The view of labor as a contemptible activity has its origins in the practice of slavery and was certainly true among the Greeks and Romans. Further, the warriors of the Gothic tribes viewed with disdain those who drew sustenance from the soil versus the spoils of battle. Interestingly enough, even nineteenth-century U.S. history contained derisive references to "sod-busters." Introspection and nonsecular meditation were more common than actual labor among various religious sects. Shoshana Zuboff sums this up in her book, *In the Age of the Smart Machine*:

> Labor came to humanity with the fall from grace and was at best a penitential sacrifice enabling purity through humiliation. Labor was toil, distress, trouble, fatigue—an exertion both painful and compulsory. Labor was our animal condition, struggling to survive in dirt and darkness.[8]

This struggle was often captured in the types of agreements drawn up between workers and owners. Indentured servants, serfs, apprentices, and clerks were among the positions that began to be described in what became the basis for today's body of labor law. In fact, U.S. labor law makes numerous assumptions about the adversarial interests of labor and management. Some of the more anachronistic of these assumptions occasionally surface as potential impediments to more enlightened management practices involving bilateral decision making in the work setting.[9]

THE MUSHROOM THEORY

The situation facing the business under discussion required open discussion of issues that heretofore had been kept within a relatively tight circle of managers. For most of Glacier's long history, its actual financial results were not shared with its employees. As recent as the early 1980s, the financial department went to great lengths to see to it that discussions of profitability and trends were tightly controlled. Managers at high levels were allowed to show transparencies of financial results only to other high-level employees, but note-taking was discouraged and no copies of the transparencies were distributed. Only a handful of stalwart managers violated this custom. Those who did so justified their actions by claiming that "people need to know how the business is doing if we expect them to respond to our own concerns." Employees shared a sort of dark humor around this. As the saying went, "They treat us all like mushrooms around here—keep us in the dark and feed us manure."

The irony of these precautions emerged in a conversation with the head of a firm often retained to conduct legal espionage—to gather data about business competitors. This manager indicated that the most reliable and accessible source of information usually was the top managers of a business. In the case of Glacier, it was often said that all the efforts at secrecy resulted in making sure that only its top managers (and its competitors) knew what the business was doing. Its employees were kept ignorant. Even when this began to change somewhat, concern over the impact of leaks was a major consideration influencing the planning of the production and distribution reduction activity. In a risk analysis anticipating possible outcomes at affected locations, the business communication planning team came up with the following concerns:

- Unions organize plants.

- Strike occurs.

- Work slowdown, sabotage.

- Informational pickets or other picketing occurs.

- International interference occurs among major unions.

- Customers are concerned.

- Union resists:
    – NLRB charges
    –Court action
    –Arbitration

- Skilled/salaried employees leave.

- Union/employees object to not following reduction in force procedure during an extended phase-down to close.

- A major news leak occurs prior to announcement.

- Exempt employees request for transfer.

- They seek minority action group intervention.

- Nonexempt request for transfer or mass external exodus occurs.

- A local government, community, or state outcry arises over job and income loss.

- Proprietary information is stolen.

- Local/state legislation to block plant closing is introduced.

- Key legislators/community leaders not available for briefings.

- Local TV station wants to film inside a plant.

- National news organization contacts plant manager directly.

- Media crew interviews employees outside gate or on property.

- Employee group/community offer to buy plant.

- National union(s) organize boycott of Glacier products.

- Employees acquire sensitive material and reveal it to media.

- Employees accelerate Workmen's Compensation claims.

- Employees delay retirements to wait for closing benefits.

- Business accelerates prior to announcement or prior to transfer of work/people.

- Employees write letters to chief executive officer (CEO) or head of Glacier.

A PLAN IN THE DARK

It is useful to examine closely the planning around communication because it reflects the overall mind set existing at the time of this event. The main body of the communication planning team consisted of human resource managers. It should be noted that *no* managers from the locations being closed or those scheduled to receive people, product lines, or equipment were represented at these meetings. In fact, one of the general managers responsible for the majority of affected locations attempted to include representatives from these locations in the actual planning of the movement of people, product, and equipment from closing to receiving plants. He was severely criticized for this breach of security, and the process continued without the input from the operational managers who would ultimately carry out the decision. As will be pointed out later, this resulted in a number of negative outcomes from both a cost and a morale standpoint among those left out of the planning stage.

A special location was designated as a sort of "war room," which was kept locked when not in use by the team. To prepare for the task, the team was trained to use a specialized version of brainstorming called "storyboarding." This process uses a variety of cards that are pinned to walls to help present various group-produced ideas. The object was to use a process that relied heavily on a dynamic visual display of ideas to allow a maximum of group interaction without stifling dissent or discouraging creative ideas from surfacing. The group agreed to the following objectives:

- Provide a timely plant-closing announcement.

- Be sufficiently comprehensive so as to minimize the probability of an economic backlash.

- Develop material in a low-profile atmosphere to minimize leaks that could jeopardize the overall plant-closing goals.

Over a period of several months, the team met to explore numerous communication avenues that would have to be traveled and assigned specific communication responsibilities to members of the team. This led to several products reflecting the group's judgment of the breadth of communication required for the successful introduction of the plant-closing program. The actual product that emerged from the planning was quite impressive and serves as a useful model to review:

Media Relations

- Holding statement

- Rationale/overview for press kit

- Media list/national release:
    - *Wall Street Journal*
    - *UPI/AP*
    - *BusinessWeek*
    - *New York Times*

-*USA Today*
-Local television stations
-Local newspapers

- Business fact sheet for press kit

- Media list/local releases (closing locations)

- Media list/local releases (receiving locations)

- Employee benefits summary for press kit:
    -Minimum six months closing notice
    -Guarantee of pay rate for 26 months for employees who
      transfer as a result of the plant closing
    -Lump sum payment details
    -Lump sum alternatives
    -Employment assistance program: Job placement assistance was
      designed to provide job counseling, job information services, job-
      search counseling, and other related skills.
    -Continued life insurance details
    -Pension plan options

- Spokespersons for national news forums

- Media relations suggestions/ questions and answers

Government and Community Relations

- Plants affected

- Government/community contacts

- Briefing scripts

- Local tax loss impact

- Material unique to each affected location:
    -Spokespersons
    -History/program overview
    -Summary statistics of affected employees
    -Local government/community contacts

- EEO employment impact

- Corporate "800" number to call for further details

Employee Communications

- Generic script

- Middle-level management meeting

- Plant and human resource managers' meeting: This was a two-and-a-half day meeting held approximately one week prior to the closing announcement. It covered the plant-closing program overview, benefits information, and workshops on how to handle media relations.

- Human resource managers' meeting: Following the announcement, a workshop was conducted for human resource managers. The topics covered:

    –Benefits counseling training
    –Identification of communications needs
    –Identification of needed resources
    –Benefits slide tape
    –Marketing/sales communications
    –Postannouncement communications
    –Employee inquiry response
    –Business videotapes
    –Feedback systems
    –Telephone hotline information
    –Generic questions and answers
    –Syndicated news article
    –Benefits counseling plan
    –Script for a major union local meeting

Employment Assistance Programs

The following list covers the major forms of assistance offered:

- Title III outplacement/retraining model

- Job Training Partnership Act—Title III

- Trauma counseling services

- Outplacement services

- Training/retraining program

- Training/retraining needs in the 1980s

- Title III training locations

Chapter 4 will provide details on the specific programs listed here and others that evolved throughout the closing program. As can be seen, the list of communication products is extensive and was a major factor in allowing Glacier to communicate this program without creating negative reactions or panic among those affected. There are, however, some issues that received heated discussion among those affected at the plant management level.

ISSUES BASED ON LACK OF INVOLVEMENT

These issues included observations that the overriding concern for preventing leaks and effecting a manageable reaction to the closing announcement ignored at least three major issues that followed the announcement itself: avoidable transition costs, inability to respond to employee requests for information, and a perceived lack of trust of the plant management teams.

AVOIDABLE TRANSITION COSTS

At first glance, it seems nonsensical to delay discussing the redistribution of such a massive amount of people, product, and equipment with the managers responsible for making it happen. The justification given for this approach was that leaks would jeopardize the program's likelihood of being executed. Impediments could come from the media, unions, civic leaders, elected officials, or others. In fact, the concern for subsequent execution of the program itself was indeed secondary. This resulted in numerous costs that the plant management teams believed were largely avoidable.

The movement of equipment required cooperation and planning among several geographically dispersed locations. A closing plant would have to meet its production schedule *and* ensure a sufficient backlog of high-quality inventory to cover its upcoming downtime when equipment was inoperable *and* meet a shutdown schedule that might or might not be in the best interest of the plants receiving its people, product, and equipment. The lack of early involvement made it difficult to capture information soon enough to support the physical transfer of equipment and ensure its successful operation at distant sites:

- Purchasing agreements needed to be drawn up with vendors who could supply raw materials at the new location.

- Wiring diagrams for 30-year-old equipment were either nonexistent or else did not reflect modifications made over the years.

- Operating procedures existed largely in the heads of employees being terminated. Either they had to train their replacements, or else some other means (e.g., videotape, production of technical manuals) had to be found to help the new location get the equipment running appropriately.

- At some locations, a major problem was the lack of long-term production schedules and therefore of any forecast that went beyond 30 to 60 days.

One plant manager summed up his frustrations over the timing of moves and its impact both on how his numbers would look and on the ultimate quality of the product being produced:

> We'll go out looking terrible. They took out the high-volume, low-shrinkage stuff first! I resent working at a place that has been written off at home office.

INSUFFICIENT INFORMATION FOR EMPLOYEES

The assumption that a brief meeting a few days before the plant-closing announcement would suffice to explain the employee benefits available proved to be far from the mark. Plant management teams complained bitterly about the lack of preparation they had been given, the lack of responsiveness from headquarters to their requests for information, the inaccuracy of the information received, and the unresolved policy issues that immediately served to impede the overall process. Such policies pertained to issues like the company's willingness to cover the cost of transferring hourly employees' household goods to a new location, or whether nonexempt employees were to be allowed to bid on jobs at a different location.

Perhaps the weakest link was the inability to answer questions about employee benefits. Part of the reason for this was the organizational separation of responsibility for handling these matters. The finance and human resource organizations were jointly responsible, and communication between them had never been stellar. Now such flaws were under a glaring spotlight.

A second issue for closing locations was the scheduling of employee support activities without due consideration for the production schedule.

The management at the plant saw this as yet another example of their not being allowed to provide timely input.

A LOSS OF TRUST

At a personal level, many seasoned plant managers felt betrayed by Glacier. This was not just a business decision to them. It was more like a family catastrophe—a death or a divorce—that had been kept from them. And it was kept from them, they believed, because they were not viewed as trustworthy to handle the information properly. A common postannouncement response was, "I wonder what *else* they aren't telling me." These were people with long service, following even longer service by family members over the years. Their identity with Glacier went far beyond economic support, and many of them had made sacrifices for the company without request and without the expectation of acknowledgment.

It would not be an overstatement to say that the success of many of Glacier's plants over the years was attributable as much to the dedication of the people employed there as to the technical improvements made through capital investments. These managers who had made such deep commitment were stunned to find themselves treated as outsiders and frustrated at the lack of hope offered to them for the future. In nearly all cases, to present to the media an image of fairness, these managers were treated as though they had been hired yesterday—no future employment offers were made. Further, these managers were restricted from seeking openings at other locations.

DEBUNKING THE "LEAK" MYTHS

This is a troublesome area. Under certain business conditions, the hoarding of information can be seen as prudent. Giving away trade secrets or communicating strategic plans for the future could be the equivalent of economic suicide. Informing plant managers in advance that their location would be closed could also be seen as risky. In the absence of facts, such assumptions go unchallenged and wind up being woven into the fabric of policy and myth that combine to influence such decisions without serious debate.

Here are some myths about leaked information that guided the plant closing activity:

- If the plant management teams were informed in advance, they would leak the information to others.

- Leaked information would prove damaging to the plant-closing program.

- Managers above the plant management level will not leak information.

- No one except those receiving explicit communications about the plant closing will know what is coming.

Now let's look at some actual events that serve as counterpoints to each of these myths.

PLANT TEAMS WOULD LEAK INFORMATION

All of the top-level plant managers were brought together to hear the announcement of the closing approximately one week prior to the general communication. They were instructed not to reveal their direct reports until the day of the general announcement. All did this—except one, who chose to take his staff into his confidence. When asked later about this, he said,

> It was just ridiculous to turn my back on a team of professionals I would need to help me close this place over a two-year period. By giving them as much notice as possible, I wanted to send them a signal that they were trusted, needed, and special.

Follow-up conversations with this manager's staff supported his point. The staff believed their early involvement helped them prepare themselves psychologically for handling the emotional surge that came on the day of the general announcement. They served as a support group for one another and were given enough time to decide collectively that they could manage through this.

Information about this plant's closing *was* leaked, and state officials were made aware of it. An investigation of the source of the information was conducted immediately. As might be predicted, the plant management team was suspected and the decision by the top-level manager was severely criticized. However, subsequent investigation found that the source of the information was a manager at another plant, a manager who had since left the company.

This is an important point. An *entire* team of managers was given advance notice that their plant was to close, *and* no one was offered any future job opportunities. In the face of this, not one person communicated this information to anyone outside the team. For those who opposed the top-level manager's decision to share the information, the leak was viewed as vindication of their position. After the source was traced to someone outside the team, the opponents responded that this was just an unusual situation. Thus does the myth live on.

LEAKED INFORMATION WOULD DAMAGE PLANS

The information that did leak out at this location was contained, and the overall damage was considered slight. This was not the case at a second plant, which was located in a small rural town and was both a primary source of employment and a large contributor to the local economy—not to mention the tax base. Here, when rumors began to spread about the closing of the location, a delegation of town representatives traveled to the corporate head-quarters to discuss the rumor with key executives.

When the group of representatives had the rumor confirmed by corporate officials, they expressed disapproval. The representatives then began a series of contacts to open negotiations with the company with the aim of either keeping the plant open or seeking alternatives, including leasing the plant to another business. The result was the decision to "give" the physical location to the city, in effect, so it could be used by the city as an inducement for future business opportunities.

Again, the information *was* leaked, and external stakeholders in a position to impede the closing decision were involved. Yet, the closing took place as scheduled. The net results were stepped up local efforts to get job offers for the employees at remaining businesses and the ultimate disposition of the plant facility in a manner agreed to by all parties. Those promoting this particular myth were appalled at the openness of the communication and remained convinced that the business was lucky that things didn't turn out worse. And so the myth lives on.

ONLY EXECUTIVES CAN BE TRUSTED WITH CONFIDENTIAL INFORMATION

The last plant leak came from corporate executives themselves! It was so simple that it seemed to defy logic. Anyone who has ever worked at a pro-duction plant is aware of the raft of rumors that are part of the daily routine. A primary topic is always the anticipated demise of the place. Within Glacier's plants were numerous informal networks, with "nodes" planted deep within the total organizational structure. To check out rumors, a few strategically placed phone calls usually did the trick. In this case, it took only one call to corporate headquarters for the plant-closing rumor to become fact.

The other source of information came from competitors who had been monitoring the marketplace and found that there was an inexplicable shift in the distribution of raw materials. They learned this because they were also "customers" for some of this material on occasion. When they asked why the change was occurring, their "suppliers" told them.

The leak police ground their teeth over this and stood ready to amend the myth to read, "No one but me can be trusted."

NO ONE WILL KNOW UNTIL WE WANT THEM TO KNOW

Corporate secrets—the ultimate oxymoron. In the case of Glacier, the assumption that only the movers and shakers know what's happening proved to be ludicrous. Here is an abbreviated list of sources who knew that a major downsizing was in the planning stage:

- The nonexempt clerks who handled the invoices for raw material orders

- The dock workers who oversaw the physical movement of finished products to the warehouse or to distribution points

- The secretaries who typed, read, or filed every piece of correspondence between the plant and headquarters

- The service businesses (e.g., janitorial, refuse) whose contracts had to be renewed

- The competitors who monitored the marketing, sales, and distribution activities of the business

This is quite likely only the proverbial tip of the iceberg, but it does serve as a reminder of just how conspicuous this carefully cloaked activity was to all these people. There is a lesson here for all those executives huddled in their war rooms, deluded into believing that their decisions can be "stealthed" from those on the outside.

SUMMARY

This chapter has first looked at what sort of pressures lead up to the organizational practice of information gatekeeping. These include costs, market competition, market share, disasters, loss of business, and the improbable occurrence of Philosopher Kings who fix things that ain't broke.

An example of a business, Glacier, Inc., facing a major downsizing decision was used to show how communication and planning were handled. The positive side of the "products" was contrasted with the negative effects of withholding information from key implementers of the decision to close plants. This logic was traced to historic examples of how the labor side of an enterprise has been held in various forms of contempt for centuries.

Finally, an examination of a series of myths used to justify hoarding of information included counterarguments based on actual events. This final point shows that the lack of involvement actually creates bigger problems for the business than do the leaks of information about the secrets—that really aren't.

Notes

1. John A. Pearce II and Fred David discuss their research in support of the belief that investing in the development of mission statements is related to a business's subsequent superior economic performance. *Academy of Management EXECU-TIVE*, May 1987, pp. 109-116.

2. I was struck by Alvin Toffler's position in *The Third Wave* (New York: Telecom Library, 1980) that the most dangerous time is during the point of overlap between waves. There we find people struggling to preserve the order of the older wave, insurrectionists attempting to establish the new one, or confused people whose behavior essentially cancels out both efforts. Upon reflection I believe that much of the content of my own work is drawn from observations of this struggle, as well as from my experiences within it. The rulers of the dying wave play pivotal roles in impeding business change required for survival in the emerging one.

3. I can't remember the first time Noel Tichy described the "boiled frog" metaphor, but I have always found it useful and have found that managers readily identify with the underlying message. Noel makes reference to the frog's plight in a recent book he co-authored with Mary Anne Devanna, *The Transformational Leader* (New York: Wiley, 1986).

4. Robert D. Gilbreath, in *Forward Thinking* (New York: McGraw-Hill, 1987), underscores the point that organizations strive to adapt to their environment and, in fact, can trace their success to the efficiencies associated with such a process. Unfortunately, they pay the price in terms of their ability to be adaptive to changes in this environment. Gilbreath goes on to say that such organizations lose their

immunity to the impact of change by striving for what they regard as optimal adapted solutions.

5. This notion of deliberately crafting a systems-oriented change is very appealing to me. Much of my thinking along these lines was influenced by Ralph Kilmann's book *Beyond the Quick Fix* (San Francisco: Jossey-Bass, 1984), and by Noel Tichy's work cited in note 3. In both cases, the authors provide specific examples of how organizations will have to expand their change process to include numerous stakeholders and several interlocking systems affecting their business in order to make any changes really stick.

6. Michael E. Porter and Victor E. Millar, in "Five Forces Model," *Harvard Business Review*, July–August 1985, pp. 149–160, describe various influences felt by a business in its competitive environment. These include: (1) threat of new entrants, (2) bargaining power of suppliers, (3) bargaining power of buyers, (4) threat of substitute products or services, and (5) rivalry among existing competitors. While I concur with these categories, I find the lack of specific reference to political influence somewhat troubling.

7. I remember being frustrated and disgusted by this at the time. I wondered if what I was seeing was anomalous, but I have come to learn that such behavior is much more common than I realized. In his book *Managing on the Edge* (New York: Simon and Schuster, 1990), Richard Pascale highlights several examples of this across well-known companies. He concludes that internal debate is often taken as a sign of organizational ill health. Taken further, he believes that constructive conflict yields many benefits to an organization. It fuels the engine of enquiry. That is, asking questions not only generates answers, but also reveals possibilities not previously considered. In direct line with the concept held by the present book— managing within change—the organization that encourages internal variety has a much better chance of coping with external change drivers.

8. I have found Zuboff's work very impressive in this area. Although the overall thrust of her material is aimed at the impact of technology per se, her well-developed backdrop of management history and the detailed examination of the distinction between managers as "brain" and employees as "body" is superb.

9. Jane Hass Philbrick and Masha E. Hass, in the *Academy of Management EXECU-TIVE*, November 1988, pp. 325–330, examine the statutory and case law related to employee committees. Their examination points out significant legal barriers to allowing the collective input of employees. They conclude that a reasonable interpretation of sections from the National Labor Relations Act supports the position that the use of employee involvement, where people are allowed to contend with issues reserved for management, constitutes an unfair labor practice and is prohibited.

Chapter 3

THE PARADIGM SHIFTS INTO TURBODRIVE

This is like a military tactical retreat. They seem to be saying, "Here's 20 clips of ammo—good luck!"
   —Plant Manager

It took me a long time to get here and now they want to take it all away. I've paid my dues and played by the rules. Took all their crap and kept my mouth shut. When others wouldn't put out extra effort or stay late or volunteer for overtime, I did. And I watched my manager to see how it's done. And, by God, I'm doing just what he did—maybe even better. Nobody ever asked my opinion or gave a damn about my feelings. I'm the first one in my family to wear a necktie to work and not come home dirty. My family is proud and I guess I am too—or was. Now they tell me I gotta "involve" everyone and be more of a "coach" than a boss. They're even training my people better than they trained me—to do stuff that I'm supposed to do. If they're serious about it, why does all this participation stuff seem to end just above me? Man, they just changed all the damn rules and I hate it.
   —Production Foreman

To cope with life, people carry around in their heads a set of rules or models that help them maneuver through the various minefields they encounter. But what happens when these tribal instincts simply are wrong? Today's managers are facing just such a calamity. Modifying behavior is nothing compared with trying to change someone's fundamental beliefs, and nothing short of that is what managers will have to do to survive the coming impact of change on them and their organizations. We begin by looking at the enormity of the challenge and how managers have dealt with it.

In Chapter 2, Glacier, Inc., was seen struggling to protect the status quo amid the turmoil of a significant organizational change. Its planning process reflected the overall management mind set at the time. The time frame, the mid-1980s, occurred when many business leaders, as well as thought leaders in management literature, began to describe an overarching change in the basic philosophy of how to manage successfully in the turbulent times ahead. A phrase that came to describe this movement was paradigm shift.

What *is* a paradigm? One top-level manager asked this recently, reminding me that it is used too often without any commonplace reference. It has become a shorthand change label whose limits are beyond the scope of casual discussion. It is fair to consider a paradigm a kind of model, ideal, outline, or prototype. I like to think of it as a mirror that reflects not only what is and what should be, but perhaps what already has happened while everyone was too busy to notice. A paradigm shift, then, is nothing short of changing an organization's entire way of being.[1]

AGING REVOLUTIONARIES

In the businesses I visit, I am constantly confronted with a mind-numbing array of policies and regulations shoring up an archaic status quo that often has all but lost its primary reason for existence. Instead, it survives only to survive—thus sustaining those who cling tenaciously to the ancient rules, roles, and beliefs they treat as some sort of inviolate religious truth. Ironically, these same people often played a part in changing these same rules, roles, and beliefs earlier in their careers. Either they have forgotten, or else they have convinced themselves that the change they brought about will endure for all time—or for as long as *they* continue to hold their positions. As one manager put it, "They'll never get me."

A paradigm shift is not something bloodless that can be discussed rationally, after which everyone says, collectively, "Oh, I see now. That makes perfect sense. I'll change the way I am behaving immediately." No, this one is here for the long haul. Some years ago I wrote:

> [T]here exists today an historic and slowly diminishing conflict in most organizations. Those responsible for managing organizations would have other members—the employees—become more closely aligned with the organization's purpose, products, and services. They believe that others do not appreciate the "big picture" of the work to be done. These other members view their membership as but a part of a larger scene, a scene encompassing all life activities. Unlike these other activities, however, those related to work appear largely outside one's personal control. We are witnessing a fundamental change in the way employees view the legitimacy of having greater influence over their work lives. Conflict arises when management resists relinquishing what it views as its traditional decision-making prerequisites, while other employees (including other managers) insist that further commitment on their part should be exchanged for a relaxation of these prerequisites.[2]

The shift from a decentralized First Wave agricultural-based society to a centralized Second Wave industrial-based society was predictable and justifiable. Putting the genie back in the bottle is proving to be very difficult as we move into a Third Wave service- and information-based society with the technological capacity to once again decentralize much of the day-to-day decision making.

FROM THE STREET TO THE SUITE

Toffler cites numerous examples of how the members of a Third Wave society, based on information and service, are seeking ways to take more control over their lives.[3] However, much of this thinking is predated by at least a decade in David Riesman's book, *The Lonely Crowd*.[4] In this work, talking about the troublesome transition from an industrial to a postindustrial society, he states, "Problems arise when a society becomes psychologically post-industrial long before the economic infrastructure is sound enough to bear the weight of steadily rising expectations." Herein lies what I believe is the crucible of the paradigm shift—a belief that the "what's in it for me?" equation needs to be revisited. Daniel Yankelovich pursues this further:

> Throughout most of this century, Americans believed that self-denial made sense, sacrifice made sense, obeying the rules made sense, subordinating the self to the institution made sense. But doubts have set in, and Americans now believe that the old giving/getting compact needlessly restricts the individual while advancing the power of large institutions—government and business particularly—who use the power to enhance their own interests at the expense of the public.[5]

The irony of denying employees a voice in work-related decision making within the boundaries of one of the world's premier democracies has not been lost on either participants or observers. For decades, management literature has challenged businesses to address this disparity, but the forces for change were relatively weak. Today their combined effect can no longer be ignored. But history—and the marketplace—will treat businesses harshly for their delayed response to the changes around them.[6]

A TAYLORED SUIT FOR THE MINDLESS

The credit for laying the groundwork for today's typical control-oriented management approach often is given to Frederick Winslow Taylor.[7] Taylor's stated goals and apparent motives stand in stark contrast to the legacy left behind by those who have performed work in his name. He wanted to reduce the burden of the laborer, create more efficient ways of performing tasks, introduce enlightened compensation schemes to reward increased production, and help forge a bond of unified purpose between those who worked and those who managed.

Taylor acquired a cultlike following that transcended politics. Even Lenin became a believer in such standardization. But almost from the start, these lofty goals were tarnished by the not-so-enlightened words of Taylor and his followers. These give insights into how the person doing the actual work was viewed. One engineer was quoted as saying that "the laborer has only to follow direction. He need not stop to think what his past experience in similar cases has been." Taylor's own words give one pause for their evidence of how individuality was regarded: "I can say without the slightest hesitation that the science of handling pig-iron is so great that the man who is fit to handle pig-iron and is sufficiently phlegmatic and stupid to choose this for his occupation is rarely able to comprehend the science of handling pig-iron."

A basic tenet of "Taylorism" was that careful analysis of work performed would help break it down into its essential elements. By simultaneously retaining only the most efficient steps and enforcing strict adherence to such a process, productivity was certain to increase. The first part was relatively easy to pull off, but the second was another matter entirely. From the start, people were regarded as both a source of labor *and* a source of inefficiency. For example, insights gained from experience, far from being viewed as a boon, were prime targets for removal. Having dismissed the worker's "mind," it now became necessary to control the "body." There followed a rigid code of instruction and behavior to be obeyed in order to take advantage of all the altered work steps based on "scientific research." Individuality, creativity, and innovation were systematically removed from the work setting. The key objective was to keep people from straying from their assigned tasks and the prescribed methods of performing them.

The ubiquitous clipboard and stopwatch of the efficiency experts could be found around the world in all types of organizations. Top management's contribution was in the construction of an infrastructure to support the direction of Taylor's work. "To monitor and control effort of this assumed caliber, management organized its own responsibilities into a hierarchy of specialized roles buttressed by a top-down allocation of authority and by status symbols attached to positions in the hierarchy."[8]

Complementary philosophies predating Taylor can be found in the history of military and religious organizations. This notion of a straightforward rational approach is still a persuasive elixir. Although much of the management literature of the 1950s and 1960s called for more enlightened forms of management, the core of industrial engineering practiced in some of today's leading industries continues to perpetuate Taylor's "scientific method."

If one accepts the argument that the control-oriented paradigm that emerged from the work of Taylor fit the existing business and social conditions of the time, a change in conditions should be associated with a shift in paradigms. Four major factors are currently influencing such a shift:

- International competition has made it imperative that U.S. businesses organize and manage their people to gain greater efficiencies that can have bottom-line impact in the marketplace.

- Whereas in the world of Taylor, the atomization of the work could be justified because of the relative lack of need for specialized knowledge, the U.S. economy is now making a transition to the Third Wave of service and information. People need to think for themselves, make decisions, and diagnose problems in ways once reserved for managers.

- The work force is changing. Workers are better educated, have increased expectations of using their education at work, and are expressing ambivalence about authority itself—they don't revere it and don't particularly aspire to it.

- The most recent precedents to democracy in the workplace came in the consumer movement of the 1960s and 1970s, when people began to see that the rights of the individual needed further protection. Subsequent legislation has been enacted to protect employee rights. Overall, there is a growing dissatisfaction with the polarity of societal democracy and organizational autocracy.

PARADIGM IN THE MIRROR

What does this emerging paradigm *look* like? In a seminal piece of work, Richard E. Walton compared and contrasted what he called a "control" versus a "commitment" model, and this work serves to define some basic tenets of the new paradigm.[9] To begin, the new paradigm operates on these principles:

1. The control and coordination of work are based on shared goals and expertise within an organization.

2. Management acknowledges the legitimate claims of multiple stakeholders.

3. It is assumed that gaining people's commitment will lead to enhanced performance.

4. In contrast to being viewed as variable costs, people are seen as appreciating assets.

Starting from this position, one finds an altered work environment that supports this paradigm. Here are some of the more "dramatic":

- Work is being designed to emphasize the whole task instead of separating thinking from doing.

- Adaptability and ingenuity are being viewed as desirable on the job.

- Shared goals, values, and traditions are taking precedence over rules and procedures as ways of gaining commitment.

- Bureaucratic structures are being flattened as people take on the problem-solving responsibilities of disappearing layers of management, and symbols of status themselves are disappearing.

- Rewards are being based more on the mastery of skills and on group-oriented performance than on Lone Ranger grandstanding.

- Greater effort is being made to give employment assurances.

- Training and retraining are becoming major avenues to support the transition to the new paradigm.

- Employees are being given greater access to information and being offered numerous ways to voice their views and suggestions.

- The enemy-within viewpoint is being exchanged for one that sees more clearly that true competition lies outside the organization. In this climate, unions and management are working to redefine their respective roles.

All this clearly suggests that we *are* between waves. But a question remains: Is the paradigm currently shifting, or is it merely catching up?

IS THE REVOLUTION OVER?

Amid all the confusion inherent in the overlapping of waves is an increasingly clear sign that the organizational models in place today need to be revised. It is not at all unusual to find structural hierarchies, management philosophies, and even day-to-day business language (e.g., references to introductory training as "boot camp") reflecting antiquated models. Although their origins can be traced to military and religious organizations, these models came into their own throughout the Industrial Revolution.

Given what is happening all around them, those who continue to create and support such models present a pathetic image. Many years ago, the owners of trucks were chastised for using them as though they were mechanized horses. Truck routes, for example, continued to reflect the need to rest one's horses every so many miles. The routes were designed for a source of transportation that was fading from view. Likewise, current organizational models might better be found in museum cases, alongside other relics and artifacts.

The leaders who will succeed in escaping from this historic bondage are those who take a completely different approach toward the future. Rather than continue to persuade people that it will be necessary to make changes to prepare for the future, they need to promote the idea that the future is now past:

> Long before . . . leaders reached the pinnacle of organizational power, while they were still considered fugitives by those who ruled, they knew they had succeeded. All that remained, however great the task and whatever the cost, was to execute whatever steps were necessary for others to accept the new reality. From the position that the revolution has already occurred, and that a return to the earlier time is impossible, hardships are taken as tests and signs that strengthen rather than diminish the new order.[10]

This "future perfect" logic holds that the only way to succeed is to start from the position that changes have *already occurred*, even though the majority of people have not yet caught on. This is a very powerful notion and deserves special attention here.

Anyone who picks up a magazine featuring "adult toys" and looks at all the gadgetry available can be excused for thinking that the rate of technological change has gone off the deep end. Yet these items reflect only a small percentage of what is available and don't even hint at those in the pipeline, destined to emerge in the near future. Even the most "progressive" consumer is actually obtaining outmoded goods at the time of purchase. Similarly, organizational models are currently being created whose utility has already passed by. The trick in avoiding this is for the leader to convince followers that the model has already changed and that they need to adjust their behavior to fit it! By so doing, the followers actually cause the transformation from old model to new model to occur. One irony here is that creating a strategic plan around changing to a new model militates against the very innovation needed, because such plans operate under the assumption that nothing has happened yet, but it is likely that something *has* happened and the leader must bring about changed behavior based on this assumption.

In the final analysis, the outmoded organizational models, management philosophy, and other symbols that have served to support timeworn operations are all ignoring the paradigm shift that has *already* occurred. We return to Glacier, Inc., undergoing downsizing and the redistribution of its assets, to provide examples of how the paradigm shift and the business change came to interact.

NEW PARADIGM COMPETENCIES

Glacier had long since defined the role of its first-line managers and those directly above them. Although some modest changes had occurred over time, their day-to-day activities reflected a top-down hierarchy and a fairly autocratic model. The following list of key skill areas outlines the typical first-line management role:[11]

- Has technical knowledge
- Maintains standards
- Demonstrates concern for others
- Maintains positive image
- Ensures needed training
- Cooperates across units
- Plans and allocates resources
- Is persistent in achieving goals
- Keeps accurate records

- Accepts responsibility
- Shows loyalty/commitment
- Uses effective communications
- Motivates through example
- Provides performance feedback
- Introduces innovation
- Delegates appropriately
- Acts promptly in crises

This list is only a slight modification of what supervisors have been expected to do for decades. Such modification has always come in the form of reduced power and influence within a formal hierarchical structure. The conflicts inherent in this position have been well documented over the years, perhaps nowhere so pointedly as by Roethlisberger in 1945:

> Nowhere in the industrial structure more than at the foreman level is there so great a discrepancy between what a position ought to be and what a position is. . . . Separated from management and separated from his men, dependent and

insecure in his relation to his superiors and uncertain in his relations to his men, asked to give cooperation but in turn receiving none, expected to be friendly but provided with tools which only allow him to be "fair"—in this situation of social deprivation our modern foreman is asked to deliver the goods.[12]

Of course, the assumption behind these prescriptions and descriptions is that the organizational environment is relatively stable and that the normal production fluctuations, perhaps driven by the introduction of new equipment or a shift in demand, were taken into account.

At Glacier, the foremen were facing a major transformation both in terms of closing facilities and in making the transition of people, products, and equipment to new locations. Under these conditions, increased demands were placed on these managers, who found themselves having to develop and employ additional competencies that many found difficult to master, even in the best of times:

- Market–customer understanding
- Leadership skills
- Interpersonal skills
- Work innovation
- Self-management
- Technology

- Strategic thinking
- Business financial understanding
- Group development skills
- Diagnostic skills
- Business communications

RESISTANCE FIGHTERS

Some prior efforts to introduce such activities as quality circles and the involvement of employees in incentive plans requiring group-oriented planning activities had been tried at several of Glacier's locations. For the most part, the foremen did not embrace or support these efforts. Their resistance tended to fall into the following categories:[13]

- *Perceived loss of power and control.* Many saw these programs as just another effort to reduce their status and further diffuse their ability to govern their areas.

- *Distrust of employee's/union's commitment.* The difficulties many of the foremen experienced with employees and, in some cases, with their union representatives, originated prior to the foremen's arrival on the scene.

They merely entered into an insidious cycle of distrust between management and labor. As a result, they often drew upon "concrete examples" to justify prohibiting any deviation from past practices. They weren't going to be the first ones to blink.

- *Distrust of upper-level management's motives.*   One of the most bitter points underscoring the foremen's resistance was their bedrock belief that upper management did not truly endorse these programs. This was based on past experience of having to manage the aftermath of fads mandated from above. Further, foremen were keenly aware of the contradiction between how they were asked to manage and how *they* were managed. In short, they saw nothing in it for themselves, either from a reward standpoint or in terms of seeing such changes modeled by upper-level managers.

- *Lack of experience and skill in "new" management areas.*   Two elements militated against the foremen gaining any experience or training in how to manage differently under these new conditions. First, the crush of the daily production demand during the closing period was overwhelming. Second, upper management had yet to accept the argument that training was necessary. Many still viewed such training as a soft area, peripheral at best to the demands at hand.

- *Disagreement with underlying philosophy of changes requested.*   Finally, many foremen simply did not agree with the management changes that were being suggested. They had been groomed to manage in a more straightforward manner that had its power vested more in their position than in terms of persuasive skills, and this whole shift was anathema to them. This was not just an academic debate; it went to the very core of their beliefs about people and about themselves. They were "hard-wired," and this was not going to change.

As Glacier's plant-closing program progressed and the transition of resources began to have its impact, the managers indicated that their overall efforts were diluted. They stated they had to bond together out of frustration but that a team effort resulted. They had a "do-it-right attitude," supported one another in fighting for resources, and developed good relationships with the people under them.

The foremen and managers' comments reflected their struggles:

Managers become more like individual contributors—hope people do what's needed without direction. People seem to resent the lack of management contact. Now it's mandatory to delegate more. We are evolving to a new managerial style.

We developed a "buddy system" so that good people from the closing locations could be paired up with good people from our location. This reduced training time and was a good introduction to our plant and what we expect.

We have developed more trust in the hourly people. For example, our high-skilled hourly employees helped in the installation and debugging of equipment. The early involvement of machine adjusters helped during a major breakdown earlier.

At all locations, it was found that the managers viewed themselves as working harder at communicating than ever before. Ironically, however, the employees indicated they were not receiving enough information. Clearly this was an area where the managers saw a no-win outcome. One manager offered interesting insight into the difficulties facing him:

Plant managers are used to communicating facts. Now they are having to communicate probabilities. This is not an easy transition to make.

It can be seen from these comments that once the managers were caught up in something real, the "soft" lessons so easily ignored in the past became the hard realities of what it was going to take to manage throughout this change. Perhaps the ultimate testimony to this point came in the form of a question.

PLANT CLOSING IMPACT ON EMPLOYEE PARTICIPATION?

At locations where employee participation activities (e.g., quality circles) had been in place, it became clear that managers had come to depend on them. Employees were asked to focus on closing issues, such as outlining the need for process documentation and operator training. Several managers indicated that having the employee involvement activities in place prior to the closing announcement was beneficial in terms of communication and the exchange of people's concerns.

The movement of equipment was assisted to a substantial degree by having operators and mechanics become involved in the planning and execution of these activities. There was an "ownership" issue that got translated into faster startup time with fewer mechanical problems at the receiving plants. When pressed on the definition of "mechanical problems," a manager further explained:

Let me put it this way. Every time we had the operators and mechanics in-volved in dismantling, shipping, and installing equipment, everything was fine. Otherwise, parts and tools seemed to grow legs and walk off.

Perhaps the most important point is that such involvement activities both proved to be resilient in the face of this turbulence *and* served the managers well in their task of having to oversee the intricacies of such a transition.

THE EMERGING ROLE OF LEADER/MANAGER

Some years ago I was present when an annual review of key executives was being conducted within Glacier. I found it fascinating to hear the labels attached to people. One in particular stuck with me: tentstakes. People so labeled were considered essential to a business but were not likely to reach the highest positions, nor were they expected to introduce innovation or suggest new business directions. Instead, as the sobriquet suggests, they were the people who kept the superstructure from blowing away. I reflect on this often these days when the management literature is filled with descriptions of "leaders" and "leadership," giving the impression—if not stating directly—that managers are less important than they were and may actually be part of the problem.

I would contend that managers are to leaders what tentstakes are to tentpoles. This is not to deny that a vacuum of leadership exists—it does, to too great a degree. This also does not ignore the need to upgrade the overall role of managers. But it does serve as a reminder of the interdependencies that too often get lost in the rhetoric. There are examples of organizations that have removed a layer of middle management only to find increased costs due to poor decisions, decreased morale, frustrated people at all levels, and often utter chaos—the tentstakes are no longer there to keep the lid on. With this in mind, we should look at the role of leader/manager as a contrived combination for discussion purposes, and then examine how this role was played out in the present example.

THE LONELY PARADE OF ONE

The wife of a successful and wealthy man was asked, "Is he happy?" "No," she replied, "and I don't think he remembers what 'happy' means."

Striving to meet the challenges of today's business environment means making sacrifices that most people would view as outrageous. It means giving up so many of life's little pleasures that life itself has to be redefined. Stories of geniuses like Edison or the Kellogg brothers or Frank Lloyd Wright usually exclude any reference to their checkered personal lives or to what it was like to work *for* them. They were driven by an inner vision that often resulted in reprehensible behavior insofar as their families and colleagues were concerned. I paint this picture because the near-idolatry surrounding the image of "leaders" needs to be tempered by a more realistic view of the total person in this role.

When F. Scott Fitzgerald commented, "The rich are different from us," Ernest Hemingway replied, "Yes, they have more money." Leader "differences" may not be so easily dismissed. I'm not sure that a continuum connecting leader and manager can be stated unequivocally. It does appear that the line between strengths and weaknesses is finely drawn for leaders. At Glacier, a key executive was finally "kicked upstairs" after having made numerous decisions that both alienated co-workers and resulted in massive financial losses. The executive's boss mused over the situation and summed it up:

> It was like going out and buying a thoroughbred and finding out after the fact that the sonovabitch can only run backwards. . . .

The current management literature is very helpful in identifying characteristics of leaders and examining what sets them apart from others.

A LEADERSHIP LITANY

Recently a somewhat elderly researcher was awarded the Nobel Prize. An interviewer reviewed the scientist's past, including references to the fact that much of her work had been both criticized and dismissed by colleagues for decades. The scientist was asked how she managed to keep going under such negative circumstances. Her reply: "I knew I was right." It is a point worth considering further. Those who step out in front often do so in the face of daunting criticism, as described eloquently by Machiavelli in 1513:

> It must be remembered that there is nothing more difficult to plan, more doubtful of success, nor more dangerous to manage, than the creation of a new system.
> For the initiator has enmity of all who would profit by preservation of the old institution and merely lukewarm defenders in those who would gain by the new ones.[14]

When Thomas Edison was trying to convince the city fathers of New York to convert from gas to incandescent street lighting, Edison's opponents would gather in Central Park each day of the deliberations. Precisely at noon, they would electrocute a dog to demonstrate the danger of electricity. To be a leader means forging ahead, like Edison, despite sometimes feeling more like the unfortunate dog.

What keeps these leaders going? Here are some attributes that they appear to have in common:[15]

- They are their own source of reward and recognition, allowing them the freedom to decide without plebiscites.

- Their courage comes from deeply held values, which often cause others grief because they are articulated without regard for the protection of myths or the status quo.

- They harbor a near-irrational hatred of inaction. They are convinced that they can and must use tools like information, resources, and support to— at a minimum—take advantage of change.

- As in the joke that goes, "I like people—in the abstract," leaders believe in building environments that allow people to grow and to rise to their own levels of contribution. This is an area that is generally misunderstood because although their actions often result in benefits for people, humanitarian goals were not necessarily primary. Rather, they see the empowerment of people as necessary to bring about a new order of things.

- Their view of a situation is often removed from its nuances. They may take a sort of out-of-body perspective in order to expand their total view. This approach often includes wrenching introspection as well. The net effect is the ability to see patterns where others see none and to tolerate— if not revel in—the random fragments of order that surround them.

- Bureaucracies are anathema to them. Kryptonite to Superman. They constantly strive to move away from the dead hand of sameness to create new models that thrive on a better balance of entrepreneurial autonomy against patriarchal dependency.

Finally, Toffler describes the kinds of skills people need in order to lead/manage successfully:

The new Third Wave economy . . . rewards certain traits . . . but they won't necessarily be the same. Clearly, it pays big rewards for cognitive skills and education. . . . The Third Wave economy will also reward people who are quickly adaptable to change; who are flexible, able to work for more than one boss . . . for people who are curious, inquisitive, eager to find out what is going on and to influence it; people who can keep their heads in the midst of disorder and ambiguity. It will pay for people who may not have the skills of a life-long specialist, but rather experience in several different fields and the ability to transfer ideas from one to the other. It will reward individuality and entrepreneurialism.[16]

MEANWHILE, BACK AT THE CLOSING

Glacier's plant closings serve as a discussion point around leadership. In this case, the circumstances required very difficult decisions. Yet, one could argue that the decision to close the manufacturing facilities and transfer assets to remaining ones was not a *transformational* change for the business. The product lines, customer base, and overall competitor arena were not changing dramatically prior to the decision, nor were they appreciably different afterward. Therefore, the change of the existing order could be described as a *transactional* one, requiring a less dramatic leadership role.

This is a difficult distinction to make with certainty because Glacier may be passing through an evolutionary stage to an altogether different state. I think there is a yet-to-be-defined stage between transactional and transformational change. But even this middle ground has a continuum of severity. I would argue that the extreme end could be represented by the type of changes experienced by Navistar over the past few years.[17]

Navistar—previously called International Harvester Company—was the Grand Old Man in its marketplace in 1979 at the age of 132. It was a name known to generations of people around the world whose livelihood involved agriculture and construction. At its peak in 1979, it employed 95,000 people and had sales of $8.4 billion. But a series of external events, coupled with its management's internal hesitancy to take appropriate steps, proved near fatal. The external events included two recessions, government deregulation of the trucking industry, a deteriorating farm economy, and a major strike among its employees. When the leadership of the business finally agreed to act, its steps were dramatic and extremely painful for everyone. Surely the most difficult one was the selling off of its agricultural equipment operations to Tenneco, thereby severing its linkage to the original founder, Cyrus McCormick, who incorporated the business under his name in 1847. The remaining decisions included selling off or closing 35 of its 42 manufacturing operations and reducing employment from 95,000 to 13,000.

The strategy shift was based on management's realization that they would have to target mature nongrowth markets. Further, they could no longer count on a growing economy to excuse inefficient operations. Instead, they would have to take market share away from competitors.[18]

For Navistar, the step not taken—a step that might have been defined as transformational—could have been to exit its current business lines altogether and pursue a totally new market, one that would require such additional changes as new players and new locations. By comparison, Glacier has yet to reach a stage requiring the degree of change that engulfed Navistar. Still, both businesses represent this middle ground between the improvement of "what is" and the metamorphosis to "what never was."

I witnessed some interesting leadership decisions throughout Glacier's plant-closing process. Some leaders demonstrated courage; others did just the opposite. Here are a few of the more courageous examples:

- The decision to close both non-union and union locations despite a long history of carefully supporting non-union status

- The decision to reverse historic vertical integration trends by contracting out such activities as the manufacture of its own operating equipment

- The decision to move ahead without knowing if the process technology would be able to advance fast enough to meet financial goals

- The decision to commit sufficient funds to keep the operating locations running at optimal conditions until the actual day of closing (this ran the gamut from general housekeeping to major capital investment)

- The decision to share confidential information with subordinates despite explicit instructions from top management not to do so

- The decision to go forward with a relatively large-scale project of this type when the justification was not obvious and would become so only at a distant point in the future

On the other hand, other decisions reflected a different and less positive orientation:

- The decision not to offer job security to key managers at closing locations so as to present an image of fairness to the media

- The decision not to involve top management teams at the closing locations in the planning process prior to the closing announcement

- The decision not to allow skilled union workers at closing locations to transfer to non-union locations, despite years of emphasizing that "poor *management* leads to unions"

- The decision not to allow nonexempt people to bid on jobs outside their immediate geographic location

Glacier was struggling with a paradigm shift and its consequences, but the key point of resistance nearly always came from deep-seated philosophical differences between the leadership/management requirements inherent in the new paradigm and the practices of the Glacier's top executives. Someone has said that innovation rolls downhill; in this case, such momentum was meager at best, and any effort to challenge it met with strong internal resistance.

PARADOXES ARE KING

The titles of two books serve to underscore a major paradox facing organizations—how much change and how soon? In one, *Beyond the Quick Fix*, the emphasis is on a series of stages that need to be addressed so as to increase the probability of a successful change. These steps can be seen as drawing from a more systemic view of organizational issues. The other, *Thriving on Chaos*, subtitled *Handbook for a Management Revolution*, generates a tone of almost desperate immediacy in its recommendations for steps needed to fix things.[19]

This is an area that has intrigued me for years. I have been told of a plant location that was operating at such a low level of efficiency that the decision to close it was imminent. A drastic last effort was made to "shock" the work force. On Friday afternoon all of the people were gathered together and summarily fired. They were told their jobs were going to be offered to the general public on Monday morning and that they were free to come in and interview for them if they thought they could meet the future increased demands of these positions. The result was quite startling. People interviewed for and acquired their previous jobs. The productivity and efficiency of the plant increased to levels never achieved. This appears to be an example of immediate and total change.

A case can be made for such a change if one argues that the resulting organizational environment would be so radically different that comparisons between the old and the new would not be possible because they represent totally different philosophies. For example, instead of comparing this change to a move from driving a truck to driving a sports car, it might be more akin to driving a truck versus flying a helicopter. On paper it sounds logical that such dramatic differences don't allow for much of a wait-and-see approach. In the helicopter example, once you left the ground, the experiment was over.

Still, I continue to be impressed by the paradox of human ability to absorb change and the rate of change demanded by environments surrounding organizations. The drivers of change—technology, government, and so on— seem to support the *chaos* perspective while the all-too-obvious limitations—

the retraining capability of adults, emotional links to past conditions, and the like—argue against the likely success of *quick fix* approaches. Herein lies one of the simplest yet thorniest issues that this shift in paradigms makes clear: power sharing.

In Eastern religions, one finds the paradox, "To find yourself, you must first lose yourself." Its organizational equivalent, which supports the new paradigm, would say, "To gain power, you must give up power." When dealing with managers inside Glacier, I would occasionally ask if they were considering starting employee involvement programs. Often I would encounter much nodding and be told how selected employees were already planning the plant picnic. A more telling remark came when I asked if the managers would consider training production line people in statistical methods to assess product quality. The answer was, "Hell, even our process engineers don't understand that stuff. How can you expect the workers to do it?!" A few years ago, when Frank Borman headed up Eastern Airlines, the unions asked to be represented on the board of directors in exchange for significant wage concessions and production improvements that could lower labor costs. Borman's response was reported to be, "I don't want the monkeys to run the zoo."

I am not suggesting that leaders/managers abdicate responsibility. But I do believe that a key impediment to an organization's introduction of rapid and successful change is the low level of ability and willingness of people to accept change imposed on them. Training people to use new skills is only one part of the issue because, as any educator will tell you, the difference between hearing and listening is often the determining factor in learning. People who are constantly reacting to change find themselves confronted with a world that is both threatening and outside their control. Those in positions of authority above them further serve to escalate these feelings by prohibiting meaningful involvement in decisions that affect the work they do.

The previous chapter gave an excellent example of closed-systems planning, when the key plant managers were systematically excluded from participating in the planning of the closing of their locations. In contrast, open-systems planning deliberately acknowledges the legitimate right of stakeholder contribution and further assumes that ultimate plans and results will be enhanced by such an approach. This comes from having both a broader perspective represented in the planning stage, and a broader endorsement of changes crafted by the participants themselves. Although I believe this, I still worry that managers need to be able to distinguish between events that require immediate unilateral actions and those that would allow for a more careful process involving others. The *chaos* will not wait, but I continue to see situations where power sharing is denied in the name of expediency, but more likely because of an individual's personal comfort level with an old paradigm.

THE HR PYGMALION

It would take Solomon's wisdom to separate the demands of the new paradigm shift from the human resource issues implied therein. This opens up a major issue for most businesses: the metamorphosis of business support functions from being primarily administrative to more strategic in their operations. Of these, the "people" function deserves some discussion.[20]

Beginning in the 1920s, personnel officers were responsible for hiring and firing. They ran a payroll, meted out discipline, and administered benefits plans. From the 1930s through the 1950s, with the growth of the union movement in the United States, this function required its members to be skillful labor contract negotiators, as they were often in the forefront of labor–management disputes. But since the 1960s this function has been asked to provide advice on selecting and grooming key people for promotion to top posts, and on promotions and transfers. Human resources (HR) managers became involved in strategic planning through their analysis of the impact of demographic, social, and political trends on their organizations.

The HR function, however, has not evolved to its present state without some major problems that, themselves, can impede an organization's adaptation to the demands of the paradigm shift. Some of the more troublesome issues are:

- HR is viewed as relatively soft and "primitive" by the line managers. They tolerate this weak sister but are careful in their commitment to HR programs they view as only peripherally related to business demands.[21]

- HR has been described as the organizational equivalent of the "roach motel"—people can enter from other functions, but they never return.

- HR's mission, planning, staffing, and structure are often viewed by line managers as serving to perpetuate the function as opposed to providing service to the organization as a whole.[22]

- HR people often do not understand the business. They don't know the financial goals or the competitive market, they can't read a balance sheet to determine how well things are going, and they don't appreciate the constraints and demands placed on line management.

- The lack of organizational power has led to some very dysfunctional game-playing between the line managers and HR. One of the more insidious forms has been described as follows:

> Personnel people can be the conscience of the corporation; they can say, "the King has no clothes"; they can call bluffs, speak truths, speak out for good against evil, and care for people. They can do all of this with support and impunity because, even though they don't acknowledge it to themselves, they have made a psychological contract with the corporation that they will never win. [23]

Too often, the net result for an organization is a random mosaic of policies and practices that reflect attempts to patch over past crises, appear "trendy" with the latest jargon, and satisfy the idiosyncratic preferences of specialists. There are a number of steps that an organization can take to address HR problems, but the direction should *not* be focused solely on "fixing" the function. Surely there are specific improvements that can be made, but a more fundamental issue stems from the question, "Who *owns* HR?"[24]

The paradigm shift is occurring in the midst of an intolerant marketplace, where a misstep could mean the difference between survival and bankruptcy. Potential missteps include an organization's policies for managing its human assets. Unfortunately, most organizations have abrogated line responsibility for such human decisions to HR. The messy business of dealing with human conflict, government regulatory agencies, and third-party representation, among other uncomfortable situations, has been delegated to HR. Not only has this de facto given HR a source of "negative power"—they are the ones who get to say "no"—it also has moved the actual ownership of human resource management policies and systems away from general managers. This is a potentially dangerous condition. In addition to "fixing" HR, then, the line managers need to insert themselves directly into decisions about how to attract, select, promote, motivate, train, develop, retain, and exit people—all in support of their overall business strategy.

Managers in Glacier found themselves thrust into a world requiring them to balance three key assets: financial, technical, and human. It is this revitalization of the concept of general management's responsibility to handle all three that is a key success factor inside the new paradigm. Yes, it means having to speak about "probabilistic" versus "deterministic" outcomes of certain decisions, and it also means having to play God with people's careers. But the downside of avoiding these responsibilities can be devastating.

Of course, HR is not the only function undergoing a major strategic overhaul. For example, the purchasing function is now being viewed as playing a major role in its capacity to save money, ensure high-quality raw materials, and establish partnerships with suppliers in such new areas as Just-in-Time inventory efforts. The information systems function is being invaded by so-called hybrid managers, who often have more of a business than a technical background. In what many regard as a perverse role reversal, people in this function must themselves absorb new technology (e.g., computer-assisted software engineering tools) that they sometimes believe deskills them in the name of efficiency. Above all, the impact of organizational change often intrudes on their technical world with demands that they play a far greater role in offering strategic support.[25] But the pygmalion effect will not occur in any of these functions without direct intervention by line managers, including their "taking a turn in the barrel" themselves. In the HR situation, a good place to start is for line managers to create a rotational assignment process that requires HR and line managers to swap assignments on a regular basis. The influx of line thinking would be a step in the right direction,[26] and the "people" perspective on the line could help move policies and practices away from the negative aspects of scientific management's control-oriented philosophy.

WHAT'S IN IT FOR ME?

The jarring impact of the paradigm shift generally produces two questions: How can we get there, and is it worth the trip? The "how" is a subtheme that will recur throughout this book. The answer to the second question constitutes what I believe will be a major impediment to the new paradigm taking hold. We have already seen some of this in the decision not to hold out job security for key managers who had to keep plants running until the last day. They were given no hope of future employment, and paradoxically, were told to make sure that the same lack of job security among the people on the line did not hurt production goals.

The calls for eliminating middle management, delayering throughout organizations, creating self-directed work teams, and shifting the role of supervisors from directive to consultative lack corresponding advice on what to do for those whose lives are going to be put in the cosmic blender. Here are a few of the challenges:

- How to "rewire the heads" of people who behave as they have been rewarded for behaving for decades.

- How to handle the fact that a shift in management style is no more voluntary than would be a choice to enter into bankruptcy.

- How to convince people that retraining is not a temporary respite until the good old days return but, rather a critical junction in their work lives.

- How to get people to accept job responsibilities that were once reserved for managers above them when they would prefer to avoid this.

The closing of Glacier plants had a dramatic impact on how the first-line managers were viewed by those they managed. We will explore this in depth later. The point here is that historic relationships, both positive and negative, were in a state of constant flux, and neither side was pleased with the turbulence. Previous roles were being challenged, avenues for redressing grievances were ineffective, and personal survival had ripped the mask off many parent–child relationships at the lowest levels in the organization. The reality of losing one's livelihood suddenly made it necessary to end the pretense of helpless servitude. These "child" employees became fathers, mothers, homeowners, makers of legal contracts, taxpayers, voters, elected local officials, heads of households, school board members, and many other things that had always been conveniently set aside in order to play the game inside their organizations.

The new paradigm requires that adults bring all their skills and talents to the organization and that leaders/managers provide a work environment that allows this power to be channeled in ways to help meet strategic objectives. This is not a humanitarian gesture. It is a main bulwark against a society losing its ability to sustain an enviable standard of living.

SUMMARY

The presence of a new organizational and management paradigm has appeared, and its differences from previous ones are substantial. This chapter reviews past management literature and more recent thinking to demonstrate the challenge this new paradigm poses for today's organizations. The transition from a control-oriented to a commitment-oriented operating philosophy is a difficult one, and often contradicts the very essence of what many leaders and managers have believed to be the right way to run organizations.

The irony is that the complaints may not be of a new order about to arrive but, unbeknownst to those complaining, of one that has already happened around them. This change will require new competencies from all people in organizations. The implication goes beyond skill building to include a change in logic as well as acknowledgment of a global shift in how human assets should be managed. The resistance to be overcome is most obvious at the lowest levels of management in organizations, and the loss of prestige and power head the list of issues raised by this group when faced with changes in their current roles. Those below them are ready for a change—have been for quite some time—and demonstrate their tenacious willingness to sustain involvement in decision making, even in a plant-closing environment.

The role of leader/manager needs to be examined carefully so that we do not conclude that managers are unnecessary and that leaders alone will suffice. The myths of leadership should be dispelled and put into proper context in order to position leaders more appropriately and to foster more realistic expectations among those supporting them. Examples of leadership—and the lack of it—were discussed in relation to the activities stemming from the decision to close plants and transfer assets elsewhere. The concept of transitional versus transformational leadership situations was reviewed. A middle ground was suggested as being more descriptive of organizations that stop short of changing their total business focus altogether. Yet, their situation still requires strong leadership, perhaps bordering on the demands that exist during certain phases of total transformation.

The paradoxes facing leaders/managers were discussed, and the balance between the need to move quickly to be effective in today's marketplace versus a need to move cautiously in order to address the difficulty in getting people to accept the necessary changes was covered. A key ingredient—meaningful participation in decision making among all organizational members—was held up as a means of managing the fast/slow paradox.

The paradigm shift and its influence on organizations' support functions was discussed, with the human resource function held up as a prime example. The issues facing this function in terms of changing its overall operating philosophy were examined, along with the need for line managers to reassert themselves in the setting of appropriate policies and practices to support their strategic business objectives.

Finally, a discussion of how to answer the question, "What's in it for me?" looked at some of the key challenges to the new paradigm in terms of required changes in the way people both act and think. Many of these are directly linked to a shift in how people's roles are perceived once they enter organizations. The childlike dependency of the past is giving way to a more egalitarian sharing of both goals and responsibilities—an approach that requires adult-to-adult interactions that often did not typify management within the old paradigm.

Notes

1. Thomas Kuhn, in *The Structure of Scientific Revolutions* (Chicago: University of Chicago Press, 1962), is often credited with coining the phrase "paradigm shift." Although I still get a few raised eyebrows when I use it in certain management circles, I remember getting the same reaction to "vision" a few years before we all decided it was acceptable. Tom Peters's book, *Thriving on Chaos* (New York: Knopf, 1987), provides many good examples of how such shifts can and should be brought about in such areas as dealing with customers, handling the blistering pace of innovation, moving toward more power sharing at lower levels, embracing versus shunning change, and trying to tie all this together.

2. This material is found in *Matrix Management Systems Handbook*, edited by David I. Cleland (New York: Van Nostrand Reinhold, 1984), p. 679. At the time this was written, I was trying to describe some changes I was witnessing and to show how such "new" approaches as quality circles could become stronger entities if they received broader organizational support. That such efforts largely failed was predictable because, as the book chapter describes, they were never woven into the working fabric of the overall business.

3. I hope readers will be tolerant of my occasional reference to Alvin Toffler and his work, such as *The Third Wave* (New York: Telecom Library, 1980). Toffler has been a beacon for me because he not only anticipated many major changes, but also wrote persuasively about what should be done to take advantage of coming opportunities. In a sense, I regard him as our generation's H. G. Wells and Leonardo DiVinci combined.

4. David Riesman et al., *The Lonely Crowd: A Study of the Changing American Character* (New Haven: Yale University Press, 1969), pp. xvi, xviii.

5. I am indebted to Daniel Yankelovich's insights into the changing "equation" that people are bringing into the workplace. As he points out, the work ethic is not dead, but the new entrants (indeed, even some of the current incumbents) are demanding that this equation be rebalanced. They will not be silenced with stern admonitions like, "Just be glad you have a job here, kid!" They are much more likely to seek out another opportunity that allows them more input into decisions affecting their work. I highly recommend Yankelovich's book *New Rules* (New York: Random House, 1981). The excerpt is from page 231.

6. I was interested in how John Naisbitt, author of *Megatrends* (New York: Warner Books, 1982), treated this area. Naisbitt says, "People whose lives are affected by a decision must be part of the process of arriving at that decision." He further examines the roots of much of this democratic shift in consumer activism and political activism. His point is that this seeking of a voice through political decisions is having an impact inside corporations, such that emerging structures will allow various internal and external stakeholders to have greater influence over how the organization will operate. He sees an emerging altered concept of workers' rights and of their ability to participate in decision making that more closely

approaches the democratic principle stated. Naisbitt and his co-author, Patricia Aburdene, return to this area in *Re-inventing the Corporation* (New York: Warner Books, 1985), in which they state, "One of the best-kept secrets in America is that people are aching to make a commitment—if they only had the freedom and environment in which to do so" (p. 256).

7. Taylor has, for years, been a sort of management theorist's whipping boy, and I have probably just become the most recent voice in the chorus. The material used for this discussion was taken from Shoshana Zuboff, *In the Age of the Smart Machine* (New York: Basic Books, 1988), from Ed Lawler, *High-Involvement Management* (San Francisco: Jossey-Bass, 1986), and from Toffler, *The Third Wave*. The most important point to keep in mind, however, is the one Lawler makes regarding the matchup between Taylor's "solutions" and the *Zeitgeist* or spirit of the times. Taylor was acceptable under then-current conditions. The critical issue now is the perpetuation of outmoded ideas.

8. Richard E. Walton, in "From Control to Commitment in the Workplace," *Harvard Business Review* (March–April 1985), comments on how it was necessary for management to build several interacting pieces of their organizational infrastructure to support the prescriptive behavior Taylor suggested. Several "we–they" symbols became a part of these decisions. I was reminded of this recently when a general manager indicated that the views and sentiments of the first-line foremen were too closely aligned with those of the people they supervised. To counter this, white shop coats were purchased for the foremen to create a visible symbol of their "difference."

9. Again I beg the reader's indulgence, but I regard Dick's work as a stake in the sand insofar as the paradigm shift is concerned. He has clearly articulated some critical things to look for when one is inside an organization. I have used these comparisons many times and have yet to have an audience *not* squirm a bit as it became clear that many if not all of them were either members of or builders and sustainers of control-oriented organizations.

10. Occasionally a book comes along that is not terribly long, but compensates for its brevity with its elegance in expressed thought. Stanley M. Davis has done this in his book, *Future Perfect* (Reading, MA: Addison-Wesley, 1987); the excerpt is from page 36. He and I met recently at a conference in Boston, and I listened as he challenged his audience to think and act in the future perfect tense. Further, he charged them to confront the inevitable "deaths" of their present organizations! It was not the traditional light after-dinner speech, but it certainly energized the crowd, and I enjoyed the controversy.

11. Marvin Dunnette, "The Hawthorne Effect: Its Societal Meaning," in E. Cass and F. Zimmer (Eds.), *Man and Work in Society* (New York: Van Nostrand-Reinhold, 1974).

12. Fritz J. Roethlisberger, in "The Foreman: Master and Victim of Double Talk," *Harvard Business Review*, 23(3) (1945), pp. 284, 293, captures the essence of a foreman's paradoxical world. Having been a foreman in a former life, I found much of his description disturbingly accurate—made all the more disturbing by the fact that my own experiences came about over thirty years after he wrote the

article! Either I am a slow learner, or else there is something about such positions that makes it difficult to effect change unless the surrounding infrastructure is changed as well.

13. Fortunately, two very fine articles serve to guide us in labeling the sources of resistance among first-level supervisors. Michael H. Schuster and Christopher S. Miller wrote about this in their *Personnel* article, "Employee Involvement: Making Supervisors Believers" (February 1985). Mike and I have worked together over the years, and I believe this work shows his skills of observing the sometimes less obvious behaviors within a manufacturing setting. Janice A. Klein's *Harvard Business Review* article, "Why Supervisors Resist Employee Involvement" (September–October 1984), draws upon her experience in General Electric's manufacturing settings to help identify the sources of first-level resistance. In addition to these articles, Steven Kerr, Kenneth D. Hill, and Laurie Broedling have reviewed the relevant literature to address a question that served as the title of their article, "The First-Line Supervisor: Phasing Out or Here to Stay?" in *Academy of Management Review*,11 (1) (1986). Their answer is "Here to stay," but not in the traditionally defined role. The resistance, as one might expect, is as much a reflection of the system demands of the foremen as it is of the individual's beliefs.

14. Niccolo Machiavelli (1469–1527) is often quoted for his amoral precepts regarding leadership—for example, "To be feared gives more security than to be loved." However, he was well aware that leadership needed to go beyond clever planning. People require both a rational plan *and* some emotional "pull" to persuade them to follow. The quote used in the text is taken from Machiavelli's book *The Prince*.

15. Noel Tichy and co-author Mary Anne Devanna describe many of the characteristics of effective leadership in their book *The Transformational Leader* (New York: Wiley, 1986). Warren Bennis and Burt Nanus, in *Leaders* (New York: Harper & Row, 1985), base their descriptions of effective leadership behaviors on numerous observations of these individuals across multiple organizations representing both public and private sectors of the economy. Additional material with quite a punch can be found in Warren Bennis's recent book, *Why Leaders Can't Lead* (San Francisco: Jossey-Bass, 1989).

   Rosabeth Moss Kanter's book *The Change Masters* (New York: Simon and Schuster, 1983) provides some key tools that are needed by people who assume not only the mantle of leadership but also the role of change agent—the catalyst for the change itself. I was also intrigued by Peter Block's *The Empowered Manager* (San Francisco: Jossey-Bass, 1987), because he explores more deeply the notion that "positive political skills" require leaders to recognize the need for a much more effective balance between the childlike dependency of people inside organizations—largely a rational response to the organization's design and implied management philosophy—and an adult autonomy that encourages deep contribution and commitment by former children.

16. While on a business trip to Puerto Rico some years back, a colleague there brought to my attention a book by Toffler that had not received much attention. The book, *Previews and Premises* (New York: William Morrow, 1983), draws from his earlier

major themes and adds a bit more prescriptive detail, as can be seen in the quote used here, from page 156. In the years since I read Toffler's words, I have found a number of leadership gurus catching up with very similar ideas.

17. Occasionally one comes across an event that underscores how easy it is for good organizational work to go unnoticed. On August 11, 1987, I listened to Carole K. Barnett, Thomas E. Kent, and Thomas F. Ernst discuss a paper titled "Organizational Decline: The Challenge of Institutional and Individual Renewal at Navistar International Corporation" at the annual meeting of the Academy of Management in New Orleans. In the wisdom of the academy's planners, this presentation was timed to coincide with at least one major internationally known speaker. The result was that those on the dais outnumbered their audience. I have drawn from my notes to try to capture some of the lessons learned by the presenters.

18. For more details about this strategy and its implications, the reader should see Noel Tichy and Carole Barnette's article, "Profiles in Change: Revitalizing the Automotive Industry," in *Human Resource Management*, 24 (Winter 1985).

19. Ralph Kilmann, *Beyond the Quick Fix* (San Francisco: Jossey-Bass, 1984), and Tom Peters, *Thriving on Chaos* (New York: Knopf, 1987), are used here as counterpoint examples.

20. This is somewhat of a confession. The material in this section is taken from a white paper I wrote for a CEO to read. I wrote the paper out of frustration because this CEO seemed to revel in extolling "people" values and had endorsed a "key values" philosophy emerging in his business. Yet I could not seem to persuade him of the need to address his underdeveloped and underused human resource function. He discarded the idea, even going so far as to ensure that the paper never was read by others in his organization. The whole episode made me realize that organizations undergo evolutionary steps in their development, and that it is nearly impossible to jump ahead of this process—certainly that was my experience.

21. My interest in Chris Argyris's writing has grown. When I was in graduate school, my professors occasionally denigrated his work because he "didn't bother to gather data." Since then, however, I have come upon example after example of real-life situations described earlier in his work. The point made in the text is such an example. It was taken from his article, "Organizational Defensive Routines: An Unintended Human Resources Activity," in *Human Resource Management*, 25(4) (Winter 1986).

22. The source of most of these insights comes from the article by D. E. Bowen and L. E. Greiner, "Moving from Production to Service in Human Resource Management," *Organization Dynamics*, 1986. In this article the authors identify a major source of conflict between line and staff representatives: "Line managers and top corporate officers report that HR responds more to the demands of their own technologies than they do to the needs of their clients." They go on to show how an HR organization's mission, planning, staffing, and structure reflect either a product or a service orientation.

23. I have referenced Stan Davis's work earlier. Some of these remarks were also made earlier in "Transforming organizations: The key to strategy is context," an article he published in *Organization Dynamics* (Winter 1982, pp. 32–33). It is an interesting issue, however, because it points up the weakness in support functions when the actual profit and loss responsibility is treated as outside their immediate influence. The king may be predisposed to kill the messenger, but not the court jester.

24. This whole debate about the ownership of HR begs yet another question: Where is the fix most in need of being made? Some might argue that the fix should come in the form of external forces. Michael Beer, Bert Spector, Paul R. Lawrence, D. Quinn Mills, and Richard E. Walton argue, in *Managing Human Assets* (New York: Free Press, 1984), that the responsibility for the fix falls primarily on general managers. Charles Fombrun, Noel M. Tichy, and Mary Anne Devanna, in their book, *Strategic Human Resource Management* (New York: Wiley, 1984), suggest that those in the function itself need to address their own levels of competence and their overall need to make the transition from a purely administrative role to one with a greater strategic orientation.

25. David Kaye's book *Gamechange* (Oxford: Heinemann Professional Publishing, 1989), describes in some detail—backed by business case examples—the "information revolution" drivers that are forcing organizations to confront information technology in terms of its strategic importance. These forces are transmitted immediately to the information systems functions. I was particularly impressed with David's treatment of the area he calls *Teamchange*, a discussion of the impact of information technology on organization structure and management.

26. Peter Drucker underscores this point in a piece published in The *Wall Street Journal* in May 1986, titled, "Goodbye to the Old Personnel Department." Although I agree overall with his point, I have also seen some fairly stupid assignments of line managers to HR functional positions. Actually, I saw a near identical problem while doing work for the U.S. Navy. Officers on ships were rotated to shore-based assignments, but always as the head—never the deputy. The problem was that the base of functional knowledge existed only in the heads of those below the person assigned to lead them. Asking former line executives to head up HR runs the risk of ignoring the need for special skills and knowledge to be effective. I'd be more inclined to hire a top-notch HR professional with keen business acumen and then open up rotational assignments for line managers to fill within the function.

Chapter 4

STUCK IN THE SAFETY NET

I think the company is going out of its way to give me help. But don't expect me to be glad about losing my job.

—Production Worker

When one has been threatened with a great injustice, one accepts a smaller as a favor.
—Jane Welsh Carlyle

To understand the magnitude of the challenge behind managing the impact of change, it is necessary to balance the macro and micro points of view. Thus far the macro organizational perspective has received more attention than has the micro Glacier, Inc., example. This chapter, however, deliberately tips toward Glacier's approach to giving support to its employees as they faced the impact of the plant closing. Much of this was particularly well done and serves as a useful framework for examining how to provide some infra-structure to cushion the impact of change. Before moving into the details of this area, let us examine briefly a larger context within which such assistance has gained attention within the past few years.

MASLOVIAN BASELINE

It's hard to "self-actualize" when your stomach is growling. That's the intuitive sense behind the hierarchy of human needs presented by the psychologist Abraham Maslow (Figure 4.1).[1] Maslow said that we move from basic needs like food, shelter, and security to higher order needs, culminating in a sort of best-you-can-be state. I have no intention of entering into the academic debate over the soundness of this model, or considering whether one can jump-start a higher set of needs ahead of lower ones. Rather, I open this chapter with reference to Maslow's work because I believe that major organizational transitions must be accompanied by a set of answers to people's question: "What's in it for me?" These answers, particularly in situations with severe economic impact, must address some basic security issues before expecting a work force to pay much attention to other more lofty game plans.

Figure 4.1   Maslow's Hierarchy of Human Needs.

It is worth examining the philosophical arguments behind the economic and psychological safety nets used by organizations. For purposes of discussion, I'll put them in five categories: historic momentum, humanitarianism, fear of reprisal, cost reduction, and bribes.

Historic Momentum.   This may be the easiest of the approaches to understand because the organization has not wrestled with much debate or may not have considered the potential changes to be even remotely challenging to past employment practices. Therefore, the approach is business as usual, with little, if any, departure from past practices. By this logic, a plant closing would be treated as an extended layoff—somewhat akin to viewing bank robbery as a long-term loan.

Humanitarianism.   This is the currency of the Philosopher King discussed in Chapter 3. Rather than trying to balance individual and organizational needs, this approach often represents the worst nightmares of managers responsible for running a business. The cause of their grief is having to subordinate business decisions to each individual's particular needs at the moment. Hard-nosed managers who pay attention to customer needs, market shifts, and being reasonably innovative within moving-target budget constraints may wake up one morning to find themselves running the Salvation Army. The net effect can be a series of assistance programs that run rampant over prudent and necessary business operations. The irony is that such practices can actually place people in more jeopardy by weakening their organization's ability to compete and sustain itself.

Fear of Reprisal.   This philosophy is easy to identify: It is a risk-avoidance approach. Its primary driver is the expectation that stakeholders who have been kept at bay year after year will seize the moment to take their revenge against the organization in its time of crisis. Employees will sabotage operations, unions will strike, the business community will shun cooperative gestures, the community will enact punitive legislation, the government will seek legal redress, and so forth. Assuming the stakeholders will act primarily on the basest of instincts, this philosophy often generates a bewildering array of practices. They can range from a sort of "let 'em eat cake" defiance to an untargeted cornucopia of efforts that "sound good." The former approach engenders the type of collective animosity that investigative journalism exploits. The latter often makes an organization easy prey to would-be consultants with quick-fix, albeit high-cost, elixirs.

Cost Reduction.   At least this approach doesn't pretend to be something it's not. Saving money is the prime driver. Interestingly enough, this approach is often mistaken for humanitarianism because it generally includes practices that help people weather the storm of change reasonably well. It is likely to be adopted by managers because organizations have come to recognize there are all sorts of costs, some better hidden than others. In particular, this approach seeks to avoid such costs as paying for stress-induced health care, extended unemployment compensation, layoff benefits, and early pension programs, among others. With these challenges as starting points, the organization begins to ask somewhat traditional cost–benefit questions: "How much counseling does it take to increase the likelihood of rapid reemployment?"

Bribes.   In a "kinder and gentler" vernacular, these might be called "incentives" but the key motive is to get people to do something you want them to do, even if it is not in their best interest. The more innocuous form of bribery may take the form of overstated probabilities, "This is surely a career-enhancing experience that will look good on your resume." A more fact-based and less subtle approach comes in the form of delayed "pots of gold" if one is willing to suspend job-seeking effort for a designated period of time. However, delaying a job search in times of economic downturn so as to reap an exiting bonus from the present organization often brings an individual face to face with a saturated job market by peers who gambled for future gold.

Of course, these categories are for discussion purposes only and are certainly not exhaustive. In fact, as we begin to look at Glacier's program, it will be clear that a mixture of these—and possibly other—philosophies influenced their ultimate decisions.

THE GLACIER NET

Glacier used an extensive support package for people who lost their jobs as a result of the plant-closing program. To help focus attention on its major parts, I have divided the overall program into four segments: income protection, health protection, occupation transition, and advance notice. Where possible, I will augment the description of Glacier's segment details with information from other sources to allow some comparisons and contrasts to be drawn. An evaluation of the various safety net options is offered at the end of each segment.

INCOME PROTECTION

Age and service were the main factors considered in the protection of an individual's separation payout. Here are some details:

Severance Pay

People with 2 to 14 years of continuous service were entitled to a lump sum payment at termination equivalent to 1.5 weeks' pay per year of service. A partial year of service was considered as well. For each additional three months, an additional sum was added that reflected a week's pay multiplied by 0.375 for the additional service period. A minimum of four weeks' pay was guaranteed.

Fifteen years of continuous service or more resulted in a lump sum payment at termination equivalent to two weeks' pay per year of service, plus half a week's pay for each additional three months of service.

Alternative Severance Pay Option

For older employees, the lump sum option was often not a preferred choice. Therefore, an alternative allowed them to receive a monthly payment. This program had the following age/service limits:

Age	Years of Continuous Service
55	10
54	13
53	16
52	19
51	22
50	25

The monthly amount was equal to 2 percent of a person's monthly earnings times the full number of years of service—a maximum of 50 percent of monthly earnings. This monthly amount was reduced by company pension payments, unemployment compensation, Social Security or disability benefits, or company insurance payments. This program ran until the person either turned 60 or became reemployed. If, by age 60, the monthly payments had not equaled what the person would have received under the regular lump sum payment option, the balance was paid to the employee upon reaching this age.

Protected Service Option

Some employees wanted to protect their accumulated service and opted for a third choice. A weekly payment was calculated on the basis of one week's pay for each full year of continuous service, plus 0.25 times each week worked within an additional three-month period at the time of the closing. Under these conditions, employment service would be protected for one year.

These persons received 60 percent of their weekly pay, consisting of unemployment compensation received plus the balance from the protected service fund. Several other suboptions were available for those who exhausted unemployment compensation funds or could not obtain them for various reasons.

Pension Plan Options

If a person was eligible for optional retirement when the plant closed (age 55 to 60, depending on time in the pension plan), he or she could take an optional retirement or defer receiving a pension until a later date. Individuals were informed that pensions taken between ages 55 and 60 were subject to a substantial reduction factor.

If a person was within a *year* of being eligible for optional retirement when the plant closed, the individual's service would be protected for that year, and afterward the employee could choose one of the options cited above. In both cases it should be noted that the pension at age 60 was not reduced. Also, the time for pension vesting—normally 10 years—was reduced to 7 years if the person elected to receive the plant-closing benefit package.

Finally, for people aged 50 and over with 25 years of pension plan participation, a special benefit package was offered:

- Supplemental payment of $7 per month per year of pension plan participation, up to a maximum $175 per month. This was payable until age 62 for retirement at age 60 or later.

- The pension plan benefits were unreduced for retirement at age 60 or later.

- A 50-year-old employee with 25 or more years' pension qualification service who elected to retire at age 60 could pass on a lifetime income to a spouse if the retirement resulted from the plant closing. This preserved surviving spouse pension benefits that were available to all active employees.

Other

In addition to the more obvious elements of a financial package, several other pieces were added. Some of these were planned, but others resulted from lessons learned after the initial benefits package impact was understood by recipients:

- *Transfer pay guarantee*   People on an hourly pay plan who elected to transfer to a receiving plant were guaranteed that their current rate of pay would be unchanged for 26 months.

- *Retirement counseling*   For people considering their retirement options, a special counseling session was offered to help them sort through what seemed to many a bewildering set of calculations and trade-offs.

- *Unemployment compensation*   Government representatives were brought in to discuss what employees would need to do to qualify and receive their unemployment benefits, if necessary, after the plant closed.

- *Financial counseling*   For a substantial number of employees, Glacier had been their only job for over 15 or 20 years. Throughout this time they had contributed to a pension plan, had participated in Glacier's savings plan, and were quite concerned about what to do with the money they would receive when the plant closed. For most, this was the largest single amount of money they had ever seen at one time—and they wanted help. Outside experts from banks and/or financial planning businesses were brought in to offer financial alternatives for the people to consider.

Comparisons and Evaluation

Based on published reports,[2] the financial package offered by Glacier was moderately generous. Businesses like GTE, Ford, Navistar, and others appear to have offered similar formulas when figuring the actual severance amount to be offered. Specifically, most businesses offer one week's salary for every year worked at the time of separation,[3] considerably less than Glacier's offer. The flexibility offered to older employees who were less likely to become reemployed is of particular note in Glacier's package.

The Glacier pension options reflect some recent thinking about the need to accelerate vesting of pension funds, the protection of pension benefits prior to "retirement age," and the need to consider survivorship issues.

The additional forms of assistance were well received by people affected by the plant-closing program. The guaranteed hourly pay rate for transferees received somewhat mixed reactions because it protected only wages, not accumulated service. Thus, seniority was lost upon transfer, subjecting the employee to shifts in assignments, and possibly a future layoff, based on such criteria. In fact, this is precisely what happened to a number of people who transferred.

The unemployment compensation information was welcomed, but the combined effect of the financial and retirement counseling was by far the most positive aspect of the added benefits in this segment. It is worth noting that Glacier agonized over the financial counseling because it wanted to avoid the appearance of a conflict of interest in advising employees how to handle their severance pay, but they also recognized that external experts often used such opportunities to sell their services. Ultimately, the decision as to whom to allow in was made by a consensus of people including the transition center manager, the plant manager, and Glacier headquarters' program managers.

The retirement counseling deserves special attention because of the individual chosen to offer this service. He was a retirement-eligible Glacier employee who was extremely well versed in the complex maze of retirement options. Something of a local curmudgeon, with the tenacity of an English bulldog, he would not only provide general counsel, but also offer individuals a blend of no-nonsense "facts" and his legendary perseverance—including an occasional phone call to Glacier's chief executive officer if necessary. Understandably, the recipients of this service were stunned, pleased, and very grateful.

Overall employee reaction to the financial assistance was very positive, particularly in locations where previous businesses had closed their facilities and the details of their severance packages were known. During one small-group session, an hourly worker commented, "I *know* we are getting a good deal because my husband was laid off last month and he lost all his pension money and got no severance pay at all!" It took very few of these comparative testimonials to convince people that the financial separation package was not an issue.

In Glacier's benefits materials one finds the following statement:

> Employees are expected to remain at work until their designated termination dates following expiration of the notice period in order to qualify for various Plant Closing or layoff benefits.

The overall drivers behind this portion of Glacier's safety net included a mixture of historic momentum of past practices, some cost reduction concerns over extended unemployment, and a certain amount of bribery to keep people on the job until Glacier determined that they were no longer needed.

HEALTH PROTECTION

Medical Insurance

Medical insurance was extended 12 months after the termination at no cost to the employee or dependents. For people aged 50 with 25 years' continuous service, the coverage was provided for the individual and dependents until the person reached age 65. Coverage for the employee after 65 was provided at no cost, but dependent coverage was provided at the prevailing rate.

Life Insurance

Like medical insurance, life insurance was also extended 12 months after termination. People aged 50 with 25 years of continuous service received life insurance coverage until age 65, providing twice the employee's normal annual earnings until that age. After that, the normal monthly reduction that applied to pensioners would occur.

Dental Plan

For all but the more extensive dental coverage areas (e.g., endodontia, periodontia, oral surgery, and accidental injury), dental coverage was *not* extended beyond the date of termination. Dental work in progress would be covered for a period of 90 days after termination. A somewhat more liberal option, available only to employees within one year of optional retirement age, included full coverage until age 65 for the person and dependents.

Comparisons and Evaluation

Studies like the one summarized in Table 4.1 have shown that most companies offer extended health benefits to people affected by a plant closing.[4] Only a relatively small percentage, including Glacier, offered a minimum of a year's coverage after termination. The same point can be made for extending coverage to the person's dependents.

The literature is less specific about insurance coverage as a distinctly separate area from "health benefits," but there is evidence to suggest that Glacier's approach was in line with what other companies had done.[5]

An interesting outcome of the dental plan was that people began to take advantage of the coverage when they realized that the benefits would end upon termination. This reaction has occurred in previous businesses as well.[6]

Employee reaction was sometimes difficult to assess because the combination of separation pay and health benefits was part of an overall package in the minds of most people. The quote at the beginning of this chapter sums up the sentiment most often expressed. Given Glacier's past practices of continued employment and above-average pay scale in most communities, this part of the benefits program probably appeared to be what most would have expected, and therefore not worth much more comment than has been presented. Historic momentum of past practices was the key driver behind this part of Glacier's package.

Table 4.1   Continuation of Employee Health Care Benefits (*N* = 224 companies)

Availability and Duration of Coverage	Number of Companies	Percentage
Benefits available for:		
• Less than 3 months	57	25 %
• 3–5 Months	54	24
• 6–11 Months	36	16
• 1 year or more	27	12
Depends on location or position of employee	4	2
Benefits not available	46	21
Total	224	100 %

Source: The Conference Board, 1986.

OCCUPATION TRANSITION

This very interesting part of Glacier's safety net, like other forms of assistance, evolved to a more efficient state over time. Although created in a hodge-podge manner, with various types of assistance coming from several directions, it eventually came to resemble a hub that could be called a "transition center," with numerous spokes representing facets of support. This actual "hub" never was formally created at the outset, but de facto the services often came to be offered in this way. An overview of these services follows:

Trauma Counseling

The purpose was to help people and their families deal with the anger and anxiety felt after the plant-closing announcement. Outside therapists conducted general employee meetings and employee/spouse workshops, and also provided a 24-hour employee advice/assistance telephone service. Individual counseling was made available to employees as well. *This activity began within a week following the closing announcement.*

Placement Services

The objective was to provide the highest level of placement services available to all of the closing plants' employees. Some of the key activities included the following:

- Psychological support

- Resume preparation

- Interview skill building

- Job search guidance

Outside consultants conducted two- or three-day workshops during business hours for approximately 20 employees per workshop.

Employee Assistance Program

The local assistance program was managed by a steering committee consisting of six to eight members, including both union/hourly and management representatives. The major purpose was to serve the needs of employees through a broad representative base with access to both internal and external information/assistance.

Transition Centers

The assistance centers became the hub of employee assistance activities in most locations. Government funds were used to hire external staff and to equip each center. The major activities conducted at these centers included the following:

- Typing and copying of resumes

- Newspaper help-wanted ads and job postings

- Job search directories and resource materials

- Aptitude and interest testing

- Career counseling for groups and individuals

- Counseling for training programs and educational courses

- Special on-site retraining courses

- Job search assistance (e.g., job clubs, support teams)

- Job development and OJT contract sourcing

Training/Retraining Program

The purpose of this program was to provide people with a new set of skills that would enable them to acquire a job. The program was set up to offer training for skills that were in high demand. The delivery systems included local community colleges and local vocational schools, outside consulting firms, and Glacier facilities. Specific activities included:

- Educational "fairs" held on site

- Educational/career counseling

- Specific programs/courses:
    –GED and remedial training
    –Off-site vocational courses and special training programs
    –On-site special training courses

Comparisons and Evaluation

This is a complex and critical area. Glacier attempted to put together a reasonably comprehensive package. Often it appeared jury-rigged because the sources of assistance were only loosely "federated" at the outset and the day-to-day integration was difficult to accomplish from a distant headquarters office. Over time, the hub described earlier began to form. To do justice to the areas covered, each will be examined separately.

Trauma Counseling.   According to a *Conference Board* report,[7] over half of the companies studied offered counseling to displaced employees. Glacier's program contained some distinct components: on-site group-oriented meetings, private individual counseling, and a 24-hour phone number to call for help.

The private counseling and the phone number were reasonably well received, and the confidentiality surrounding both served Glacier and its people well throughout this time. On the other hand, the group-oriented meetings raised more than a little dust. At times, this became an updated version of the old joke about the Boy Scout so intent on earning that final merit badge that he began forcing old ladies across the street against their will. On the surface, few could argue with the idea of offering people the opportunity to unburden themselves of the fears and concerns associated with such a major life event. As always, however, the rub came in the execution of this ideal.

The timing, content, and staffing of this part of the program generated some controversy among the closing plants. From a timing standpoint, the plants indicated that the program schedule had a narrow focus. The support functions insisted that people attend introductory sessions, with insufficient regard for the plants' operating schedules. The content of the meetings was quite upsetting to some people. A typical comment was, "I felt better *before* I attended the meeting." People apparently felt they were not ready to deal with the emotional side of the plant-closing issue, that this approach came at them too soon and made them very uncomfortable. In some instances, the staffing of the program was considered questionable by the audience. They saw some counselors as being "out of touch with working people" and others as being "flaky." I would conclude that people were preoccupied with the meat-and-potatoes issues of benefits and unemployment options, and that they simply couldn't handle this onslaught at such an early point in the process. Recall that this event occurred within one week of the closing announcement.

Some people did express appreciation for the group meetings, and several plant managers indicated that the use of counseling picked up toward the end of the plant's scheduled operation. As for the "flaky" counselors, I will return to them in Chapter 11.

Placement Services.   This is a tough area, second only to the retraining of adults. Much research has shown the numerous obstacles that get in the way of people taking advantage of this type of help.[8] For some, it is nearly impossible to get past the shock of losing their source of income, despite their historic loyalty and hard work. For others, some of life's realities such as age, gender, educational level, lack of job-seeking experience, and membership in a specific working group (e.g., blue-collar), form what seems an insurmountable barrier to finding another job. Many had to get past a sense of shame and loss of self-worth before they could even begin to take rational steps toward reemployment.

This activity was not without its moments of irony. Many saw Glacier's severance package as so generous that they decided it was safe to delay their job search. Some "took the summer off"; others "went to Florida"; many just waited until their unemployment benefits ran out before getting "serious." This meant that the placement service representatives had to work hard at convincing people that they would be less likely to find acceptable jobs if they delayed the search. This admonition met with only mixed success.

Another irony was the "internal comparison" issue that people carried around with them as they looked at other jobs outside Glacier. Many employees found it difficult to work for non-Glacier firms. They had become accustomed to a certain level of managerial skill and overall employment practices. When their expectations were not met, they often turned down offers or else quit after a very short period of time.

I sat in on several of the sessions for people going through this process and was impressed with the stages of emotion through which the participants passed. Over a two- or three-day period, they expressed many of the classic "grief process" emotions of denial, anger, despair, resignation, and hope. I would concur with those who see placement, under these circumstances, as having to focus primarily on rebuilding the diminished sense of self-worth above nearly all the other, more rational lists of things-to-do-to-get-another-job.

The placement professionals summed up much of their frustration by saying that most employees were not interested in the job search process— they just wanted another job. They were emphatic about it and did not mince words:

> You took away my job. You should find me another one.

Most employees were reluctant to accept the reality that Glacier had been paying above community rates for some time and that the job market offered them little chance of matching their current hourly wages. Employees who had earned from $8 to $12 per hour found the job market offering only $4 to $6 per hour. Some might argue that Glacier's past pay practices had been a mixed blessing, to the extent that the plant-closing decision was economically based. Some dark humor emerged around this issue. One man, referring to his World War II days, likened his terminated status to the short life spans expected on hazardous assignments:

> They used to complain to me about fighter pilots being paid more money. I told them they weren't being paid more, they were being paid sooner. . . .

Glacier also did a lot of common things like helping employees type resumes, and providing them with phones and a desk to organize their materials. Some see this as offering "false security."[9] I take strong issue with this viewpoint. The evidence I witnessed suggests that the recipients grew to recognize a truer source of false security to lie in accepting organizations' assurances of sustained employment in the future. In many cases, the period of delayed job search was a legitimate psychological sabbatical needed to assimilate the impact of change. To challenge this with an outplacement equivalent of the educational theory of formal discipline ("All students must take Latin to strengthen their minds") seems to me an example of misplaced logic and possibly harmful.

Employee Assistance Program.   This was an interesting "shadow organization" concept that worked better than many expected. The official description of this program was of a group of organizational representatives who met to try to help people affected by the plant closing get the appropriate assistance they sought. In actuality, it was much more.

The full measure of what this piece of Glacier's package meant requires a bit of history. One location stood out over the years for its labor–management strife. When it was placed on the list of locations to be closed, a general expectation of various forms of retaliation arose. Two events occurred, however, to ameliorate these concerns. The first came when the plant manager was replaced by a lower level manager who did not share his adversarial viewpoint or his role in the plant's history of union confrontation. The second was the involvement of the most militant union representatives on a joint labor–management steering committee to provide employee assistance. The lack of acrimony was, itself, historic. Even the community noticed, as evidenced by these editorial words in a local paper:

> Glacier is showing compassion and responsibility by easing the pain for its employees and the community while closing its plant.
>
> Its approach is doubly appreciated by a community that has seen corporations give short notice, if any, idle hundreds and stagger the economy without a fare-thee-well. The bruises still hurt.
>
> Glacier took a positive approach from the beginning and what happened here was typical. After it was determined that competitive factors required the closing here and at many other plants, the corporation made the announcement early, giving employees and the community time to prepare.

These "steering committees" began to appear across all of the closing plants, union and non-union. The "children" who had been allowed to plan picnics and suggest the paint color for the lunchroom were now sitting at the table with the managers, making "grown-up" decisions destined to affect most, if not all, of the people in the plant—including those making the decisions. No pain, no gain. Over and over we see that the innovative use of human assets comes most easily in times of duress. I'd like to think that such examples paved the way for more of the same in Glacier—but they didn't. I'd also like to think that the innovative Silicon Valley type firms are creating new organizational approaches that will design in broader participation as part of their overall fabric. Some evidence suggests otherwise.[10]

I grow impatient with organizations and managers whose lack of vision, stunted management philosophies, or inexperience keep their organizations moving inexorably toward an economic abyss. More than any other single factor, I find this one to be a real show-stopper. Even Glacier's own example was not embraced by itself after the plant-closing events passed. So much for one-trial learning.

Transition Centers.   The genesis of these centers can be traced to the availability of government funds. These Title III funds were available as a result of an 1982 law called the Job Training Partnership Act (JTPA), a federal commitment to train and find productive employment for persons with serious labor market barriers. Title III of the act authorizes a new program to assist experienced workers who have permanently lost their jobs as a result of technological displacement, foreign competition, and other structural changes in the economy. This federal funding is provided for state-administered programs to help dislocated workers adjust to changing labor market conditions, acquire new skills, and find new jobs. Although few strings are attached, the law requires that at least 35 percent of the funds be spent for training or related services. The intent is to encourage opportunities for experimenting with different approaches.

This was an interesting aspect of Glacier's program because it became so clear that the impact of the overall change management effort hinged upon relatively few variables, some as clearly defined as the skill level of transition center managers. Time after time, these people either proved their resourcefulness in often ambiguous circumstances, or else demonstrated remarkable stupidity in the fruitless and empty gestures offered up in the name of assistance. I'll let someone else write the list of "Ten Criteria for Selecting Effective Transition Center Managers." Instead, let me point out some that seemed to be crucial.

Experience.   Having gone through this before in one or more situations, the managers were prepared in many ways. They knew what assistance was available, at what cost, and how much inconvenience it would cause the organization, the managers, the workers, and themselves.

Temporariness.   The Glacier people who were losing their jobs were impressed by the fact that the transition center manager's job would last only as long as theirs did, or maybe a few months longer to help clean up some details. Several employees commented that they could trust someone from outside Glacier to talk to and found these outside people better able to identify with the concerns of those about to lose their jobs. I have talked with managers from other companies who used internal people who were to be terminated in these kinds of jobs. That approach might work but it brings me to the third and final criterion I'll discuss.

Professional Competence. The best transition center managers I dealt with had a combination of experience and either training or formal education in areas directly related to dealing with people in need of a measured blend of personal counseling and a figurative "whack on the head." These skills, I believe, are not commonly found inside organizations. Further, I have some difficulty believing that the walking wounded themselves would be in the best position to lead such efforts without such a background—or even with it.

As I listened to many of these managers, it became clear to me that Glacier would have been better served if the plant management had used each of the transition center managers as a clearinghouse for the many services that were offered via the center. Instead, each "vendor" was expected to approach the center manager, the plant manager, and perhaps others. This reminds me of another old line: A camel is a racehorse designed by a committee. The lack of control over timing, staffing, and content can be attributed to not vesting the transition center managers with sufficient authority over the various service providers.

Finally, the transition center managers themselves pointed out several problems with using Title III funds. Their views are shared by others and can be summed up with the following points:

- Overabundance of paperwork and record keeping

- Dealing with inefficient state bureaucracies

- Overcoming the stigma of using government money in the eyes of recipients

- Dealing with changing regulations without sufficient notice

- Employee resistance to filling out required forms

- Recipients' resistance to state requirements for "personal information"[11]

Another issue was in the measurement of program effectiveness. Too often, the criteria centered on things that could be counted easily, such as interviews conducted. That's like evaluating a surgeon on the number of operations performed. Perhaps the most damning comment came from an executive at Glacier headquarters:

> If I had to do this all over again, I think I'd argue against using Title III funds. Frankly, I believe we would find it less expensive as a company to fund all this activity ourselves. This is particularly true if we ever count up all the time, effort, and money spent on gathering, recording, and distributing all the information required by the state agencies handling the funding and program evaluation.

Training/retraining program.   In the words of the transition center managers, "Most employees were not interested in going back to school, they just wanted another job." I believe that the whole training/retraining area, as it relates to "rewiring some heads" as well as providing new skills, is the most difficult change impact challenge. Although there were some small successes in Glacier and elsewhere, there are systemic and human nature problems that get in the way.

It has been pointed out that a number of significant impediments must be dealt with if significant progress will ever be made.[12] Here are a few of the major issues:

- The psychological strain of training as well as the lack of sufficient financial support to sustain the trainee during the training have been common, as can be seen in the following quote:

> Training is generally an arduous experience for the unemployed worker, and can scarcely be considered institutionalized malingering. Even with the financial support available to trainees in Sioux City, many men and their families were forced to make genuine sacrifices in order to capitalize on this opportunity for self-improvement. Moreover, the hard economic facts indicate that this price of low support in a lengthy program is a high dropout rate, which wastes the resources already invested from public or private funds and by the trainee himself.[13]

- In response to government criteria for continued funding, criteria focusing on numbers of people placed, the practice of "creaming" occurs. This means that people who are poor readers, don't have a high school diploma, or can't type are often turned away because they constitute a group considered too high-risk for posttraining placement.

- The training time for equipping people with enough knowledge to master a technical skill is often grossly insufficient.

- Training and retraining lead to unrealistic expectations among participants regarding job opportunities and pay levels.

The most telling set of statistics are those summarizing the percentage of displaced people who seek retraining and the percentage of businesses that offer it. On average, about 15 percent of people affected by a plant closing will enter retraining. Glacier's numbers were substantially higher, at 32 percent. In a study of over 224 companies that reported a closing, only 11 percent offered retraining.[14] This is a disturbing statistic in view of the material presented in Chapter 1 regarding the future demands to be placed on job holders in just a handful of years.

There are *no* easy answers to this problem. From a government standpoint, better criteria for evaluating program success can be found—for example, longer term retention of jobs gained through retraining and special funds for remedial skill training. From an organizational standpoint, the practice of pushing out the door people who are poorly equipped to master new jobs will only fall victim to the adage, "What goes around, comes around." When the newer cadres of managers can wrest control from the hands of the short-sighted, perhaps such practices will decline. Finally, from a human nature standpoint, much of the resistance is based on unrealistic expectations. Extrapolations from the past ("The good old days are just around the corner") are a way of denying reality. As hollow as it sometimes seems, particularly in the face of a major economic dislocation, people need to consider the concept of lifelong learning as a critical bulwark against becoming victims of redundancy. On the other hand, I would encourage critics to also take a long, hard look at what passes for adult learning materials and practices. These often stop just short of being intellectually insulting and socially degrading. Unfortunately, the model of education to which most of us were exposed in school too rarely is questioned when the retraining of adults is planned. Adult learning requires a more contemporary model, along with some contemporary attitudes on the part of the learners.

Recalling the philosophical arguments behind safety nets, I believe that Glacier's motivation in offering assistance in this area was about two-thirds humanitarian and one-third cost reduction. The imbalance accounts for the grumbling by some plant managers regarding the poor timing of assistance insofar as production schedules were concerned. The latter reflected the need to get beyond the point of needing external assistance as quickly as possible.

ADVANCE NOTICE

Not counting its distribution center consolidations, Glacier announced its intention to close 10 manufacturing locations over a three-year period. Two closed after the first six to seven months, but the rest had at least a 12- to 18-month notice. One employee commented:

> Glacier, Inc., has allowed us substantial lead time to prepare for the plant closing. This has been to our advantage.

It may appear obvious that advance notice should be considered part of a safety net. However, I was surprised by the number of comments like this one:

> Close the plant and get it over with. People are going nuts waiting now that Glacier has turned its back on us. It's time to turn mine on Glacier.

As the plant closing program progressed, Glacier passed along some lessons learned by managers at locations that had closed, to those managing plants scheduled to close.

Comparisons and Evaluation

A good place to start is with a study that examined the policies and practices of approximately 350 companies that had experienced a major reduction in employment.[15] Of particular interest was the amount of advance notice each gave employees of the coming event. The following figures show that Glacier's program was in the extreme minority.

Days of Notice Given	Percent
0	12%
1–90	70%
91–180	9%
181+	9%

There appears to be general agreement that, on humanitarian grounds, advance notice is a good idea. It allows people to prepare for their future, and some believe there is an implied contract that obligates an employer to inform people if such a dramatic change is coming. In the past, however, employers have resisted giving notice for several reasons. Here is a sampling:

- Reduced morale will lead to lower productivity.

- Sabotage and thefts will occur.

- Management will be targets of employee aggression.

- The best people will leave.

- Business will be unable to obtain credit.

- Customers and suppliers may be lost.[16]

Looking at Glacier's situation, let us address each of these:

1. *Reduced morale will lead to lower productivity.*   The short answer is, "Didn't happen." I will be returning to this point with much detail to show the actual impact on productivity and product quality and the employees' views of these two outcomes.

2. *Sabotage and thefts will occur.*   Again, no. In fact, this point was handled in some innovative ways. One of the more interesting ones took the form of an auction of items the plant would not be needing. People were offered an opportunity to bid on items that included such things as their personal chair at nominal prices. Thus, the employees acquired some things with intrinsic value to them at very little cost. The plant manager indicated that there was no incident of theft and credited this to the auction.

3. *Management will be targets of employee aggression.*   As others have found, the predominant emotion was sadness at the loss. Managers were viewed as experiencing the loss along with them. The anger that occurred was aimed at first-level managers' inability to provide useful information.

4. *The best people will leave.*   Past research has shown that blue-collar and white-collar workers have distinctly different views of their job situations. The former group views the alternative to the current job as unemployment or a lower paying job. Hence, they perceive no real need to leave a good-paying job until it is gone. The latter group, upon sensing trouble, gears up for a search and prepares to exit as soon as it is practical. Glacier experienced both of these scenarios. As was pointed out earlier, however, Glacier also set the stage for some of the professional turnover by not offering any hope of future employment at the outset. Also, there

is some evidence to suggest that the skills of the people who stay are not significantly different from those of the people who leave.[17]

5. *Business will be unable to obtain credit*   This did not happen because of Glacier's size and its long-term history of economic strength.

6. *Customers and suppliers may be lost.*   Again, because of its size and history, Glacier did not experience this problem.

Overall, I believe that Glacier was motivated by a belief that sufficient notice was given for the business to accomplish its objectives. The period of time was viewed as long enough for support programs to have the desired effect of preparing people and reducing long-term unemployment for most employees in the closing plants. One question that remains, however, is, "How much notice is enough?"

After talking with plant managers, their management teams, people who offered transition assistance, and those losing their jobs, I found a general agreement that six months to a year is about as long as most people need. This assumes that the support programs are ready to be rolled out at the time of the announcement. A sizable number of those with whom I spoke indicated that an announcement more than one year in advance began to be dysfunctional in that people either lost a sense of urgency or began to believe that the plant was not going to close after all.

NUCLEAR WINTER

Glacier, Inc., joined a number of other organizations in breaking an unstated bilateral contract of commitment between the person and the person's employer. The net effect was described as the occupational equivalent of nuclear winter. The survivors came to view themselves as the real victims. In the case of Glacier, the effect of the plant closing was nearly always discussed in terms of its impact on the people losing their jobs and the locations scheduled to close.

WHO GOT WORK?

As for the people who lost their jobs, approximately 60 percent of those who were seeking a job were reemployed within six months of the plant shutdown. This figure, however, masks some major swings in reemployment numbers for rural versus urban locations. A reemployment figure of somewhere between 50 and 70 percent appears to be common across some of the reported studies done by Ford, Levi Strauss, Armco, Strohs, and Navistar. One should be careful, however, because factors influencing these statistics include plant geography, current local and national economic conditions, work force demographics, and the overall mind set of the people affected.

REACTIONS TO THE NET

An interesting part of the Glacier program was an effort to track some of the people who left a closing plant and determine their job status, how they viewed the assistance given to them, and some of their coping strategies throughout the closing time frame.[18] The study came up with some very interesting results. First, there are data pertaining to the relationship between the use of the outplacement assistance and subsequent reemployment, as shown in Table 4.2.

Over 70 percent of the people seeking employment signed up for the services available. At first glance, one might be tempted to conclude that people would be better off without such help. The demographic data, however, showed that people who *needed* help were more likely to seek it. In particular, young single females with children made up a substantial portion of this group. The study suggests that people may have jumped too soon to get a job they later regretted. The unemployed group tended to continue to deny the reality of the closing, and many expected that Glacier would call them back. From these figures, I would suggest that offering outplacement assistance is like trying to create a level playing field: Those whose potential for reemployment is less than that of others are given a chance to strengthen themselves prior to the search.

For those unemployed, the services may not have been enough to counter

Table 4.2   Reemployment Data for Glacier Employees

Group	Used Outplacement Services	Did Not Use Outplacement Services
Happily employed	25%	14 %
Unhappily employed	20	1
Unemployed and miserable	38	1

Table 4.3   View of Outplacement Services by Former Glacier Employees

Service Category	Helpful	Not Helpful	Not Used
Job search workshops	81%	2 %	12 %
Transition center visits	79	3	5
Resume assistance	78	2	11
Training classes	64	7	3
Follow-up calls	52	9	21
Job listings	23	9	23
Placement agencies	22	16	36

several other factors, including their own mind set—for example, a coping strategy of denial, blaming others, withdrawing, or taking on a pollyanna attitude of blind faith.

Another interesting set of figures (Table 4.3) shows how the people who used the outplacement services viewed them some six months after the plant had closed.

The transition center manager and others offering assistance found that individuals would not complete a resume on their own because they were blocked by their own self-doubts, fears, or confusion. This suggests, again, that a combination of counseling and the "laundry list" of assistance is necessary.

THE GRATEFUL DEAD

There have been some references made in the literature to the use of ceremonies in organizations.[19] In particular, there appears to be a growing awareness of the value of orchestrating "closing ceremonies."[20] At Glacier, one location held such an event and invited all the people affected by the closing, as well as several other stakeholders, to attend. The event itself had been described as follows:

. . . a parade of production workers led by the plant manager, all wearing V-necks with company logo, and carrying signs reading "CELEBRATION" and

"NEW BEGINNINGS." The parade ends in the balloon-filled cafeteria where the group enjoys food, dancing, story telling, and expressions of gratitude and encouragement for future pursuits.[21]

To some, the idea of having a party to mark the end of one's job seems, at minimum, a bit mawkish. Yet, humans do make use of ritual and ceremony in many situations—happy and sad—to help manage the impact of change.

The Glacier ceremony was well attended and, according to those who participated, offered an opportunity to achieve closure on a particular chapter in their lives and say farewell to people who had been a part of their social setting, in many cases, for decades. I attended this event and was struck by a single symbolic gesture made by the plant manager to signal the precise moment of closing. An inflated plastic replica of one of the plant's major products was held up by the plant manager in front of all the people and was deflated slowly until all of the air was gone. It was a poignant, emotional, and highly symbolic moment for the people in attendance.

THE WALKING WOUNDED

The final point to be made regarding the plant closing impact deals with the so-called survivors. As mentioned earlier, scant attention was paid to those who were going to be left. Many simply assumed that the survivors would consider themselves lucky, and that was that. The actual events tell otherwise. Survivors were found to need nearly as much assurance as did those who lost their jobs.[22]

The most dramatic demand placed upon the management team at the receiving plants was for communication about the impact of the closing. In fact, communication was considered by receiving plant management to be a prime ingredient for smoothing out this transition. This took many forms: bulletin board announcements, birthday meetings, round table discussions, staff meetings, box lunches, off-site dinners, one-on-one conversations, newsletters, and the like.

The impact of the closing announcement itself on the receiving plant was quite different from what many outside the plant expected. According to the plant staffs, the following were the main reactions:

- Fear that this could also happen to them

- Empathy for other Glacier employees who lost their jobs

- Guilt over being "survivors"

The management teams at the receiving plants spent considerable time reassuring their people that their plant was not going to close and that the new machinery, people, and products would help ensure job security for them if the transition went smoothly and if productivity, efficiency, and quality could be demonstrated within a reasonable period of time. Managers reported that people began to express hope for the future and to feel excitement about the new changes coming.

MANAGING THE DILEMMAS

DOLLARS AND SENSE

Among the key issues facing managers who attempt large-scale organizational change are the likely costs associated with the impact. At Glacier, it was quite expensive to plan and bring about the closing of ten production units and to provide the assistance described earlier. How much should the human side of this change cost? The literature does not give exact figures, but Table 4.4 provides some comparison numbers taken from published summaries.

One cannot help but be struck by the minimal amount of variation in placement percentages compared with the wide range of per-person costs across these different companies to achieve these results. Further interpretation must be made with caution because it may *take* $3,000 to place a person in one set of circumstances and only $325 in another.

Table 4.4   A Comparison of Costs Associated with Plant Closings for Several Companies

Company	Program Cost	Placement Percentage
Armco	$820/person	67%
Ford	$3,060/person	61%
Glacier	$816/person	60%
Navistar	$325/person	55%
Strohs	$2,597/person	67%

MOVING THE UNMOVABLE

I was sitting in a group of production line people as they discussed the difficulties they faced in making the decision to relocate in order to keep themselves employed. They talked about the difference in cultures, the difficulty of reorienting themselves to new sports team loyalties, and in some cases the extreme hardship they faced because—instead of moving—they continued to commute between their old location and the new one. The stress of having to make new friends, learn new store locations, and so on was articulated clearly. At one point I asked, "How far is it from here to your previous location?" The answer: 32 miles.

Someone once told me that the overwhelming majority of Americans do not move more than 70 miles from where they were born. I was reminded of this as I listened to the travails of these people. The point could not have been clearer to me: Geographic distance is judged very differently by different groups of employees. I also listened to the "intransigent" group discuss the impact on their families and the hidden costs of relocating to a new city.

The willingness to relocate will no doubt be driven by the adage about the pain of change being less than the pain of staying the same. However, there do seem to be a few things that managers could address: family counseling, trial positions, and guaranteeing seniority rights as well as salary. Nevertheless, I remain unconvinced that any large-scale geographic movement can be expected among people faced with economic dislocation.

TRADING ON THE LOGO

Some Glacier people still joke about having the company logo tattooed on their backsides. A lot fewer now than before, though. Something happened in the past few years at Glacier that severely challenged the whole concept of loyalty. It might be called "trading on the logo" because a sort of last-ditch exchange of that type took place.

In effect, the company was able to bank on a relatively untapped reserve of loyalty from employees who sometimes cited three family generations of commitment to the company to explain why they worked there. When Glacier needed to close its locations and yet keep them running until the very last day, it encouraged people to stay on the job by offering them a generous severance check *and* by appealing to their sense of loyalty in this time of crisis. Most people bought in and, in effect, exchanged the value of the logo for a lower paying job after the closing. It is only speculation that an earlier job search would have resulted in a higher rate of pay—but the possibility exists.

The trouble with this is that such deals can be made only once. After that, one is faced with a very different work force. Next time they will ask the time-worn question of mercenaries: *What's in it for me?*

"IMMINENT" DOMAIN

Glacier and other companies have been busy sweeping out large numbers of employees. Yet they seem to be able to only place about 60 percent of them. What will happen to all of the other people? I have had several occasions to speak with people in this category, particularly the "too old" bunch. They have said that the companies will rue the day they allowed so much corporate memory to walk out the door. They predict that the demographic curve and time are on their side. All they have to do is to hang on for a little while, and their skills and abilities will once again be needed—but this time it will be on *their* terms. According to a recent *Wall Street Journal* article (April 25, 1991), the future is now . . .

> **Not Forgotten: More companies call retirees back for temporary work.**
> Travelers Corp. figures it saves $1 million a year in employment-agency fees by keeping tabs on retirees and recalling them as needed. At any one time, 60% of its temporaries are retirees, from Travelers as well as other companies. Of a dozen workers who retired last year at Hershey Foods Corp. headquarters, half already have been recalled for temporary assignments: "They're better workers," it explains. J. C. Penney Co. routinely asks retirees each Christmas if they want to help with the annual rush.
> PHH Corp. calls on retirees because "we need their brains and experience." Coleman Co. taps a former executive secretary for a temporary secretarial job because "you can't get someone off the street who knows the foreman of the north plant when you've got to get hold of him." Armstrong World Industries uses retirees to fill gaps created by an early-retirement program last fall.
> *Chili's Inc. has to pass on this approach. "We've never had a retiree," the restaurant chain says.*[23]

SUMMARY

The impact of change has, as a central focus, human assets. Paradoxically, the greatest catalyst and impediment to change is the management of these assets in the face of major organizational transition or transformation. This chapter focuses on a specific set of actions that can be taken to reduce the turmoil that naturally occurs when people find themselves on shifting occupational ground.

Beginning with reference to some basic human needs, a range of motives for organizations to provide a safety net to people faced with major transitions is explored. These include such categories as simply extending past practices, operating under humanitarian principles, avoiding possible reprisal, reducing costs, and offering "bribes." With this backdrop, a detailed look at Glacier's safety net offers an opportunity to understand how such programs are put together and why certain elements are offered. This package, offered as part of a plant-closing program, is divided into four categories: income protection, health protection, occupation transition, and advance notice. For each of the package elements, a detailed description is given, accompanied by an evaluation of its utility. Further, a comparison is made against actions taken by other organizations in similar circumstances.

In looking at the aftermath of Glacier's decision, our attention turns to what has been called the organizational equivalent of nuclear winter. An examination of reemployment statistics is offered, followed by some research findings that capture reactions to Glacier's assistance offered during this transition—who used the various forms of assistance, how useful they were, and how ceremonies were used to help move people through this difficult period. The survivors of this nuclear winter are also discussed. A description of the dynamics of managing people who remain behind after a major organizational change is offered. In particular, some insight is given into how managers handled communication.

Three major dilemmas facing managers under circumstances similar to those of Glacier are reviewed: balancing the cost of assistance with the benefits, confronting the issue of the immobility of large numbers of people whose jobs and careers are being affected, and acknowledging the final exchange of company loyalty for a delayed job search.

Finally, a glimpse of the future is offered. Recent information is reviewed, showing that people who were released from their jobs in the early 1980s via downsizing, early retirements, and the like are now beginning to be drawn back by their previous employers, largely because of the gap in availability of people *and* because of the need for their corporate memory.

Notes

1. Abraham Maslow, *Motivation and Personality* (New York: Harper and Brothers, 1954), discusses each of the types of needs shown in the diagram. Physiological needs are as basic as hunger and thirst. Safety needs focus on avoiding physical harm. Social needs include a desire for friendship, love, and affection. Esteem needs surround self-respect, positive self-evaluation, and high regard for others. Self-actualization is, in the simplest explanation possible, fulfilling one's life goals.

2. I have drawn upon several sources here for comparison purposes. They include *Plant Closings and Economic Dislocation* by Jeanne Prial Gordus, Paul Jarley, and Louis A. Ferman (Kalamazoo, MI: W. E. Upjohn Institute for Employment Research, 1981), a report by Ronald E. Berenbeim titled *Company Programs to Ease the Impact of Shutdowns* (New York: Conference Board, 1986), a *Personnel Administrator* article titled "Easing the Pain" by Joseph J. Franzem (February 1987), and a presentation made by Carole K. Barnette, Thomas E. Kent, and Thomas F. Ernst at the 1987 annual meeting of the Academy of Management, titled "Organizational Decline: The Challenge of Institutional and Individual Renewal at Navistar International Corporation."

3. Despite the disclaimer on the inside of a report by the National Center on Occupational Readjustment, Inc., titled *Managing Plant Closings and Occupational Readjustment: An Employer's Guidebook*, I found this work, edited by Richard P. Swigart (Washington, DC, 1984), to be an excellent how-to manual containing many "in the trenches" insights not found elsewhere.

4. This information comes from the Conference Board study, cited in note 2, by Ronald Berenbeim. It contains not only good summary results, but excellent case studies as well.

5. I believe the work done by the National Center on Occupational Readjustment (NaCOR) and the research cited previously in reference to Navistar show that Glacier was about the same as the companies cited in these works as far as health benefits were concerned.

6. The NaCOR work included reference to the fact that people began to realize that a sort of window of opportunity was closing and that they had better use certain benefits, such as dental plans, or lose them. This is certainly food for thought for businesses contemplating the impact of change announcements.

7. Earlier I made references to the Conference Board report. Here it can be seen that the companies studied showed a growing awareness that the impact of change can be so severe as to require some form of third-party assistance. Specifically, displaced workers need assurance that something can be done to sustain themselves in the future.

8. Quite a lot of research in the 1960s and 1970s is accounted for in *Plant Closings and Economic Dislocation* by Gordus, Jarley, and Ferman (1981). Here they speak about

the impediments to reemployment found among various employee groups. A somewhat more recent view, in H. G. Kaufman's *Professionals in Search of Work: Coping with the Stress of Job Loss and Unemployment* (New York: Wiley, 1982), also picks up on this theme.

9. An article in *Personnel Journal* by James E. Challenger (February 1989) titled "When Outplacement is a Sham," states: "Providing an office for the job seeker insulates that person from the job market. The office becomes a place to go every day, a safe warm nest." Having spent a good deal of time talking to people in such situations and to professionals providing help to them, I find this logic troubling. The underlying premise is that speed in getting reemployed is a well-accepted goal for everyone. Frankly, I have seen these facilities used as both a staging ground to pull together one's thoughts, a place where one can speak privately to others who may be in the same fix, and—above all—a sanctuary that allows for some internal reflection and adjustment to being ripped out of one's former frame of reference.

10. In his most recent book, *Why Leaders Can't Lead* (San Francisco: Jossey-Bass, 1989), Warren Bennis takes a broadside against the ersatz "leaders" in today's organizational settings. He names names and, at times, *calls* names. I was both surprised and pleased at his candor, as I have dealt with some of these same characters and admire Warren for speaking out so forcefully. He is to be congratulated for also identifying a well-kept secret about Silicon Valley—marginal human resource practices stemming from a management mentality that has been hidden by the marketplace pyrotechnics. These have distracted what would otherwise be a more penetrating look at the day-to-day operations of these so-called model organizations. The stories I hear are far from encouraging and back up Warren's observation that these companies are only emerging copies of established whipping-boy organizations cited often in the management press.

11. The Conference Board report cited above has a good section in it dealing with the benefits and detriments associated with the use of Title III funds. The transition center managers and headquarters program managers I worked with agreed with the overall findings from this report but felt it may have been a little softer in its tone than they would have been.

12. In her *Wall Street Journal* piece, "Manager's Journal" (February 9, 1987), Karen Blumenthal talks about the use of federal funds to help in the retraining effort of displaced workers. She points out that much of the effort is off target because the program is underfunded and the criteria for measurement lead some providers to accept only those who can be placed easily following whatever training they receive. Similar points are made in the Conference Board report and in the previously cited work by Gordus, Jarley, and Ferman.

13. For more details in this area, a good reference is *Strategies for the Displaced Worker* by George P. Shultz and Arnold B. Weber (New York: Harper and Row, 1969).

14. These statistics, first cited by Berenbeim in the Conference Board report, have appeared elsewhere (e.g., the *Wall Street Journal*) and should be of great concern to those looking to the future. The hands-off attitude among too many in

organizational settings is deplorable because our current trends point to a desperate need for retraining and an overall revamping of how adults are prepared for future job demands.

15. In 1986 the Congressional Office of Technology Assessment in Washington, D.C., published a report titled "Plant Closing: Advance Notice and Rapid Response." Among other items, it focused on the practices of a large number of organizations regarding the provision of early notification of intentions to close or lay off large numbers of their people. I recommend this work for its depth and apparent attention to research detail—not a common finding.

16. For a complete review of all the reasons that have been given for not providing advanced notice, I would recommend the following sources: (a) the NaCOR work cited earlier, and (b) the book by Gordus, Jarley, and Ferman, the congressional report cited above, and an intriguing article by Robert I. Sutton, titled "Managing Organizational Death," *Human Resource Management* (Winter 1983).

17. Ann Howard's article in *The Academy of Management EXECUTIVE* (May 1988) is titled "Who Reaches for the Golden Handshake" and represents one of the few efforts I have found to investigate whether the "best people leave." Her research seems to indicate that such a truism needs to be seriously reconsidered. In my own observations, personal mobility is far more complicated an issue and is tied to many more variables than one's personal competence and worth in the marketplace.

18. At the 1987 annual meeting of the Academy of Management, Debora Sholl Humphreys presented a paper titled, "Decline as a Natural Resource for Development." This interesting piece of work deserves attention because it examines the impact of change on people who lost their jobs as a result of a plant closing. The people are tracked over time, and Humphreys was able to gather data describing their views of the assistance offered to them, with particular emphasis on its utility. Further, she offers insights into the coping strategies these people used.

19. Some of the earliest references I have found regarding the use of rituals and ceremonies were in Terrence E. Deal and Allen A. Kennedy, *Corporate Cultures* (Reading, MA: Addison-Wesley, 1982).

20. A fuller treatment of the use of ceremonies in organizations that were undergoing decline or "death" can be found in Stanley G. Harris and Robert I. Sutton, "Functions for Parting Ceremonies in Dying Organizations," *Academy of Management Journal*, 29 (1986).

21. I return to Humphrey's work because she was instrumental in setting up a closing ceremony I myself was able to attend. Her insights represent both the view of an architect and those of one who experienced the impact of the event as well.

22. In a *Wall Street Journal* article (December 5, 1985), Larry Reibstein takes a look at the people who survive the impact of cutbacks. This is an impressive article because it focuses the reader's attention on an issue that grew to be of major proportion for Glacier, Inc., namely the unexpected turbulence among those on whom the organization must rely to move ahead in the future.

23. The *Wall Street Journal* article was printed on April 25, 1989, and I have kept it because it represents the first time I saw reference to the "pea in the python" issue that will undoubtedly emerge throughout organizations currently patting themselves on the back for making their short-term measurements look so good by pushing masses of people out the door in record time. Reprinted by permission of *The Wall Street Journal*, © 1989 Dow Jones & Company, Inc. All Rights Reserved Worldwide.

Chapter 5

CHANGE: A HEALTH HAZARD

Increased blood pressure among employees who are coming into my clinic. Increased cases of ulcers. Increased incidents of TIA [tension-induced attacks]. There are more injuries and recordable injuries occurring. Some employees report that the injuries occur because their senses have "dulled" due to additional work load.

Upper management is conspicuously absent in the health and safety world. They need to get more involved, particularly during this time of great change.
   —Health & Safety Professionals at Glacier, Inc.

Even Bob Wilson wasn't sure what killed him. The medical records would show liver cancer. The cancer came after he had survived a major heart attack only a short while earlier. Preceding all this was the plant closing. As plant manager, Wilson was in a unique and unenviable position: having to close a plant he had turned around only a few years earlier. As he liked to point out, his "numbers" were good, employee morale was high, and he was proud of being able to see the connection between these results and his personal intervention.

> I know that they say the pressure of something like this plant closing can make you sick, but I'm really not sure this is the reason for my heart attack. I just don't know.

But there was more to Bob's source of stress than his having to close a plant. At least two other factors existed: his fierce loyalty to his staff and his debate with headquarters over his own future employment prospects. Before examining this further, it is helpful to understand what the experts say about the connection between stress and illness under such conditions.

A MODEL OF CHANGE SICKNESS

A few years ago I came across some research that suggested a format for thinking about the relationships between external events and the ultimate

Figure 5.1   Relationship between External Events and Individual Health

impact on individuals.[1] A model for capturing the chain of events is shown in Figure 5.1. A lot of emphasis here and elsewhere is placed on macro issues surrounding businesses. The model points to one of the major outcomes of these issues—job loss—and leads to both the economic and psychosocial impact of such change. As the double arrow indicates, there is a possible interaction between economic impact and psychosocial impact. Either or both are seen as related to potential illness and mortality for an individual. The final point, however, is that the individual's condition may, itself, have an impact on either the psychosocial or economic effects. Herein lies the rub. Despite many attempts at researching this area, the experts cannot conclude that the direction of causality is from impact to pathology, or the reverse.

LITANY OF CHANGE SICKNESS

This is not to say that the area of change impact research lacks effort, scope, or rigor.[2] In fact, much is now known about how change affects such areas as:

- Individual and family costs
- Income loss and retraining
- Unemployment issues
- Economic dislocation
- Psychiatric disabilities
- Stress and suicide

Out of this work come several important findings showing the impact of change as strongly linked to individual well-being:

- Economic deprivation has been shown to be more closely related to health problems than to variables such as education, age, and skill level.

- The availability of financial resources during times of stress is probably most crucial because it is seen as evidence of control over one's life.

- Although reemployment takes longer in rural settings affected by such changes, urban employees' lives are found to be more disrupted. Most likely this is due to the community support found in more rural environments. For urban workers, the closest thing to community had been the plant itself.

- Periodic employment may be more harmful than prolonged unemployment in terms of the destruction of health. This is particularly true if the new employment is viewed as downwardly mobile.

- White-collar employees are more susceptible to stress and health-related issues than are blue-collar workers. It appears highly probable that this is because the former group has more of a psychic investment in their work, whereas a less valued social role is attached to the work for blue-collar workers. This, incidentally, is not necessarily an inherent trait. Over the years, blue-collar employees have systematically been placed in positions that do not lead to forming such connections.

Related to this last point, the loss of social standing may be less critical for blue-collar workers. This could be related to their unwillingness to accept the blame for circumstances beyond their control. Paraphrasing a quote heard often by a Glacier manager, "If you want to blame me for the crash, you should have involved me in the take-off."

The feeling of guilt over these circumstances falls much more heavily on those who have carried the day-to-day management responsibilities. In the words of one of the affected people within a closing Glacier plant:

> I strongly feel if we had better management in the past five years things might have been different.

Recalling Bob Wilson's confusion over the source of his illness, consider the following quote from researchers in this area:

> On the whole, there is already considerable evidence that occupational stress is a factor which increases morbidity and mortality from physical disease, especially heart disease.[3]

THE CAREGIVERS

An unusual opportunity was provided during a meeting of all of Glacier's safety and health professionals. At that meeting, four groups of 20 persons each were asked to respond to three questions:

1. What evidence of employee stress do you see in your capacity as a health or safety representative?

2. What are some lessons learned from the health and safety point of view?

3. What messages would you like to send to upper management?

It is important to note that, second only to first-line supervision, these people had extremely close—and often quite personal—interaction with people at the closing plants. In general, the themes that emerged from these sessions are as follows:

EVIDENCE OF STRESS

Increased blood pressure among employees who are coming into the clinic. Increased cases of ulcers. Increased incidents of tension induced attacks. There are more injuries and recordable injuries occurring. Some employees report that the injuries occur because their senses have "dulled" due to additional work load.

Increase in requests for counseling by clinic staff. Employees are reporting greater feelings of anxiety over the closing and frustration over increased responsibilities and excessive overtime.

Increase in emotional problems, divorce rates, and absenteeism.

LESSONS LEARNED

Health and safety costs are greater than management anticipated. Employee perceptions of stability and security have been shattered.

The increase in uncertainty reflected in the clinic visits indicates that the level of communication needed for this change to be successful has been grossly underestimated. Employees perceive inconsistency in what is being communicated.

MESSAGES FOR TOP MANAGEMENT

The communication efforts need to be improved. This means having more one-on-one conversations, using multiple forms of media, and putting more substance in the message. There is a need to put the messages in laypersons' terms.

Upper management is conspicuously absent in the health and safety world. They need to get more involved, particularly during this time of great change.

The health and wellness programs being promoted throughout Glacier may be in conflict with the stress being caused by working lean—a direct outcome of the plant-closing change.

Many people in the plant clinics are not prepared for the level of counseling demands being made on them. More training is needed to handle the emotional problems brought on in a plant-closing situation.

Many employees equate the plant closing with business press articles describing corporate-level "meanness" that starts with Glacier's chairman.

Finally, a medical report issued two years after the initial announcement of the plant-closing program noted that the number of people treated had remained relatively stable, but the types of problems had changed significantly. The changes included:

- Alcohol/drug problems: Up 39 percent

- Financial setbacks: Up 35 percent

- Mental/emotional issues: Up 22 percent

In all, those who provided the health and safety support for Glacier's people offered strong qualitative information that underscores the impact of such change on individual health.

EXECUTIVE MONKEYS

Several years ago some research on animals provided new insights into the effects of stress.[4] Pairs of small monkeys were placed in restraining devices with a small lever within each monkey's grasp. At regular intervals, a moderate shock was administered to both animals simultaneously. The shock could be avoided if one of the switches was pressed. Only one switch was actually connected to the power source. Over time, the monkey with no control came to ignore the lever. The second animal, called the "executive" monkey, learned to control the situation by pressing the lever at the appropriate time. As the research points out, the executive monkey was able not only to sense the shock personally, but also could observe the reaction of the "nonexecutive" to the same shock.

It was discovered that the executive monkey developed ulcers, and the researchers attributed this to the constant alertness demanded to avoid the shock. The nonexecutive could only take the shocks, and thus became less reactive—and also less disturbed.

Research on humans has shown the relationship between stress and ulcers as well as other disabilities. But what seems worth considering in the executive monkey example is an interpretation that goes beyond the stress-induced ulcers. Another factor—having to witness the impact of stress on another—was present. It doesn't seem that surprising that people who are viewed—or view themselves—as having control over the well-being of others will be subjected to more stress.

At Glacier's operating level, it is easy to understand why groups of production workers could avoid feelings of guilt over an economic calamity that was being imposed on all of them indiscriminately. First, the events were viewed as stemming from a source outside their world. Second, never having been involved in the decisions leading up to this action, they felt that nothing they could do would affect the outcome. Finally, most seemed to trust the system to do the right thing and preferred to wait for someone else to act. All these conditions were somewhat different for the management team.

In Bob Wilson's case, he worked tirelessly to ensure that each member of his immediate staff found employment by the time the plant closed. As might be expected, some people were more marketable than others. The more difficult cases became a constant source of concern to Bob, who went to great lengths to contact his network of associates developed over the years for help. In the end, he was able to find a place for everyone, but this took a tremendous toll on him, as witnessed by the grateful but concerned staff.

BOOK OF REVELATIONS

Around the time of Glacier's plant-closing activity, a book made the rounds among managers in the plants scheduled to close. The book, by Alfred Slote, is titled *Termination: The Closing at Baker Plant.*[5] The striking thing about this book, for Glacier's managers, was not so much its unusually readable style or even that it covered a topic of immediate interest to them. Rather, it was its uncanny capacity to predict what was going to happen within Glacier plants: the dynamics around union negotiations, conflict with headquarters, employee concerns, and the impact of such a change on the health and safety of the people at the plant.

The first reactions to this ranged from neutral to positive. People were genuinely surprised to find that the book's rich description so closely paralleled their own day-to-day experiences. After all, the events described had taken place almost 20 years earlier, in a plant that produced totally different kinds of products with substantially different processes. Further, the union–management relationships within Glacier were nowhere near as rocky as those at the plant described in Slote's book. Despite these obvious facts, the similarities began to haunt some of the managers. One said, "I wish I had never read that damn book. It keeps telling me things I don't want to come true—but they do!"

Someone once told me that the difference between quantitative and qualitative data is volume. Slote's work cannot be dismissed because of the lack of quantitative controls and statistical acrobatics; those were provided later by others who also worked on the project. Instead, the book is powerful because of its extraordinary attention to detail and its ability to draw attention to the subtle nuances of a plant-closing environment.

DISAPPEARING INK

Bob Wilson was faced with more than a plant closing, a heart attack, and helping his employees find new jobs. He also had to contend with a "mistake" that Glacier made. As was pointed out in a preceding chapter, Glacier decided not to give any of its managers assurances of future employment at the time of the plant closing announcement. This was a deliberate effort to present a "we're-all-in-this-together" face to the media. In Bob's case, however, a headquarters general manager made an exception. Not only did he assure Bob he would have a job, but the job would be at a location and level that was mutually acceptable—and he put it in writing.

Over time, the general manager fell out of favor, and Bob's new boss began to do some serious back-pedaling on this agreement. Bob sought legal counsel and quietly asked several of his trusted friends within Glacier what they thought he should do. Just as this whole issue was about to come to light, Bob discovered he had liver cancer.

Glacier became magnanimous. Bob was given a ceremony during which he was thanked for his contribution toward a successful plant closing. He was given an increase in salary and was subsequently provided with financial counseling for his survivors. This was very reflective of the overall Glacier culture, in which open disagreements were a sign of poor breeding and people's problems could be solved by giving them a big check.

Over a period of several years, I came to know Bob and saw behind his "tough plant manager" façade. He was a risk-taker. He openly solicited critical feedback of his operations and himself by those he led. He experimented with ideas like innovative compensation schemes and employee involvement. Finally, he was the only plant manager who defied the headquarters authorities and shared the secret of his plant's fate with his immediate subordinates as soon as he knew about it.

What I found truly admirable about Bob was his ability to draw back from his day-to-day pressures of running a closing plant and contemplate the big picture of what was happening. He used a unique form of debate with me. He would lean back in his chair, raise his eyebrows and ask, "You don't *really* believe that, do you?" Time after time he forced a deeper investigation of many issues that otherwise would have gone unchallenged. With his death, Glacier lost a lot more than a plant manager.

Having been drawn close to the health problems Bob faced, I found myself becoming even more frustrated at not being able either to identify the cause or to reverse the effect. Somehow, I think my consternation over this puzzle would have suited him just fine.

THE CAUSAL ARROW

The Glacier plant-closing program did not include any purposeful research into the health-related problems associated with the impact of its decision. What is available comes in the form of recollections from the caregivers, a doctor's memo with summary statistics, and my very unscientific "sample-of-one" observations of a plant manager who died.

Unfortunately, we are no closer to being able to point to a definitive direction of causality now than we were before Glacier closed its plants. This is a troubling point because, as has been pointed out, the closing of plants is only one of a wide range of organizational changes that are taking place today. Just as we have accepted the reality of giving financial and career assistance to people adversely affected by such changes, there is a moral imperative to recognize the need to address health-related issues as well.

A noted medical researcher has labeled such impact a "social emergency,"[6] and such a crisis is all the more critical because, up to now, we have adopted a sort of macho perspective on those "executive monkeys" involved. The actual health impact may well fall most heavily on those in positions of authority and responsibility. Although I am willing to acknowledge that some groups are disposed to react more negatively to change than others, the fact remains that too few acknowledge the problem in the first place.

It has occurred to me that the lessons learned about the negative impact of change will receive little attention from executives and others who would prefer more upbeat "one-minute solutions." The health-related issues described here are even more likely to be destined for obscurity, because they are frightening, produce great feelings of guilt, and can't be solved by writing out a big check. Before solutions can be offered, a general awareness must exist to prompt appropriate questions:

- Who is most likely to suffer health-related problems because of this change?

- What options are available to minimize the health-related impact?

- What resources are needed to manage the impact?

SUMMARY

The impact of change is often considered in macro terms, but the ultimate endpoint can be at the other extreme of that continuum: a hospital bed or a cemetery. To set the stage for such a discussion, a model is offered to show how the events triggered by a macro force can lead to individual pathology. Debate continues over whether change causes sickness or whether it is only that sick people are intolerant of change.

Much research literature exists, and a number of published studies point to a series of reasonably clear points: Economic deprivation is linked to health issues, people need financial control most during such times, urban dwellers suffer from such change more than those in rural settings, having no work is sometimes better than having occasional work, and managers are more susceptible to such changes than are those with less responsibility.

Glacier, Inc., provides information in this area. First, there are observations from its health and safety professionals. In particular, they offer insights into the types of problems they saw during the plant closings, some lessons learned, and a few messages they believe Glacier's top management needed to hear.

Past psychological research on "executive monkeys" was reviewed to show some possible connection to the debilitating effects on managers who undergo the kind of stress found during Glacier's plant-closing program. A comparison of the differences between individual contributors and their managers is offered to explain why the latter group is likely to experience significantly greater stress under these conditions. The case of one manager was highlighted to show such impact.

A brief discussion follows of Alfred Slote's book, *Termination: The Closing at Baker Plant*, and how Glacier's managers at closing plants viewed its uncannily accurate predictions of what they would be going through. Glacier serves as a further example of how an organization can add insult to injury while introducing major change. A description of events surrounding the management of change expose its cumulative effects and how Glacier reacted to its own mistake.

The chapter concludes with a call to accept the likelihood that organizational change will have negative effects on the health of some people and offers some questions that should be asked and answered before introducing such change.

Notes

1. The original model was created by Louis A. Ferman and John Gardner in "Economic Deprivation, Social Mobility and Mental Health," included in a book edited by Louis A. Ferman and Jeanne P. Gordus, *Mental Health and the Economy* (Kalamazoo, MI: W. E. Upjohn Institute for Employment Research, 1979), pp. 193–224. I also found reference to this model in an additional source, *Plant Closings and Economic Dislocation* by Jeanne Prial Gordus, Paul Jarley, and Louis A. Ferman (Kalamazoo, MI: W. E. Upjohn Institute for Employment Research, 1981).

2. Although they are certainly not exhaustive, I am including a series of citations that will help the interested reader get up to speed quickly on some of the more frequently cited work in the area of change-related health issues:

Individual and Family Costs

Dooley, D., and Catalano, R. "Economic Change as a Cause of Behavior Disorder." *Psychological Bulletin, 87,* 450–468 (1980).

Farran, D. C., and Margolis, L. H. "The Impact of Paternal Job Loss on the Family. The Economic Context: Consequences for Children." Detroit, MI: Society for Research: Child Development, 1983.

Unemployment Issues

Aiken, M., Ferman, L. A., and Sheppard, H. F. *Economic Failure, Alienation and Extremism.* Ann Arbor: University of Michigan Press, 1968.

Dorsey, J. W. "The Mack Case: A Study in Unemployment." In Otto Eckstein (Ed.), *Studies in the Economics of Income Maintenance.* Washington, DC: Brookings Institution, 1967.

Ferman, L. *Death of a Newspaper: The Story of the Detroit Times.* Kalamazoo, MI: W. E. Upjohn Institute for Employment Research, 1963.

Young, E. "The Armour Experience: A Case Study in Plant Shutdown." In G. Somers, E. Cushman, and N. Weinberg (Eds.), *Adjusting to Technological Change.* New York: Harper & Row, 1963.

Income Loss and Retraining

Dorsey, J. W. "The Mack Case: A Study in Unemployment." In Otto Eckstein (Ed.), *Studies in the Economics of Income Maintenance.* Washington, DC: Brookings Institution, 1967.

Foltman, F. F. *White and Blue Collars in a Mill Shutdown.* Ithaca: New York State School of Industrial and Labor Relations, 1968.

Stern, J., Root, K., and Mills, S. "The Influence of Social Psychological Traits and Job Search Patterns on the Earnings of Workers Affected by a Plant Closure." *Industrial and Labor Relations Review, 28,* 103–121 (1974).

Wilcock, R. "Employment Effects of Plant Shutdown in a Depressed Area." *Monthly Labor Review, 80,* 1047–1052 (1957).

Economic Dislocation

Gordus, J. P., Jarley, P., and Ferman, L. A. *Plant Closings and Economic Dislocation.* Kalamazoo, MI: W. E. Upjohn Institute for Employment Research, 1981. (*Note:* This work is a 20-year summary of research in the area.)

Psychiatric Disabilities

Brenner, M. *Mental Illness and the Economy.* Cambridge, MA: Harvard University Press, 1973.

Catalano, R., and Dooley, D. "Does Economic Change Provoke or Uncover Behavior Disorder? A Preliminary Test." In L. Ferman and J. Gordus (Eds.), *Mental Health and the Economy.* Kalamazoo, MI: Upjohn Foundation, 1979.

Marshall, J., and Funch, D. "Mental Illness and the Economy: A Critique and Partial Replication." *Journal of Health and Social Behavior, 20,* 282–289 (1979).

Slote, A. *Termination: The Closing at Baker Plant.* New York: Bobbs-Merrill, 1969.

Stress and Suicide

Dublin, L., and Bunzel, B. *To Be or Not to Be: A Study of Suicide.* New York: Smith and Haas, 1933.

Gore, S. "The Effect of Social Support in Moderating the Health Consequences of Unemployment." *Journal of Health and Social Behavior, 19,* 157–165 (1978).

Kasl, S. V., Gore, S., and Cobb, S. "The Experience of Losing a Job: Reported Changes in Health, Symptoms and Illness Behavior." *Psychosomatic Medicine, 37,* 106–122, 1975.

Lopata, R. "Failure Can Be Hazardous to Health." *Iron Age,* August 1981, pp. 59, 63, 65.

Theorell, T., Lind, E., and Floderus, B. "The Relationship of Disturbing Life-Changes and Emotions to the Early Development of Myocardial Infarctions and Other Serious Illnesses." *International Journal of Epidemiology, 4,* 281–293 (1975).

Yoder, D., and Staudohar, P. D. "Management and Public Policy in Plant Closure." *Sloan Management Review, 26*(4) (Summer 1985).

3.   James S. House makes these comments in an article titled, "Effects of occupational stress on physical health," in *Work and the Quality of Life.* Cambridge, MA: MIT Press, 1974.

4.   The research was performed at the Walter Reed Army Institute of Research in Washington, D.C., and was reported by Dr. J. V. Brady in an article titled, "Ulcers in 'Executive' Monkeys," in *Scientific American, 199,* 95–100 (1958).

5. I have already cited Alfred Slote's book, *Termination: The Closing at Baker Plant*, and would add only that it had a dramatic impact on many Glacier managers who were desperate for help in understanding what might happen to them and their plants as the closing program proceeded.

6. Dr. Sidney Cobb, a member of the Institute for Social Research at the University of Michigan, made this observation, dated June 10, 1969, in the Foreword to Slote, *Termination: The Closing at Baker Plant*.

Chapter 6

TRUST ME ON THIS ONE

Close the place and get it over with. People are going nuts waiting now that the company has turned its backs on us. It's time to turn mine on the company.
—First-Line Manager

You become what you think about. You are what you do. As one approaches adulthood, it quickly becomes obvious that people are judged according to what they do for a living. Despite a few intrepid folks who dare to say, "That's not who I am, it's just what I do," the stubborn criterion exists. Surrounding this truism is the growing realization that one's control over the definition of what one "does" is in serious jeopardy. In the past, people went to extraordinary lengths to be seen as working hard in order to gain the support of their employers. They would demonstrate unflagging loyalty to their organization. In this chapter, we look at the impact of change on loyalty and at some ideas for making decisions that will result in more effective management of human assets during periods of change.

PUNISHING LOYALTY

Loyalty is often punished by the impact of change. We have seen some evidence of this in Glacier, Inc., but numerous examples can be found throughout organizations today. The outcry comes from all levels within organizations and from external stakeholders as well. Examples:

- An Oklahoma community rises up in anger when jobs are threatened by a potential hostile takeover of Phillips Petroleum by a corporate raider, jeopardizing a business that had supported generations of employees.

- The top 25 executives of Borden, Inc., pledge that all will quit if any one of them is fired after the company is acquired.

- McDonald's severs a long-term relationship with a supplier after the latter was acquired by a business McDonald's didn't find compatible.

- Pilots, flight attendants, and mechanics joined forces against decisions by Eastern Airlines management to decimate their ranks.

- Jack Welch, the CEO of GE, declares loyalty to be an outmoded concept.

At Glacier, it was difficult to assure key managers that their careers would not be hurt by the plant-closing decision or by the related assignments they were asked to accept. In one example, a young, high-potential manufacturing manager was asked to assume the plant manager position at a location scheduled to close. He was assured that this would be good for his career. As the scheduled shut-down time drew near, he found upper management waffling, unwilling to displace anyone to make room for a "good soldier." A short time later, the young manager was employed by a competitor.

MUTED CANDOR

The decision to withhold information, or to disclose only partial details about the impact of change on an organization, has been defended under some circumstances.[1] When the fear of lost customers, impatient creditors, or the exodus of marketable employees is believed justifiable, management often is reticent about such matters. None of these events *is* necessarily a given, and yet organizations often wind up regarding candor as far too risky. In fact, it has been shown that customers actually will go out of their way to support businesses they want to see succeed, employees will take pay cuts to protect their jobs, and creditors will often show restraint during difficult times.

At Glacier, Inc., the tone regarding candor was often set at the top of the organization. The irony was that the source was more often the human resource (HR) organization than line executives. In fact, the top HR executive was often credited with setting the overall tone of risk avoidance. A cartoon was circulated at Glacier showing an executive dictating the closing line of a business letter, "Yours forever blameless." There was general agreement that this was a painfully accurate description of Glacier's top HR manager's overall stance. His organization was instrumental in influencing the following decisions:

- No safety net offered to loyal and seasoned top performers at any level

- No up-front involvement of plant managers in planning the closing activities

- Sharp criticism and muzzling of a general manager who wanted to discuss the plant-closing option with his plant managers to gain their input and support

The plant managers themselves found it difficult to be open with people, but for distinctly different reasons. First, they simply were ignorant of many of the directions being decided above them. Second, they were uncomfortable speaking about things that "might" happen because this was far different from the strong deterministic stands characteristic of their roles.

THREE-LEGGED PIG

Do upper-level managers know how transparent they and their actions appear to those lower in the organization? It seems ludicrous that secret "war rooms" are created and muffled debates are held—all on the assumption that no one will ever figure out what's going on until the executives want them to. Glacier, Inc., had always been a major source of revenue for its parent corporation, and many managers feared they were seeing a mosaic of decisions that added up to a "cash cow" mode of thinking on the part of management. The plant-closing program, and subsequent discussions about further jettisoning of assets, led to one apocryphal story that was circulated throughout Glacier at the time.

As the story goes, a traveling salesman is driving down a country road and passes by a farmyard in which a three-legged pig is standing. Astounded by the sight, he stops, backs up, and enters the yard in search of someone who can explain the phenomenon. Soon he encounters the farmer, who engages into the following dialogue with the salesman:

Farmer: My pig? Well sir, this isn't any ordinary pig. No sir. This is a very special and precious animal. One day the pig grabbed me by the pantleg and dragged me to the well. One of our kids had fallen in and would have drowned if the pig hadn't come and got me.

Salesman: That's amazing, but why does the pig have only three legs?

Farmer: Well, now, we're not talking about just some plain pig. This is really an extraordinary creature. One night the pig beat on the farmhouse door and woke us all up. It turned out that a fire had started and we would have all perished if it wasn't for that pig.

Salesman: I'm impressed, but it doesn't explain why it has only three legs.

Farmer: Sir, I'm surprised at your insensitivity and your inability to understand the significance of all that I have told you. With a pig this valuable, would *you* eat it all at once?

GUESS WHO IS WATCHING

Probably the single most jolting decision made at Glacier came two years into the plant-closing process. The top executive had come to Glacier several years earlier to help break into a strongly change-resistant culture. He came to be revered by Glacier employees but also was viewed as sometimes out of touch with where the business needed to go in the future. His direct reports occasionally developed business objectives that supported totally opposing philosophies, and there was a rising resentment among younger managers about their not being allowed to influence decisions that would shape the business they would ultimately have to support—and later inherit.

Despite these difficulties, a general conclusion was reached that the top executive should be encouraged to seek other opportunities in a dignified manner that allowed everyone to express gratitude for his contributions over the years. A major study had been conducted over a year or so about how to restructure the business to prepare it for the future and who the key players would be.

A large-scale meeting was planned for all key managers throughout Glacier. Its intent was twofold. First, it included a process for obtaining managerial reaction to the rationale for the change and the structure decided on. It was unusual for Glacier under such circumstances to ask managers to meet in small groups to discuss what they had heard. In these meetings they would offer views and suggestions that would be carried to the larger group by a representative. The second segment of the meeting used what was called a fishbowl approach. All of the small-group representatives, the newly as-signed upper-level management team, and the top executive would sit around a table, surrounded by the overall audience, and discuss the small-group input. This was to be an opportunity for candid exchanges and for the orga-nization to model the behavior that was expected to help support the new structure.

Less than a week before all the managers were to assemble, a corporate "hit man" flew into town and announced to the top executive that he was being removed from his job immediately. The replacement was brought in, the meeting was canceled, and Glacier managers throughout the organization were stunned by this deliberate effort to punish and embarrass their leader. The need for a new executive was not debated, but the common sentiment was that the succession process and its timing were atrocious and sent out a negative signal.

Indeed. The majority of younger managers took this as a sign that a new era was beginning, one that would be marked by far less concern for individuals, despite their contributions over time. The rag-tag dissenters to this new management philosophy were becoming the new recruits for a mercenary army. And one shouldn't forget another group of onlookers: those "encouraged" to take early retirement or otherwise moved out of the organization during earlier purges. As has been pointed out earlier, they are prepared to reenter the work setting, but with a dramatically different set of expectations regarding loyalty.

FROM LOYALISTS TO MERCENARIES: TEN EASY STEPS

The following actions can be taken to destroy employee loyalty to a company and create, instead, an army of mercenaries who will chase pay, promotions, and any other outcome that benefits themselves primarily:

1. Offer executive bonuses at a time when employees are forced to accept cuts in pay and benefits.

2. To achieve short-term financial results, treat people as "variable costs" and put them out on the street. Then rehire only those you need to speed up the operation in the next quarter—and repeat the cycle.

3. Use an economic downturn as justification for taking punitive action in the form of job displacement.

4. Trade on loyalty by asking employees to delay a job search in a glutted market until the organization is "ready" for them to leave.

5. Blame a business downturn on those most distant from the decision making that brought it about.

6. Assure employees that increased effort will result in greater job security, and then sell off or close operations once they become profitable.

7. Give no advance notice of major business changes that will result in the loss of income or continued employment.

8. Offer no outplacement assistance to those who are asked to leave their jobs because the business no longer needs them.

9. Sharply restrict employee involvement in business decisions that will subsequently affect them.

10. Ensure that internal promotions or advancements are far more difficult to achieve than changing companies or organizations, even if it means going to a competitor.

All of these actions should be carried out in a climate that operates ahistorically. That is, articulate clearly that past achievements and willingness to make sacrifices will not be taken into account. Instead, consider having a new organization slogan, "What Have You Done for Me Lately?" printed on banners, bulletin boards, and so on. Of course this is only a small sample of what can be—and has been—done in numerous organizations. However, strict adherence to this list will achieve dramatic results in a surprisingly short period of time.

A MODEST PROPOSAL

By now, most people who have taken the time to look into it realize that lifetime employment in Japan is only a sometime thing. Nevertheless, the concept provokes stormy debate because, as many Glacier managers piously pointed out, "Only the marketplace can guarantee job security." I always cringed at this homily and secretly wished everyone would go home, sit by the phone, and wait for the marketplace to call. This whole notion of playing the organizational version of Pontius Pilate has bothered me, and I was pleased to see Tom Peters take the issue on directly in his book, *Thriving on Chaos* .[2]

Peters proposes that people who do what they are supposed to do, and do it well, should be kept employed. Period. Frankly, I get more than a little tired of the same old whining about how the big guys like IBM can do this but little firms in a volatile market can't. Over time one begins to realize that small businesses don't necessarily remain small by accident. Much of their potential growth is stunted by "small" thinking. Where are the people who decide to give the market a good kick in the pants? Where is the next Henry Ford who decides to break with tradition and pay people a fair wage, or another Arthur Andersen who decides to pay apprentices for the first time? I concur with Peters and would like to go a step further.

Those who write books in the field of management are often accused of being more prescriptive than descriptive. Tom Peters makes many good suggestions in his book regarding how employment guarantees can be woven into the fabric of a business. To take an additional step, an explicit model is needed to explain how such decisions, and others regarding the use of human assets, can be made effectively.

STRATEGIC HUMAN ASSET MODEL

As we look broadly at the potential impact of change, it is necessary to acknowledge how crucial it is to focus attention on human assets. Some time ago I was asked for help by a group of people who were trying to find a buyer for several banks that had run into serious financial difficulty. The FDIC and these intermediaries were seeking ways to convince bank employees to remain on their jobs during these troubled times. The obvious point was that finding a buyer is hard enough, but finding one who would accept massive losses of key players was nearly impossible. Another request came from a major corporate CEO who wanted to review his noncore business portfolio to see which businesses should be sold and which ones kept. The problem was that any hint of such a review was likely to result in massive losses of key people.

Glacier's plant-closing program or even the layoffs as far away as Wall Street,[3] are only the tip of the iceberg when it comes to managing the impact of change on human assets. Much of the management literature—and nearly all of the business school curricula—have historically focused on the management of technical and financial assets. The need to connect these assets to strategy has been made clear. Some years ago I began to think about the connections between business strategy and the human activities that seemed to go on inside organizations. Too often these activities appeared to represent discrete events, connected neither to the goals of the organization nor to one another. From an operating manager's point of view, there seemed to be a lot of turf protection going on; "experts" were viewed as building mini-empires to support gilded-lily procedures whose elegance was exceeded only by their lack of utility. The irony is that these same procedures, if managed well, provide some of the strongest points of leverage for a business that needs to attract, retain, and develop its human assets.

In order for an overall model to be effective, there must be an infrastructure that provides support in at least two ways. First, there must be human resource systems that both feed into this process and are fed by it. Second, management practices must themselves be consistent with the overall philosophy underlying the tools and policies inherent in the model. The model I developed several years ago is being used within Andersen Consulting and has served well to help see key leverage points in managing the impact of

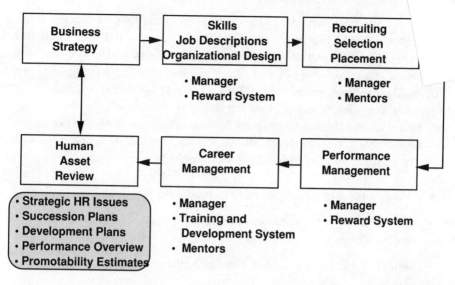

Figure 6.1   Strategic Human Asset Model

changes. As we proceed with a discussion of the model, I will conclude a review of each stage with a brief overview of the support systems needed.

Figure 6.1 graphically represents a strategic human asset model that serves as a framework for our discussion. Let us examine each of the model's components separately:

THE BUSINESS STRATEGY

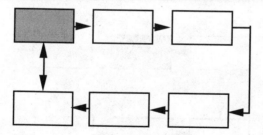

Though beyond the scope of the present discussion, the development of a business strategy is the most critical step that can be taken, beginning with a collective understanding or vision of the organization's purpose. My own experiences here have proved useful in identifying warning signs that signal the potential for subsequent business failure. In the case of Glacier, a key executive was told that his immediate subordinates were concerned that there was no clear direction being articulated for the business. They thought he should bring them together to develop a future vision to help aim their efforts. The executive responded, "I hate the word *vision* because it implies we never had one. Our vision is 14 pecent ROS."

Many successful businesses have leaders who draw from their key players a collective vision to which all are willing to commit themselves. Such activity uses as main ingredients the following:

- An assessment of the organization's readiness for change

- An agreement on some reasonable tactical directions that form a mission statement

- Identification of skills needed to sustain strategic options

- Codification of shared values that managers will use to guide subsequent decisions

All this needs to be drawn out against a hard look at the organization's current and potential marketplace and competitors. An equally hard assessment of the organization's technical and financial positions needs to be understood. The combined effort—driven by courageous leaders who regard themselves as agents of change—can produce dramatic results and sets the stage for the remaining activities in the human asset model.

SKILLS, JOBS, AND DESIGN

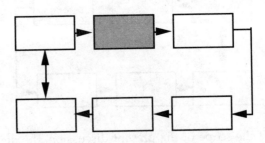

As can be seen in the model, the top left-hand box contains the business strategy activities. The next box to its right shows the first human asset challenge:

- Translate the strategy into skills necessary to achieve it.

- Translate group skills into accurate and useful job descriptions.

- Create an organizational design that supports the strategy and takes advantage of optimal work flow, communication networks, and defined roles and responsibilities.

Linking Strategy to Skills

Selecting strategic options without identifying the skills necessary to implement them is an empty exercise. But few people can readily rattle off even a hypothetical set of skills to consider. I have had success by presenting the following set as a starting point. These skills represent a reasonably contemporary group that highlights many of today's challenges:

Market–Customer Understanding.   Includes knowledge of the needs, preferences, trends, and practices affecting customers and market behaviors.

Strategic Thinking.   Involves the ability to identify future options and constraints, to assess strengths and weaknesses of product and processes, and to focus on creating a competitive edge.

Leadership Skills.   Includes influence, delegation, risk taking, decision-making skills, giving feedback, and developing others.

Business Financial Understanding.   Includes knowledge of the business as a financial system; understanding of the budgeting process and of the long- and short-term implications of decisions and actions.

Interpersonal Skills.   Focuses on providing positive feedback, listening to others, developing and maintaining effective work relationships.

Group Development Skills.   Focuses on facilitating groups, managing teams, conflict resolution, and problem solving. Also includes change management skills.

Diagnostic Skills.   Includes the ability to gather data to help in decision making, and the mapping of roles and expectations to determine how tasks fit with organizational goals.

Work Innovation.   Focuses on creating innovative management practices, work teams, redesign of work systems, and self-governing work units.

Self-Management.   Focuses on time and stress management, career development, personal goal setting, and impression management.

Business Communications.   Includes effective report and proposal writing, presentation skills, and listening skills.

Technology.   Includes job skills that are technical in nature, such as optimal use of technology, basic computer use, and the like.

There are some key issues that set this list apart from others:

- Technical competence and the ability to manage one-on-one relationships are not sufficient. Managing *groups* of people and the dynamics of these interactions are now becoming vital skills.

- Our culture is producing people who increasingly demand more involvement in decision making and want more control over their work life. This requires managers to operate in a climate where *power is shared* to a much greater extent than it was in years past.

- The successful manager must acknowledge and anticipate a broader spectrum of cultural, political, and technical forces, both within and outside the business setting, that can have significant influence on an organization and its people.

Describing Positions

There has been some significant criticism recently over the use of job (or "position") descriptions.[4] Much of this is deserved, as one can find evidence of huge collections of such descriptions that are either so detailed that their shelf life barely exceeds their insertion into a binder or else are so general that they offer no practical guidance for people looking for a little structure to get them oriented.

There are numerous position description outlines to choose from, but Figure 6.2 shows some elements that have been useful for me. Figuring out why a job or position exists, whom it reports to, what resources are available, and what accomplishments will be held up for assessment represents a major challenge for most people coming into a new organization. Having some of

Organization Relationships

Position Purpose

Quantitative Data

Responsibility

Specialized Knowledge

Working Relationships

Major Challenges

Decision-Making Authority

Figure 6.2   Position Description Elements

the information categories shown in Figure 6.2 filled in can save a lot of time and frustration—not a bad way to help accelerate the assimilation process as well.

Organization Design

Over the years I have been greatly impressed with people who are capable of designing organizations that both support the strategic objectives of the business and operate with a minimum of internal conflict.[5] The decisions that must be made require a clear understanding of key business directions. A starting point is to examine variables that can have an impact on overall organizational effectiveness. These ultimately form a litmus test against which any structural option should be assessed. A list of these variables and their related criteria follow:

1. Decision making, delegation, and control:
    –Degree of decentralization
    –Role/power/authority

–Profit-and-loss and return-on-investment control
–Control of product and functional costs

2. Responsiveness:
   –To changes in the market, technology, or competition
   –To overall company needs for cash, earnings, and capital con-
   straints
   –To changing growth objectives

3. Organization costs:
   –Management structure
   –Duplication of activities
   –Suboptimization
   –Internal competition
   –Future work: research and development, education, and so on
   –Economies of scale
   –Flexibility to move in and out of product lines, programs, and
   projects

4. Measurement and reward system:
   –Development and design of measurement and reward system
   –Breadth of application of measurement and reward system
   –Understanding of the system
   –Consistency with goals and strategies
   –Relation of product line results to measurements
   –Focus of system on market, channel, and customer-focused
   programs
   –Functional program results related to measurements and re-
   wards

5. Development and assessment of management:
   –Specialization and high levels of functional expertise
   –Multifunctional trade-off skills
   –Hands-on general management skills
   –Teamwork and negotiating skills
   –Communicating skills

As the top management team decides on a structure that meets its strategic directions, information that links each of the structural options to each of
these areas can be very useful in identifying issues that will require close
attention as the change is introduced.

I would like to add a point that has occurred to me throughout many of
the organization design meetings I have held. People do their very best—

most of the time—to pretend that such decisions will be made rationally and that seeking out data along the lines I have outlined will ultimately lead to the right decision. Aside from the fact that there is no such thing as a "right" decision, I would add that I have witnessed *no* design decision that did not ultimately come face to face with less rational criteria, such as:

- Preventing political warfare among long-time adversaries

- Creating a place to put someone so they don't hurt anybody else

- Placating some critical power-mongers by giving them mini-empires

- Ignoring the need to address more fundamental and messy organizational inefficiencies

That last point is critical. To underscore its origin, imagine that we have traveled by starship to a planet whose inhabitants were very much like us in nearly all respects, except that they have not yet perfected the wheel. In fact, the best they have come up with is *octagonal* wheels. As you walk down the street, you pass by a row of their vehicles and peek under a fender. There you find one of the most amazing shock absorbers you have ever seen—a necessity you immediately understand, given the state of development of their wheels. You run back to the ship, take out a box of round wheels, and present them to your planetary hosts. Immediately you have two groups of enemies. The first is responsible for the design, development, and installation of octagonal wheels. The second group designs, develops, installs, and maintains shock absorbers.

As I look at organization designs, I see many examples of "shock absorbers" put in place because of the inability to envision a rounder wheel or the lack of courage or power needed to confront those who deify octagonal wheels. The impact of change can make the overuse of shock absorbers a costly and hazardous road for an organization to travel. My advice is for organizations to look around them and try to identify areas whose existence is predicated on turbulence that has been buffered and allowed to continue unchallenged by upper management.

Support Systems

This stage requires managers to play a key role in helping to identify the specific skills needed to meet the organization's strategic objectives, to help create positions that will be able to make optimal use of these skills, and then to create networks of positions that form an overall structure that helps orchestrate the human talent assembled throughout the organization.

In addition to the managers, the reward system is pivotal in helping identify the appropriate level of compensation for positions and for maintaining an equitable pay structure as this process continues. In some instances, the reward system also helps create unique packages to help attract people with unique sets of skills. This is a delicate balancing act that keeps one eye on the external marketplace and the other on internal equity among current employees. If used properly, it is a major source of support within this stage and—as will be discussed later—within others as well.

RECRUITING/SELECTING/PLACING

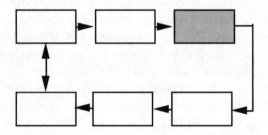

A few years ago I was working with a general manager who was assigned to a business that had been a major source of income because its products were based on a technological advantage it held over its competitors. Now the technology had shifted, and, despite a downward trend, the business still was reasonably profitable but needed to be managed in a manner that would acknowledge its ultimate fate within the next five years. It was under these circumstances that I learned the most about how to attract, select, and position people. Doing this in growth businesses was relatively easy compared to doing it in the environment this manager inherited.

The first problem was that of having to articulate the business strategy clearly in order to explain to those being recruited why they are being considered for the position. In this instance, the manager discussed the situation openly and explained that he was looking for people who not only had the technical skills required by the open positions, but also were looking for an opportunity to work in an environment that required a highly disciplined and innovative team of managers to meet profitability targets in a declining market. The result was a stream of recruits who accepted the challenge and came expecting to gain unusual experience that would serve them well in the future.

I would like to share my personal biases in this area, with the understanding that I will no doubt run into the "shock absorber" police the next time I am out on the street:

- A certain hypocrisy creeps into a recruiting arena when considerations are raised regarding equal employment opportunity (EEO) or affirmative action programs. One doesn't have to listen long before the contradictions surface. There are a lack of appropriate candidates because all the good ones are snapped up by competitors. Where is the recruiting being done? At the top umpteen schools, of course. A question I've often raised has always been met with silence, followed by a new agenda item: "If EEO goals are all that important, why aren't we looking at additional schools?" Incidentally, pointing out evidence that there is little correlation between "success" and where one goes to school has not helped.

- The interviewing skills I've seen over the years of helping clean up after selection debacles are just short of atrocious. When information is obtained (usually it isn't, because interviewers seize the moment to provide a personal history of their unsung but glorious accomplishments), the questions very often are illegal, insensitive, and—at a minimum—focused on extraneous data. This problem gets worse as one moves higher in the organization, for two reasons. First, the selection criteria are more subjective, thus demanding that the interviewer not only gather data but do so in an evaluative manner.[6] The second reason is related to a humorous anecdote about the amount of information people need to make good decisions. As the story goes, the higher one gets in the organization, the less information one requires to make decisions. The ultimate achievement, therefore, is to attain a level where one can make decisions without any information at all. Unfortunately, higher level managers often convince themselves they have "arrived." This fallacious assumption leads to some ludicrous interviews in which no useful information is exchanged, yet extremely important decisions are reached. As the old story goes, few are willing to tell the king he's wearing no clothes.

- There is only one thing worse than the lack of interviewing skill common within organizations—the decision to delegate the screening process. Options I find particularly offensive include turning to internal functional representatives who do not have to live with their choices or to external "scientific" vendors ranging from handwriting analysts to those who claim to be able to peer into the inner souls of the hapless recruits. I have witnessed this and have also experienced it first hand. I have often helped influence a decision to "throw the rascals out" before they played upon the fears of self-acknowledged lousy interviewers.

It continues to confound me that otherwise self-confident executives would submit to such nonsensical snake oil quackery, albeit disguised by computer printouts and multicolored graphics. One can only speculate on how long these managers would have lasted if they were equally careless with the technical and financial assets of the business.

The science of testing is often held up as a more accurate and more easily defensible alternative to interviewing. In principle, I agree. Adherence to the development, validation, and professional application of a testing program can add significant accuracy to the selection process. But in the hands of untrained people, unfortunately, the results can be disastrous. Here is a case in point. I was asked to review a test that had been used by a consumer products business for over 20 years to select entry-level sales recruits. Their scores also were available as a source of input for subsequent placement decisions. Over the years, a growing amount of grumbling was heard, but the head of sales and several people he had personally hired stood their ground in defense of the device, by which they themselves had been screened. A corporate-engineered removal of this manager created a period of uncertainty for which several lower level managers were waiting. Seizing the opportunity, they asked that I conduct a formal examination of the validity and reliability of this test. The results surprised and shocked everyone. The test bore some relation to performance, but not in the direction assumed—the better one did on the test, the poorer was one's subsequent job performance! For over 20 years this business had systematically discriminated against those whose test scores indicated they would be better performers.

Those who believe that the selection and placement of people can be simplified by ignoring the time or skills required are sowing the seeds of disaster in the not-too-distant future. Further, although there is nothing wrong with seeking another opinion or viewpoint, I draw the line between information based on firm business-related criteria and related data sources and the subterfuge offered by "specialists" whose bizarre logic would make for good comedy if it didn't have such harmful effects on people's careers and lives. In short, managers should avoid a crapshoot when it comes to recruiting, selecting, and placing your human assets. At Glacier, a common belief was that key placement decisions were made over cocktails at 30,000 feet.

Support Systems

This stage places a significant burden on managers to help in the recruiting process via interviewing and special presentations to potential recruits, in the selection process by helping identify criteria required for successful candidates, and in the placement process by guiding people into positions that will both meet the organization's objectives and the career goals of the individuals.

Mentors play an important role at this stage. The informal advice and counsel that can be passed along to people who may not know the ropes as far as this stage is concerned can have major benefits. Mentors should be candid about their view of the person's readiness for certain assignments and the match between the demands of the position and the person's stated career objectives, and they should offer some advice on how to gather information, attend to subtle cues during interviews, and marketing oneself successfully. Being able to point out alternatives and emphasize the need to consider longer or shorter time frames for decisions is an activity best left to mentors— a source with a high degree of credibility.

PERFORMANCE MANAGEMENT

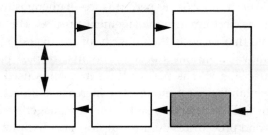

Over the years, I have encountered two recurring themes that underscore nearly all major organizational problems: inadequate communication and poor performance management systems. At times, the two share more than a common boundary, and it is critical that the management of performance not join in the folly of hoping for "B" but rewarding "A." Overall, performance management should begin by determining why it should take place at all. Some of the major reasons often cited by organizations include the following:

- Sustain or improve performance.

- Promote greater consistency in performance evaluation.

- Provide high-quality performance feedback.

- Allow for individual input during the evaluation process.

- Link evaluations to employee development.

- Link evaluations to a merit-based compensation plan.

- Form a basis for coaching and counseling.

- Allow for a blend of qualitative and quantitative evaluations.

- Recognize both the means and the end regarding objectives.

- Create a high-quality process that is easy to administer.

- Manage employee expectations of the job demands.

- Identify factors that determine how well the job is done.

Occasionally, organizations confuse performance measurement with employee disciplinary actions. The measurement process is not intended to be used as a punitive tool. Rather, it should be used as a level playing field on which judgments can be made about an individual's performance. Subsequent actions taken because of this performance—either positive or negative—are *not* part of the performance management process. This is a crucial distinction and one that protects the integrity of the overall system. A salary increase or removal from one's position because of past performance is a human asset decision that is part of the subsystems used to support the overall strategic human asset model. The increase is an activity tied to the reward system, and the removal results from a manager's reliance on established policies and procedures guiding appropriate disciplinary steps.

A good deal of research has been done in this area, and the following are some major steps that need to be handled carefully if the relationship between the organization's strategic direction and subsequent individual and group performance is to be strengthened.[7]

Goal Setting

It is sad but true that an enormous percentage of people do not know what is expected of them on their jobs. I lay most of the blame at the feet of the managers responsible for communicating this information. Such a breakdown is the primary reason for the weak link between strategic planning and subsequent organizational performance. There are many proponents of methods and procedures for setting performance goals. Some favor Management by Objectives; others prefer less structured, more flexible approaches. There is clear evidence to support the point that any method that relies solely on unilateral planning done by management—allowing no input from those who will do the work—builds in the potential for greatly reduced commitment and also silences the insights of those experts whose claim to the "expert" label comes from intimate day-to-day knowledge of what actually is done.[8]

I have used and recommended several approaches. In all cases, I have started with what I call a **SMART** model to assess the adequacy of performance objectives. The letters S-M-A-R-T form an acronym of my criteria:

- *Specific objectives.* Rather than indicate that someone should increase sales or improve presentation skills, a specific target should be set. For example, "Sales will be increased by 5 percent over the same period last year," or "The person will attend a course in professional presentations."

- *Measurable objectives.* Someone should be able to tell if the objective was accomplished. Sales can be measured directly. Other objectives may have to be observed. In either case, the objective should be stated in a way that indicates how it will be determined if a goal has been reached.

- *Attainable objectives.* Credibility surrounding the setting of work objectives is easily lost if managers talk about "stretch objectives" but employees view them as simply impossible. Setting unattainable goals undermines the overall process, conveying the message that the likelihood of being able to receive recognition or other favored outcomes based on one's willingness to perform at a high level is nil.

- *Results-oriented objectives.* A particularly important aspect of setting performance objectives involves the tracking of progress. Some refer to Gantt charts or PERT charts. Others use less formal methods but the intent is the same: recognizing the trend toward accomplishing an overall objective over time. Each work objective should be tied to interim "checkpoints."

- *Timing.* An open-ended objective insofar as a time frame is concerned offers little help in assessing importance and setting priorities. Unfortunately, most objectives have no specific time-oriented goal attached to them. This leads to major misunderstandings in a variety of areas, including the timely allocation of resources and underestimation of the impact on others who rely on having this objective accomplished.

Performance Tracking

I have been responsible for developing and reviewing numerous tracking systems, and there is more than a little truth to the claim that it really doesn't matter that much. Advocates of rating scales, personnel comparisons, critical incident techniques, behavioral checklists, and other more esoteric approaches all find themselves confronted with inexorable and persistent sources of error that do not seem to be greatly affected by clever formatting or related acrobatics.

The four biggest rating errors include the following:

- *Halo effect.*   As the old joke has it, 200 "Attaboys" can be done away with by one "Aw shit." This is the reverse side of the halo effect. Just as one glaring negative event can unfairly influence a general perception of a person's performance, so a single observation of a positive event can sway an evaluation in the opposite direction. In either case, the error is committed because little if any additional information is considered—or gathered.

- *Constant error.*   Some of the most ridiculous words employees ever hear come under this heading: "I didn't rate you outstanding in 'Communications' because only my mother is outstanding." "I don't believe anyone ever falls into the extreme categories—either they would have been fired by now, or else they would be pope." "I could have rated you higher, but this leaves you room for growth." This type of error is akin to loosening the glass rod in a thermometer and moving it either up or down a little and then tightening it back down. Reality and its measurement begin to part company. Employees resent tough graders and try to seek out more lenient ones—particularly if the organization tries to connect these ratings to pay or other personnel actions.

- *Rating restriction.*   This is actually a form of constant error, but it usually manifests itself as pretty wimpy fence-sitting behavior because, rather than attempt to differentiate an individual's performance, the rater takes a safe position. Thus, all ratings are around the middle of a scale. Unfortunately, this lack of variation not only removes any useful feedback opportunities for the employee, it also plays havoc with reward systems whose pay-for-performance impact is diluted by such behavior on the part of the rater—everyone gets a tapioca increase regardless of true differences in performance.

- *Stereotypes.*   We are becoming a bit more sophisticated—or cautious—in this area. Although raters may not articulate their biases publicly, their evaluations often reflect them. Gender, ethnic background, educational level, appearance, personality, and other aspects of an individual begin to affect the overall rating received. At Glacier it was found that ratings were biased upward according to one's level in the organization. The logic is that you must be good to be at such a high level. Unfortunately, there was little acceptance of the notion that a promotion puts you at the bottom of a higher ladder.

Having worked in this area for some time, I have concluded that the most effective method for dealing with performance tracking and the reduction of errors is a sort of checks-and-balances process. Every form I have created was designed to obtain bilateral goal setting *and* a self-evaluation from employees prior to the manager's final assessment. Also, I recommend that no discussion with an employee be held unless the material to be presented has been reviewed by an upper-level manager and a human resource manager. A review of litigation in this area suggests that the courts look favorably upon such a process as demonstrating an intent to provide a reasonably fair approach for performance evaluation.[9]

A major issue regarding the linkage of performance management to overall business strategy is the inability of the organization to recognize the need for such a connection. One research project showed that, of 248 companies surveyed, over 80 percent used some form of performance assessment, but less than 65 percent tied this to activities such as termination or layoffs, future potential, succession planning, or career management.[10] As the strategic human asset model shows, performance management is a critical link in the flow of such events. The potential outcomes from addressing this area effectively include:

- Clearer work goals and objectives in support of organization strategy

- Greater overall commitment from employees at all levels

- Improved individual performance

- Stronger link to rewards

- Stronger link to career management

- Improved managerial skills in performance management

- More employee involvement in the overall process

- Reduced administrative burden by encouraging involvement

- Improved ability to forecast human asset plans

Support Systems

This stage appears to managers to be instrumental in generating bilateral decisions regarding performance objectives. Also, the manager must encourage self-appraisals by employees and provide timely, fair, and useful performance feedback in a professional manner. This is a particularly difficult area for managers, for at least three reasons. First, they dislike playing the role of judge on some days and coach the rest of the time. Second, they fear retribution in the form of reduced commitment if they are candid. Third, they don't know how to do this task very well, they have not been adequately prepared, and they sometimes confuse performance assessment with taking punitive actions. This area has the potential for being the weakest link in the chain of events within the strategic human asset model.

The reward system is crucial here as well. The time-worn phrase "pay for performance" is put to the test at this spot. The relationship between the performance management stage and subsequent changes in compensation or other valued outcomes is the crux of the issue. It's frustrating to find that an organization has gone to great lengths to establish a reasonably effective objective-setting process and provides good performance feedback, but fails to tie the outcome to rewards in a way that captures people's attention. A few years ago I read a report that showed the general percentage difference in pay between outstanding and satisfactory employees—a figure around 3 percent. This is like buying a Lamborghini and only driving it in and out of the garage. The leverage lost because of an organization's reluctance to put some teeth into its pay-for-performance platitudes most likely reflects its true belief in its ability to discriminate across performance.

CAREER MANAGEMENT

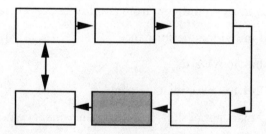

In contrast to performance management's emphasis on past performance, the career management stage is future-oriented. This is the organizational process for answering the question, "What do you want to be when you grow up?" My interest in this area grew out of my conversations with managers who snorted, "Career management my ass! They're damn lucky to even have a job!" The potential for enlightenment was overwhelming.

Some years ago, a career management seminar was created and presented to exempt employees in Glacier, Inc. The reaction was a curious mixture of shock, surprise, and anger. Most participants had never considered the existence of any system connected with managing one's career, and several were angry that they had never been exposed to the points of leverage before. More than that, a good number had joined Glacier at a time when the predominant message was, "Just do a good job and your career will take care of itself." That wasn't far from the truth during a period of predictable growth, well-known competitors and competitor strategies, and well-established career paths. But all that had changed, and so had the message: *You* are responsible for managing your career." Unfortunately, the former change preceded the latter by quite a few years.

The area of career management has received much attention,[11] and there appear to be at least three areas within career management that constitute stumbling blocks that seriously impede the strategic management of human assets:

- Career growth is confused with being promoted.

- The career management process is not widely known.

- Managers do a lousy job of guiding employees in the management of their careers.

To begin to understand the events that lead up to career planning, consider the model shown in Figure 6.3. As can be seen, this parallels much of the logic behind the strategic human asset model. The basic idea is that the activities that ultimately influence individual choices and behavior are initially influenced by information derived from the organization's strategic plan or by an understanding of where the organization is headed. With this as a backdrop, let's address each of the problem areas cited earlier.

Career Management = Promotion.

Few other myths have become so readily accepted and acted upon inside organizations. The most common expression perpetuating this is "up or out."

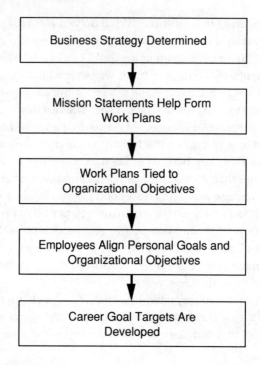

Figure 6.3   A Strategic Career Planning Approach

One need only reexamine the statistics shown in Chapter 1 and check out the front page of the *Wall Street Journal* to find references to downsizing, leveraged buyouts, restructuring, and other major upheavals that have not only destroyed loyalty but have laid to ruin any past certainties about career paths. In short, it has become physically impossible to compete in a marketplace with an organizational philosophy predicated on promotional increases as the sole option associated with career management. In fact, several options not only are possible, but may *have* to be exercised to ensure the survival of the organization itself:

Upward Movement.   This, of course, is the traditional path that has become accepted as the only true measure of career growth.

Lateral Movement.   More recently, the need for more generalist thinking has led to a broadening of people by having them move laterally to new positions both inside and outside their original functions.

Downward Movement.   Once considered just a cut above leprosy, accepting positions at lower levels has not only been required because of the impact of change, but is increasingly the movement of choice for many. The reasons vary, ranging from wanting out of the "rat race" to a desire to focus on family or other outside interests. Still others have come to question seriously whether they want to make the sacrifices necessary to hold higher positions. For example, more and more first-line supervisors indicate that it just is not worth the hassle. Older executives may want to open up a key position for a younger person and spend their time elsewhere in the organization.

Job Expansion.   For many, the worst part of their jobs is the boredom that comes from the sameness associated with any long-held position. What is desired is not necessarily a whole new job or a different career path. Instead, creative ways to enrich the job by offering new responsibilities, offering opportunities to serve as a mentor over others, or taking on some supervisory responsibilities are possible.

Special Assignments.   This is also known as the kiss of death in most organizations. Though not widely acknowledged, this career path is actually one that has gained prominence within the last ten years both because of increased sensitivity to the need to help people achieve "soft landings" outside the present organization and because a growing number of people with enviable performance histories are faced with involuntary job loss as a result of economic conditions and other factors

These assignments are largely holding spots for either a well-orchestrated job search or else the later unveiling of organizational change that would result in internal placement. Unfortunately, this category has been so long associated with the "walking wounded" that its very mention draws murmurs and knowing nods in most businesses, and certainly among recruiters.

Career Management Process

The career management process consists of at least three key elements. Each can be thought of as one of three legs that support career planning and execution. They are:

- Self-awareness

- Climate assessment

- Career management tools

Self-Awareness.   There is a whole industry in this area. The list of alternatives presented here represents only a small part of what is available. The objective is a better understanding of one's values, how one is viewed by others, one's work habits, future goals, family relationships, career preferences, preferred working conditions, interpersonal style, and how past events may have influenced one's subsequent career choices. A myriad of surveys, questionnaires, semistructured interviews, and self-assessments, as well as an assortment of graphing, charting, and other image-driven approaches, can be used to get a better fix on oneself.

Climate Assessment.   This process focuses on the surrounding environment. For those looking outside of an organization, it is somewhat more difficult to gather this information, but these are the critical areas to pursue:

- Learning the business strategy

- Translating strategy into needed skills

- Reviewing the organization's development policies

- Discovering career path histories

- Identifying "power" positions

Much has already been said about the first two points. Each organization has some kind of process for developing its human assets, and this is often found within an employee handbook or a personnel manual. Some interviewing is probably the most effective way of discovering both career path histories and getting information on the positions within the organization that can have the most influence over one's career direction and/or options.

At Glacier, this list was reviewed during a meeting of key technical people. As the conversation turned to the conduct of informal interviews, further clarification was requested. The response included a suggestion to interview people in charge of areas where one might want to work. However, the conversation would not be a job interview but, rather, an information-gathering session. One engineer, stunned, turned to another, who had made this suggestion, and said, "You can't do that kind of thing around here!" The second engineer responded, "How do you think I got *this* job?"

Career Management Tools

This area has been more than a little confusing for people. To put it in context, I will divide it into three areas: career management vehicles, planning, and tactics.

Career Management Vehicles.   The major vehicles that one can use in the career management area include:

- An organizational strategy statement (or annual report)

- Copies of position descriptions from areas of interest

- Information from an internal job-posting system

- Access to managers or a mentor

- Information about an organization's
    - compensation system
    - performance management system
    - training and development system

- Access to any internal resume format used

- Information about how human assets are examined by the organization

These vehicles can prove to be great sources when it comes to creating a mosaic of information, ultimately providing key information needed to begin one's career-planning activities.

Planning.   Planning involves three key steps. First, one needs to develop a career vision that requires a review of the job information, self-assessment, and career goals data that have been previously obtained. Second, it is important to perform a reality check to be sure one's career management skills are leading down a logical and reasonable path. This may require both additional self-assessment *and* input from others. Finally, it is important to create a written document that describes one's goals, achievements, and strengths. This will most likely take the form of a resume, either one based on an internal format or one that meets the needs of external sources.

Tactics.   When it comes time to put one's career plans into action, there are several areas to consider. It is likely that many of these will be set in motion at one time:

- Vertical, lateral, downward, or external job moves

- Gaining on-the-job training

- Gaining formal education

- Expanding current job

- Packaging oneself via
    −sponsors
    −experience
    −resume
    −altered style

- Marketing oneself via
    −networking
    −interviewing
    −taking on high-visibility assignments

Management Role in Career Management.   There are a few key objectives that should be emphasized for managers who are looked to for career management assistance. These include acknowledging that a career system actually exists, becoming an advocate, increasing one's awareness of the career management needs of others, and acquiring some basic skills in the following areas:

- Performance management

- Career discussions

- Raising and answering career questions

- Guiding employees in the use of resources

- Critiquing and testing career-planning logic

- Providing information and support

Often a manager feels severely constrained when it comes to knowing what steps can be taken to help develop people. The following list contains several useful options.[12]

- On-the-job coaching and development counseling

- Job rotation

- Project team or task force assignments

- Replacement assignments because of vacations or illness

- Planned reading in specialized fields

- Participation in community and civic affairs

- Attendance at selected conferences, workshops, seminars, and the like

- Opportunities to make presentations

- Attendance at staff meetings

- Service as instructor, conference leader, or trainer

At this point in the strategic human asset model it should be noted that a large and potentially valuable amount of information has surfaced. This includes indicators of the organization's ability to identify necessary skills, a measurable flow of human assets in and out of appropriate positions, jointly established performance goals, quantitative data regarding performance assessment, and useful knowledge about career goals and aspirations across the organization. At each stage in the model, I have tried to point out how the individual activities should tie back to the organization's strategic direction. This entire effort can now be rolled up in the final stage of the model.

Support Systems

The detailed description of events that take place in this stage underscores the need for strong and sustained management support. The career management assistance involves closer attention to opportunities for enhancing human assets. The blend of quantitative and qualitative data coming from this stage often provides critical input during times of major organizational change. To the surprise of many managers, people's concerns over future career opportunities offer much greater leverage than do their shorter term concerns over pay. Retaining key players during periods of turbulence requires a strategy that goes far beyond quick-hit salary adjustments. The stronger response comes in terms of career management assistance.

In this stage, the organization needs to be able to rely on a training and development system to support both organizational needs and individual career plans. It is encouraging to see businesses of all sizes recognizing the need to elevate the status and utility of their training and development functions. Regarded as the "weak sister" of many businesses, this function is being revamped to reflect a growing concern over the need both to reskill people affected by shifts in technology and to offer some basic knowledge not obtained prior to employment. Some key indicators to watch for in this area— indicators that demonstrate organizational commitment—include having the function headed by people with business experience as well as functional experience, placing greater emphasis on the need for instructional design skills,[13] and building in more quantifiable accountability criteria that go beyond "happy face" course evaluations.

The role of mentors is important here because they can help individuals interpret career discussion outcomes and can coach people prior to such conversations. These roles are nearly impossible to mandate within organizations but should be encouraged. One difficulty I have encountered is that people in their mid-thirties seem to lose interest in being mentored, and good mentors are hard to find among people under the age of 40. This leaves a large hole that too often is filled by misunderstanding, distrust, poor decisions, and a loss of either the person's commitment or—the person.

HUMAN ASSET REVIEW

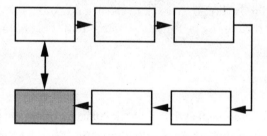

A human asset review offers a useful opportunity for an organization to examine its human assets, much as it would its financial or technical assets. For the handful of organizations who do this quite well, it contributes to their being judged to be among the best managed. These examples continue to be in the minority, however, and my patience is tested whenever otherwise astute organizational leaders lecture me about the pointlessness of trying to assess the "soft side" of any business. To these managers, the whole area appears subjective and beyond control or influence. To allocate resources in such a direction strikes them as sheer folly.

That's the trouble with ignorance: You don't know what you don't know. Furthermore, I have found that people will resist logic when it conflicts with what they are comfortable in believing. This results in sending mythical organizational armies out to battle, underestimating the impact of change, and unwittingly promoting the conversion of loyal employees into mercenaries. With this in mind, let us look at the key elements that constitute a human asset review. As the model shows, this review has five key elements:

- Strategic human resource issues
- Succession plans
- Development plans
- Performance overview
- Promotability estimates

Strategic Human Resource Issues

There are a number of subcategories here, and the inclusion or exclusion of each is highly situation-specific. A sampling, however, would include:

- Review of current organizational structure and any proposed changes
- Examination of the human asset implications of strategic business shifts
- An overview of the flow of key human asset movement
- Highlighted efforts to deal with such issues as "problem employees," "superstars," and "female and minority assets"
- Proposed changes or modification to the human asset model process

Succession Plans

Over sixty years ago the first interest in succession planning emerged in the U.S. business community.[14] The fundamental objective of this process is to identify backups for key people in the organization. Despite decades of effort in this area, numerous pitfalls can be found throughout businesses that are supposedly doing it right. Some examples include:

- Top-level management is not involved in the process and shows little interest.

- The mechanics are in place, but subsequent decisions ignore past data gathered.

- The quality of the data available is highly suspect.

- Replacement nominations are accepted without further review.

- Backup candidates are chosen only for top-level managers.

- The succession process itself is not reviewed for improvement.

The overall process requires access to information on career progress, performance over time, and somewhat less tangible information on how well the person has been able to absorb the impact of change and fit into new environments. These and other elements help set the stage for a full review of logical candidates and, possibly, for the realization that no backups exist, leaving the organization vulnerable.

Development Plans

A few years ago I was asked to estimate how much time managers should expect to spend developing themselves both on the job and outside the job (e.g., in seminars and schools). I believe that less than 10 percent of a manager's development time should be spent at any external event. The major emphasis should be on internal opportunities for growth and experience. The question I rarely get—but one that deserves to be raised—is: "Why don't organizations *ask* people what they want to be doing in the future?" The outcome is often enlightening, sometimes challenging, and occasionally disquieting. People's perceptions of their options generally are in need of a formal review, particularly in the context of a human asset review.

Some key elements that make up such development plans include:

- Career interests, both near term and longer range

- Technical, managerial, and interpersonal qualifications, as well as areas in which further development is needed

- An individual's view of development actions that have already been taken and those planned for the future

The manager's response to this input should include:

- A brief review of the person's accomplishments

- An assessment of his or her qualifications in terms of strengths and development needs

- Development and career recommendations that focus on
    - development recommendations
    - potential next assignments
    - assessment of the individual's stated career route and goals

As indicated before, development recommendations should focus primarily on on-the-job experiences, such as shifting from a staff to a line role or cross-functional exposure. However, carefully targeted external opportunities should also be included. Some of the alternatives are community activity, serving on the boards of other organizations, and attending courses, seminars, workshops, and professional association meetings.

The key issue to keep in mind is that a human asset review brings such information to the attention of managers at the top level of an organization so that developmental decisions can be evaluated against strategic objectives. The result allows insights into the current and future human asset strengths available to the organization.

Performance Overview

Drawing on the performance management results, this overview allows the organization to examine performance in a variety of ways. At times the focus is on certain functions, such as marketing, research and development, or human resources. Perhaps the focus is on certain levels within the organization, e.g., profit-and-loss managers, general managers, first-level supervision. Still other analyses may focus on a comparison of the overall distribution of performance ratings against what are found in a comparable business setting to determine if differentiation is taking place and how this compares to an external standard. Of course, individual performance is also reviewed in those instances where decisions are required:

- Performance problems

- Outstanding individuals

- Unexplained changes since the last review

Promotability Estimates. One of the more telling assessments to come out of such a review pertains to estimates of promotability. For each of the people being reviewed, an estimate of his or her promotability is provided along a continuum like this:

- Promotable to two or more higher levels

- Promotable to only one higher level position

- Good performer, no further promotions foreseen

- Performance/utilization issue

- Too soon to evaluate

Generally, such an analysis takes into account other variables, such as the time the person has been on the present assignment, his or her level in the organization, and possibly a review of performance over time, including major accomplishments.

This process often elicits surprising information. It is useful in helping to focus on people in lower profile assignments who are demonstrating strengths that could serve the organization well in times of change. The depth of the review remains an issue, but it soon becomes apparent that the discovery of future leaders requires probing below the top level of current managers.

The line connecting the human asset review stage with the business strategy stage has an arrow at both ends. This shows that the human asset review has the potential to influence strategic business plans *and* can serve such planning efforts by requesting that specific information be obtained from the human asset system feeding into the human asset review itself.

Finally, although this is not formally shown in the model itself, the organization will find it must rely heavily on a human resource information system to handle the influx of information that such a model generates. The use of computerized support has grown dramatically over the years, and only recently have managers recognized the need for a more creative use of information pertaining to their human assets. This model, to be most effective, would create a high demand for such support.

The use of a strategic human asset model can make a critical difference when it comes to managing the impact of change on an organization's human assets. The days of unlimited supply of young recruits and unquestioned, long-term loyalty are fading fast. New thinking will be required because there is little doubt that the average person will no longer accept at face value the statement, "Trust me on this one." Trust was an even earlier victim than loyalty.

A final but crucial question remains: "Who is responsible for creating, monitoring, and modifying such a model?" In the past there has been no systemic view taken in the majority of companies. Therefore, various pieces of the model became the domain of personnel specialists. These people tended to be "product-oriented" versus "service-oriented" and often built walls around themselves both to keep other personnel people from usurping their territory and to gain what might be called negative power—the power to cast a negative vote. Their right to such power resulted from the historic abrogation of responsibility by general management for messy human decisions and the need to deal with noisy stakeholders such as the government, community leaders, or labor unions. Today, we are faced with a world of change that demands a radical shift in thinking. The responsibility for managing human assets should be elevated to the same status as the responsibility for managing technical and financial assets. In both of the latter areas, general management plays a significant and highly involved role. So too should general management take the responsibility for tying human asset decisions into the strategic management process.[15] The best framework I can offer to help start this process is the model I have presented.

SUMMARY

The impact of change on loyalty serves as a barometer of how poorly organizations have managed the impact of change. Much of the problem can be traced back to a lack of candor by people specifically responsible for addressing such issues. A major unintended, but nevertheless true, outcome of all this is a deep and lasting impression made upon people that loyalty is no longer valued and that employees at all levels and of all ages are reassessing their relationships to employers.

One unfortunate result is a shift in perspective from being a loyal employee to becoming a sort of mercenary who, by such a definition, becomes solely focused on answering the question, "What's in it for me?" Organizations have taken numerous steps, often out of ignorance or in the name of expedience, that have helped people make this transition in their thinking.

Many believe that long-term gainful employment is *not* an idea to be discarded. Instead, it can be argued that the overall management of human assets needs to be cast in a different light. Just as technical and financial assets are the source of much management attention, so too should human assets be treated. Unfortunately, a model showing how this can be done has been lacking. Such a model is introduced in this chapter, and its stages are explained in detail.

This model shows the linkages between business strategy and the subsequent management of human assets, as well as the subsystems needed to support the major stages of the model. The key stages in the model include:

- Business strategy
- Recruiting, selection, and placement
- Career management
- Skills/job descriptions/organizational design
- Performance management
- Human asset review

A number of tools and techniques are reviewed to help understand how human asset decisions can be improved. Further, some myths surrounding these issues are explored, and examples of outcomes resulting from improper management of human assets are reviewed. Special emphasis is placed on management's role and on the need for strong reward systems, mentors, a training and development process, and a strong human resource information system to handle the support side of human asset management. Finally, it is argued that general managers, not staff specialists, must oversee the integration of human asset decisions into the overall business strategy and must take a more proactive stand in crafting policies and practices in this area.

Notes

1. Robert I. Sutton, in "Managing Organizational Death," in *Human Resource Management*, 23, 391–412 (1983), discusses a number of issues that must be managed during times of severe organizational crisis. He shows that many of management's fears are not borne out by actual events, nor are there past events to justify most of their bunker mentality. He does show that turnover among people does occur. In a previous chapter, however, I have cited research that casts doubt on the claim that only the "good" employees leave.

2. I have cited Tom Peters's book *Thriving on Chaos* before and would like to quote directly from page 344:

    After a probationary period of 6 to 18 months, provide a guarantee of continuous employment to your permanent work force (where "permanent" is defined as enough people to handle 90 percent of normal demand). Develop, ahead of time, a specific strategy for dealing with precipitous drops in demand, including major redeployment (to maintenance, sales). Develop an ongoing retraining program to precede/accompany the introduction of, say, new technology.

Tom develops an entire chapter around the idea of providing guaranteed employment. I believe that few organizations are going to pick up his challenge but that the increasing numbers that do will find they have harnessed a lasting competitive advantage—as long as intransigence among competitors on this issue prevails.

3. I noted recently an article in the American Society for Personnel Administration's publication, *Resource* (June 1989), that discussed a lawsuit brought by brokerage workers in New York. A class-action suit was filed against L. F. Rothschild & Co., Inc. In the suit, *Finnan v. L. F. Rothschild & Co., Inc.*, No. 89-2718 (S.D.N.Y. 4/21/89), the plaintiffs allege that more than 250 employees were laid off without the notice now required by the plant-closing law passed in 1988. The law, called WARN (Worker Adjustment and Retraining Notification Act) went into effect on February 4, 1989. This is the first test of the new law and, interestingly enough, it comes from white-collar, not manufacturing employees.

4. Tom Peters (*Thriving on Chaos*, p. 500) believes that job descriptions should be scrapped because, by their design, they serve to limit people. He cites his own experience to show that not reading such documents never hurt his career. Unfortunately, this is an area where Tom and I don't find much common ground. Position descriptions can and do serve a variety of purposes. They help managers organize their thinking about which groupings of skills make the most sense so that people are given the opportunity to make a significant contribution. They also serve as building blocks when organizational structure alternatives are considered. They contain useful information for developing performance objectives, and they give a more than reasonable first approximation of why the position exists and what is generally expected from people in that spot. Until I see a much better alternative than the one Tom suggests, "coaching," or unless these coaches demonstrate skills that exceed what I have encountered to date, I'll continue (forgive me, Tom) to recommend the use of job descriptions.

5. A few years ago I had the extraordinarily good luck of being able to attend one of Jay Galbraith's presentations on creating organizational structures. His materials were very well developed and his arguments were extremely persuasive. I highly recommend his book, *Designing Complex Organizations* (Reading, MA: Addison-Wesley, 1973). And I hereby give him credit for a phrase I've used successfully ever since that presentation: He referred to academia as the place where the "rubber meets the sky." An exceptional treatment of this area can be found in Henry Mintzberg's book *The Structuring of Organizations* (Englewood Cliffs, NJ: Prentice-Hall, 1979).

6. Several years ago I helped design an "evaluative interview process" for a group of businesses. It was based on the material in Richard A. Fear's book *The Evalua-*

tion Interview (New York: McGraw-Hill, 1984). Fear makes a number of excellent points about what one should ask during an interview and how to look beyond the immediate information, assemble pieces of input that form a pattern of the whole person, and—above all—elevate the overall process to something considerably more important than simply a data-gathering task. Of course, he also gives good general interviewing tips as well. This is a very helpful resource.

7. Of the great number of sources available, I have found two very helpful. Ronald A. Berk has edited a collection of papers in a book titled *Performance Assessment Methods and Applications* (Baltimore, MD: Johns Hopkins University Press, 1986). In this collection are some insightful sections on the assessment of performance, viewed from several angles. From a somewhat more strategic point of view, I recommend Robert L. Laud's chapter, "Performance Appraisal Practices in the Fortune 1300," found in *Strategic Human Resource Management*, edited by Charles Fombrun, Noel M. Tichy, and Mary Anne Devanna (New York: Wiley, 1984). Laud does a fine job describing research he performed in the area of how performance assessment was being done within a large number of organizations and the degree to which this process was linked to strategic organizational objectives.

8. In his book *High Involvement Management* (San Francisco: Jossey-Bass, 1986), Ed Lawler makes the following statement:

    When people participate in decisions about target performance levels and goals, it can affect their commitment to achieving those goals (p. 30).

    For anyone who has followed Ed's contribution to the area of management research over the years, these words are not taken lightly. They follow enormous research effort and evidence that point to the need to institutionalize a bilateral process wherever possible within an organization if one wants to gain the commitment of people to its goals and objectives.

9. One of the better reviews of case law in the area of performance management was written by Gerald V. Barrett and Mary C. Kernan, who published an article titled "Performance Appraisal and Terminations: A Review of Court Decisions since *Brito* v. *Zia* with Implications for Personnel Practice," *Personnel Psychology*, 489–503 (1987). They provide some specific suggestions for businesses that want to ensure that their performance management systems can be defended in court.

10. I cited Bob Laud's work earlier and would add here that it offers some insights into how few organizations have actually tried to link their human asset decisions to strategic business objectives. Bob presents a powerful and persuasive case that this is a yet-to-be-realized opportunity for many organizations. I also believe this gap is at least in part a result of the skill level of human resource people serving many organizations. This is part of the terrible paradox I have found in this area: Line management doesn't ask much beyond administrative support from HR, and HR doesn't have the skill to go beyond such requests.

11. There are a number of good references in this area. Among them are Don Super, *The Psychology of Careers* (New York: Harper, 1957); S. H. Osipow, *Theories of Career Development* (Englewood Cliffs, NJ: Prentice-Hall, 1983); Douglas T. Hall, *Careers in Organizations* (Pacific Palisades, CA: Goodyear, 1976); and Beverly L.

Kaye, *Up Is Not the Only Way* (Englewood Cliffs, NJ: Prentice-Hall, 1982). I am particularly pleased to see that Beverly's own model on page 101 of her book reflects the overall philosophy underlying my own strategic human asset model. I have tried to modify her model somewhat to fit within the context of this chapter, but the overall principles are very similar.

12. Over the years I have been privileged to work with Dr. Warren Wilhelm and Mr. Joseph Zaccaro, principals in the Human Resource Consulting Group. We first worked together on some career management materials, and the list I cite in this chapter is drawn from their work. I want to extend my appreciation to them for allowing me to gain greater insight into the career management area because of their research and practical applications.

13. Until just a few years ago, I was unaware of the existence of a discipline called "instructional design." My ignorance is more than a little embarrassing. In any event, I have gained more respect for the work done in this area. Walter Dick and Lou Carey provide an overview of such an approach in *The Systematic Design of Instruction* (Glenview, IL: Scott Foresman, 1985). One can also gain some good insights from R. M. Gagne and L. J. Briggs, *Principles of Instructional Design* (New York: Holt, Rinehart and Winston, 1979). Andersen Consulting has historically offered its clients educational assistance based on what it called METHOD/E, a methodology drawing heavily on instructional design principles. For example, its four major phases are curriculum planning, training design, training development, and training support. A major proponent of this approach is Jack E. Bowsher, recently retired as the program director of IBM's Corporate Management Development Center. Jack has written a very interesting book, *Educating America* (New York: Wiley, 1989), and speaks out forcefully on the subject of how adherence to instructional design approaches helps deliver high-quality instruction and can potentially serve as an integral part of restructuring the U.S. educational system.

14. Walter R. Mahler and Frank Gaines, Jr., have written a book titled *Succession Planning in Leading Companies* (Midland, NJ: Mahler Publishing Company, 1983) that offers useful examples and advice regarding the challenges surrounding the development, installation, and operation of a successful succession system. Walt Mahler also offers some excellent courses in this and other human asset management areas, and I highly recommend them. The materials from these courses are among the best available I have seen.

15. Some years ago I read a book that helped clarify my thinking in this area. Michael Beer, Bert Spector, Paul R. Lawrence, D. Quinn Mills, and Richard D. Walton jointly co-authored a book titled *Managing Human Assets* (New York: Free Press, 1984). Their basic argument is that human asset decisions need to be moved into a higher arena of management activity. I particularly liked this passage on page 105:

> Existing HRM [Human Resource Management] practice is all too frequently a hodge-podge of policies based on little more than outmoded habits, current fads, patched-up responses to former crises, and pet ideas of specialists. HRM practice urgently needs to be reformed from the perspective of

general management. HRM issues are much too important to be left largely to specialists. A company's policies and practices in this area (whether, for example, they are pursuing the traditional adversarial employment relationship or attempting to move toward greater mutuality), can make the difference between success and bankruptcy.

Chapter 7

CAN WE TALK?

Great ideas often enter reality in strange guises and with disgusting alliances.
—Alfred North Whitehead

Profitability, along with other measures of organizational success, can obscure a multitude of moronic management practices. Although Glacier, Inc., had several examples, none stands out more than the circumstances found in its Elderburg plant, known for its historic labor–management strife. I had an opportunity to visit the location a few times and was able to piece together some past details. Elderburg was over 50 years old, a multistory structure plant, and produced a relatively high volume of Glacier's consumer products.

MAKING THE NUMBERS

The position of Elderburg's union and its management had been adversarial for years. The need for product volume remained very high, and the distance from headquarters allowed for a certain degree of managerial autonomy, rarely subjected to higher level review. It was only a few years earlier that a plant manager in a similar Glacier location gave his security guards orders not to allow headquarters people inside the plant. This "captain of the ship" mind set was on its way out but was still endorsed by most of Glacier's plant managers. The regional human resource manager summed up the situation:

> Basically, Bob [Elderburg's plant manager] is the biggest part of the problem. He's been here for over 20 years and looks for ways to screw the union. He thinks this is the only way to deal with them and has refused all of their offers to negotiate on new work methods, flexible assignments, the introduction of employee participation, or even giving them an opportunity to speak to him. He basically has a closed-door policy when it comes to dealing with the union leadership.
>
> But nobody at headquarters really cares what he does down here as long as he makes his numbers. Turnover is low, the volume is high, costs are within guidelines, and so there is no reason for anyone to challenge the way he is handling the work force. Of course, he is a tyrant, is mostly indifferent to their needs, and borders on paranoia whenever a problem arises.

Any acts of violence, sabotage, insubordination, or other forms of resistance to his autocratic approach are all treated by headquarters as "unusual and isolated" events. So far no one has caught on that there are legitimate reasons for the employees to complain and that this stuff results from their frustration over his lack of communication. Someday this will have to change, but only if he doesn't make his numbers.

The overall philosophy of everything being all right if you "make your numbers" was certainly not isolated at the plant level. A high-level manager sat at a lunch table on a day when several key promotions had been announced throughout Glacier and its parent corporation. Others at the table remarked openly that several of those promoted were among the worst managers of people they had ever encountered and expressed surprise and disappointment that these individuals had been elevated to higher positions of authority. The manager listened to all of this and issued a summary judgment that no one challenged: "No one in Glacier, Inc., has ever been promoted or demoted because of their people management skills."

Elderburg's plant manager did find himself faced with a situation that neither he nor any of his peer managers ever expected—the closing of their plant by Glacier. This offered an opportunity for some lower level managers, both within the plant and at headquarters, to move on an action they had wanted to take for years. Bob was eased out and took an early retirement option. An interim manager was moved into the spot for a short period but proved to be as ineffectual as Bob and was soon removed. Finally, the change that many had thought would never come arrived. A younger manager named Dan was put in charge. He had worked alongside labor representatives over the years and believed they truly had the best interests of their constituents at heart and would not deliberately try to hurt the plant.

When Glacier announced the plant closing, the union at Bob's plant reacted strongly and blamed the company for taking advantage of them. Glacier headquarters was not surprised. In fact, many had expected a strike and shutdown to follow. It didn't. The removal of Bob and the "surrogate Bob" sent a message throughout Elderburg that significant changes were on their way. When Dan took over, he began a series of dialogues with union leaders. I had a chance to talk to them afterward, and they summed up the situation:

We don't believe it's necessary to close Elderburg and will do everything we can to keep it open. If that isn't possible, we'll see to it that people who want a job will get one, either at Glacier or elsewhere.

We've made all this clear to Dan and he says he doesn't want the plant to close either and we believe him. He shoots straight with us and we do the same with him. This is way different from the old days. Bob was a tired old asshole with an axe to grind. We never thought he would leave and still can't believe that Dan was given the plant.

We're working hard with Dan to set up some ways to help people get through this. Ole Bob would have died before sittin' down with us to work this out. With Dan, it's different. He always has his door open, and we have already put a committee together to help look at all our options. The hell of it is that Elderburg could have done a lot better and not have had to close if we'd been able to do this sooner. Not with Bob here, that's for damn sure.

Management practices obscured by profit often receive overdue scrutiny after a merger or acquisition. The public would be surprised at how many of these decisions overlook details that, in hindsight, would have offered warning signs. One example is the past failed merger between Dart and Kraft. At the time of the merger, Kraft was viewed as somewhat less of a "high flyer," while Dart was considered a "Wall Street darling." Unfortunately, what Dart brought to the table was far less than met the eye. On the surface there appeared to be a string of businesses that created a strong income stream. Beneath this, however, was a darker truth. Of all the businesses, only one—Tupperware—really was making significant money. In fact, the profit margin for Tupperware was so incredibly high that no one challenged a number of management practices that ultimately resulted in gross salary, perquisite, and benefit inequities throughout Dart and—ultimately, Kraft.

The Dart–Kraft merger disintegrated quickly for a variety of reasons. The point remains, however, that Dart's profitability was able to mask a myriad of business weaknesses that surfaced only after the merger. Both the Glacier and Dart–Kraft examples underscore an issue that seems difficult for many to accept. In most organizations today—top-management videos and annual report commentaries notwithstanding—making the numbers is *the* acceptable criterion. All others run a distant second. It is a shortsighted perspective and one that has already brought much trouble to organizations whose linear thinking ruled out the possibility of the major competitive market shifts that ultimately occurred.

Recently I was asked to speak to the CEO and vice-presidents of a large and profitable organization facing a year of contract negotiations with its union. The union was rumored to be interested in some new things, such as sharing in the profitability of the organization. I was asked to present examples to upper management of how other organizations had approached this issue. The "absence of pain" was more than evident. This business had earned a 16 percent return on its sales the previous year—$50 million. It employs approximately 1,500 people in its largest location and has somewhere close to 13 organizational layers between the CEO and the people on the line. As I looked out into the audience, I saw a lack of readiness for change reflected in the absence of questions and in the tone of those raised—testing the credentials of the speaker. The only glimmer of hope was an occasional voice wondering aloud whether it would be worth looking into this. But no critical mass existed to push this idea over the top, and everyone went back to business as usual.

By contrast, IBM has a stringent review committee that screens promotions against a set of criteria including both business performance *and* a track record of managing human assets. In one such session, vice-presidential candidates were being reviewed. The sponsor of one had just given a glowing tribute to the nominee's contribution to the financial side of his operations over the years. The chairman of the review committee shot back, "Yeah, but you can't give me one good example of a person he has helped develop!" The nomination was tabled.

What concerns me most about these examples is that beneath the glitter of gold was a source of untapped information that could have alerted management to the need to address the impact of change more effectively. Glacier had actually experimented with a variety of employee participation gambits in the early 1980s, but most of these were treated like unwanted skin grafts by the plant "captains." The employees were often limited to such "strategic interventions" as choosing a new color of paint for the cafeteria or planning the plantwide picnic. The plant management then expressed amazement at how well people performed when given the opportunity to participate in such things. Somehow, the magnitude of the accomplishment—adults planning a social event—escaped me.

A few plants did find employee participation to be very helpful. Some tied it to incentive plans, others tried variations on the quality circles theme, and still others just wanted to find ways to get ideas on cutting costs. As Glacier made plans to close these and other locations, a natural question arose: "What happens to employee involvement programs under such conditions?"

INVOLVEMENT UNDER SIEGE

It would come as little surprise to most people if an organization undergoing decline or total phaseout would react in ways that downplayed employee-oriented interests. In fact, there is research that found just such behavior to occur.[1] From the standpoint of the organizations themselves, it was found that their predominant reactions included:

- Stress on short-term solutions and goals

- Implementation of tighter control systems

- Elimination of people-oriented programs and expenses

In short, decision making was quickly centralized, and a widening gap between organizational and individual interests emerged. The response of most employees was to become more mercenary in their behavior. Specifically, they tended to:

- Express open distrust because of conflicting messages, such as an expressed desire for employee involvement while management increased its control.

- Blame the organization's condition on top management.

- Sharply reduce communication and openness.

- Become involved in increased conflict because of lack of cooperation, a reduction of efforts to address mixed messages, and an overall lack of resources available to handle problem solving.

This same research found evidence that change efforts could succeed under adverse conditions. Using Glacier, Inc., as an example, let us look at the criteria leading to this success, including some examples of its outcomes.

1. *Clear crisis was widely accepted.* The communication plan created by Glacier was comprehensive, used multiple media, and repeated its message over time. The message was reinforced by the behavior of the managers at the location. The arrival of various forms of assistance served as further notice that the plant-closing program was real.

2. *Plant employees trusted plant management.* In those instances where employee involvement activities succeeded, a strong bond of trust had developed earlier between people who had elected to participate in various forms of involvement (quality circles, gain-sharing committees, etc.) and the upper levels of plant management.

3. *Involvement success was visible and measurable.* Prior to the plant-closing program, the involvement activities had accomplished numerous goals. These included a reduction of cost and waste in the production process, reorganization of materials and process flow, and a more optimal use of support functions across several production lines. After the announcement, these same activities were found to have a profound effect in two areas:

- The various circles and other employee groups began to serve as major conduits of information between upper management and other employees. Changes that were coming were passed along, with explanations of the reasons for certain decisions. Employee concerns and suggestions about how to operate more effectively under these conditions were given to management by committee members.

- In most closing locations it became necessary to disconnect, dismantle, crate, and ship out a large amount of production equipment to receiving locations. In those plants where the machine operators and maintenance people worked together to accomplish this, the equipment arrived at its destination intact. In plants where this was not done, receiving managers noted that tools needed for operating the machine had "walked off" and that the overall condition of the equipment was such that extra effort was needed to install it. In a few situations, the operators and maintenance people actually traveled to the new location, helped set up the machinery, and trained new people to use it. Sometimes this training occurred at the closing site prior to removing the equipment.

4. *Concerns for people were given high priority.* This was evident from a variety of activities and efforts made by plant management and by support people brought in to give assistance. Insofar as the involvement itself was concerned, the single most telling point was that it was encouraged to continue. What had evolved into a reasonably effective medium of information exchange was put to the test under very tense conditions at times. By officially sanctioning this as "acceptable behavior," a message was sent out that the organization's needs and the needs of its people would be addressed jointly.

5. *Unofficial rule-bending was practiced.* Although Glacier, Inc., was not particularly flexible, the plant-level management team occasionally made a few Solomonic judgments as the plant-closing program progressed. On the more positive side, substantial effort was made to help people make the transition to a new job. In one location, a deliberate effort was made to hire temporary people who understood they were replacing others who needed to be released early because they had found other jobs. On the more negative side, one plant manager had to enforce discipline to communicate a business-as-usual message. A person who was causing disruption within the organization during the last month of operation was called in and dismissed. This was no small event in the eyes of those who had elected to stay to the end to receive plant-closing benefits. The plant manager explained:

I agonized over this and decided I would have to remove the person for the overall good of the plant. Also, I knew the loss of benefits would be seen as a substantial punishment by those who remained. As I weighed these thoughts, it occurred to me I could reinstate the benefits after the plant closed and just not communicate my intentions. It worked even more effectively than I had expected. People talked about how grateful they were that the person had left and thought that whatever had happened was justified.

Well, maybe the person deserved to lose the benefits, but I couldn't see it. It was just too much of a lingering punishment for behavior that was probably caused by the stress of the moment.

DISGUSTING ALLIANCES

Not all of the alliances that were formed within Glacier were "disgusting." But this idea does serve as a discussion point concerning Glacier's long-standing union relations and union avoidance position. Overall, they point out how employee interests, organizational interests, and the interests of certain functional groups can be at variance.

Historically, Glacier had built up a strong union relations department and its rules, rituals, and self-perceptions had evolved into a code of behavior that underscored a fundamental assumption: conflict is natural. They saw themselves as serving to protect the company's interests through careful and clever contract language, sharp negotiating skills, and occasional detective work combined with a bit of legal espionage. The macho image of this group was well known, and they regarded themselves as a font of knowledge when it came to making employee management decisions.

The union avoidance organization was in some ways similar to union relations, but it took on a few interesting quirks of its own. Both groups capitalized on conflict. In the case of the union avoidance group, however, the declining strength of unions and their widely publicized record of losing elections supervised by the National Labor Relations Board at non-union facilities resulted in some bizarre claims. For example, in the depths of a recession, when unions were forced to make financial concessions, were losing membership, and were being decertified by their own members, the union avoidance group arrogantly reported that the lack of organizing activity was due to their own constant vigilance.

The union relations group managed to mobilize itself only every three or four years, when contracts had to be renegotiated. In between, they served as contract interpreters and as consultants if grievances couldn't be settled locally. The union avoidance crowd, however, were always "on," forever searching for union organizers under their beds. As the years passed, they cried wolf so often that even long-time supporters began to have doubts. Some of their happier moments came when some poor local management team did something ridiculous and organizers actually did show up to capitalize on employee disaffection, however momentary. This allowed the union avoidance people to dust off all their antiquated arsenals, blow their "I Told You So" trumpets, and march into battle with nostrils flared. The hapless plant management team were muscled aside and relegated to spectator roles until the "crisis" passed.

Over time, the irony of the fact that the union relations and union avoidance groups actually disapproved of employee involvement activities surfaced on many occasions. How could they justify their existence if people began to discuss things without needing a third-party interpreter?[2] It is interesting to consider just how much commonality can be found between unions and their counterparts—union relations and union avoidance—inside organizations. Glacier's plant-closing program offered a glimpse into this area.

As might be expected, the union relations and union avoidance groups quickly jumped into the breach as local gloom dispensers, and offered the following dire predictions to management:

- Productivity and quality will decline.

- Employee sabotage and theft will increase.

- You can expect widespread defections by the "best" people.

- Employee anger toward management will not be containable.

- People will not trust management and won't accept the rationale for the change.

Research evidence does not support this, and Glacier did not find it to be the case, either.[3] Chapter 8 will focus on the actual change in productivity and quality and, as will be seen, does not offer much support for the first claim. Most of the defections were caused by Glacier either moving people around or sanctioning such movement for those who needed to seek outside employment. Much to the chagrin of both the union relations and union avoidance groups, a spate of employee–management cooperative committees emerged in the wake of the plant-closing announcement. The union relations people scrambled for their contracts to see the "limits" of what should be offered. The union avoidance people recoiled in anguish as non-union locations allowed what they regarded as "quasi-union" representatives to talk directly to management. Yes, these were indeed trying times for people whose whole purpose in life was either to use contractual language to contain insipid management leadership at the plant level, or else to cloak themselves in layers of subterfuge to thwart bogeyman organizers. Instead, they found themselves sitting on the sidelines as groups of adults facing a common and direct threat to their livelihoods stepped away from their former parent–child roles and decided jointly on ways to manage the impact of this change.

A TEMPORARY CULTURE

Much has been written about the usefulness of group solidarity during times of change, and the use of Glacier's committee structure is a good example.[4] These were only a part of the larger adjustment that was being made to manage through this turbulence. The use of such a process is an example of what can be termed a *temporary culture*.

One characteristic of a temporary culture is the emergence of a shadow organizational structure with its own communication networks, often inter-woven with those of the formal structure. In the example of Glacier, this included the embedding of the temporary culture message of change man-agement throughout many of the day-to-day work environment activities. The use of myths, rituals, joint celebrations, and carefully crafted symbolism was evidence that a temporary culture existed and was influencing daily events.

Committees were allowed to cross organizational boundaries to gather data to help shape decisions affecting the overall organization. Employee assistance programs of the past were now enhanced with outplacement ser-vices to counter the potentially negative plant-closing outcomes. Newsletters, bulletin boards, and small-group discussions were prepared or led by people whose unofficial purpose was to represent the views expressed throughout the plant at all levels.

Management soon operated within both the formal and shadow organi-zations. Their formal role helped span the boundary between the plant and the outside environment, but their shadow role served to open communica-tion channels that bypassed neatly drawn lines on charts or traversed levels within the organization. In short, the organization's temporary culture began to define and model the kind of behavior that was necessary to handle the impact of change. Cooperation and communication were escalated. Those who offered help were recognized and had their status elevated. Those who could not help gained the enmity of others.

The net effect of the temporary culture was to create new heroes, under-score emerging values, and respect the need for the passage of time to allow people to adjust to this transition, to feel their loyalty was not being taken for granted, and to move forward with confidence they would survive and even thrive under changed conditions. I have witnessed this type of cultural muta-tion several times and find that management teams who work within it can be extremely successful in getting people to channel the energy of their anxiety into more productive avenues. Shadow organizations and temporary cultures are tools to achieve an even greater and less often articulated goal: greater control over one's life. These techniques help people achieve a more comfortable balance to assure them that they can influence their environment. The astute managers and leaders will recognize the potential power of this desire, offer the appropriate mechanisms for harnessing it, and help nurture its growth. Those who fear it or fail to recognize its power will face an increased lack of employee commitment and possibly the destruction of their organization over time.

As we look at the buffer effect created by profitability and other measures of organizational success, and at the impact of change on the involvement of people, there is a point of connection that needs to be addressed. It was captured nicely in a research article:

> It is evident that employee involvement threatens the status quo and therefore may be threatening to the people that have learned to thrive in the "old" system. The employee involvement process represents decline of the status quo and is often met with the same kinds of behavioral tendencies that exist in any decline situation. [5]

We are facing a period of overlapping waves of change. For those who still feel they are going to be able to sustain their past victories with little more than increased emphasis on time-worn practices, the challenge of change is only a minor inconvenience. Their resistance to "radical" shifts in behavior cannot—in their own minds—be justified. Under these conditions, their resistance to employee involvement programs resembles the behavior of the *Star Wars* character Jabba the Hutt—a loathsome bloated figure in a somnolescent state, which mobilizes itself only when an intruder has the temerity to appear. In a grand vengeful gesture, Jabba rises up, smashes the interloper, consumes the hapless victim, belches, and falls back into a stupor. In today's world, I witness a similar act performed again and again as someone inside a "successful" organization attempts to bring about change. The sleeping giant awakens only long enough to squash innovation and protect the status quo.

For those who have managed to escape this fate, another challenge comes when employee involvement in its many forms tries to survive the turbulence of organizational change. Its enemies are those who believe their only choice of action is to restrict freedom and to oversee all decisions and those whose role in the past has been to stand in the way of such activity in order to justify their purpose. Past efforts to institutionalize involvement are sorely tested, and it has become clear that such a process results in a surprisingly robust entity that can sustain extraordinary impact while continuing to offer valuable benefits to the organization. The difference between the first scenario and the second is simply the absence of pain. As leaders confront this, they will have to consider the dilemma of having to inflict pain deliberately on their organizations to gain the attention and support of those who would otherwise delay mobilizing the organizational assets needed to reinvent itself during times of transformation.

SUMMARY

Over the years, several examples have surfaced that give us pause regarding how organizational success (e.g., profitability) has covered up poor management practices. A major criterion for most businesses—if not their sole criterion—is simply judging whether the organization or any of its profit and loss centers "made their numbers." Only after this test is failed are questions raised about how the enterprise is being managed, particularly its human assets. Not only does "success" cover such practices, it serves as a barrier to change as well. The introduction of employee involvement—or the lack of it—can be traced to the smugness associated with the head-in-the-sand attitude of those who readily recite litanies of past accomplishments and stand ready to project a linear trend of success into the future without the need for substantial changes in their approach to management.

Examples at Glacier and other organizations are offered to show how profitability can actually obscure serious problems. IBM's process for assessing candidates for promotion is held up as a positive example of how one's management of human assets can influence the direction of one's career advancement within that organization. Organizations that have used their success as justification for maintaining the status quo are shown denying the need for meaningful employee involvement in decision making. Commonly, under these circumstances, the quintessential "picnic planning" serves as the limit of "involvement" allowed for their employees.

The chapter examines employee involvement during times of change to see how it fares. Research and other evidence are reviewed to show the conditions under which such activity fades and those that favor its continued existence. Examples from Glacier are held up to show the type of impact its involvement activities had during its plant-closing program.

An examination of subfunctions within Glacier—the union relations and union avoidance groups—demonstrates that their past contributions and beliefs put them at odds with the goals of employee involvement. This issue is explored to show how they reacted and to give warning to leaders who are trying to manage the impact of change. This is a political form of resistance that must be addressed directly. The predictions of this group are contrasted with actual outcomes to demonstrate further just how far their predictions were from the reality of the plants.

Much to the chagrin of such subfunctions, temporary cultures often emerge and are made up of adults who eschew past inequitable relationships in favor of open dialogue without the use of intermediaries. In Glacier's case, plant committees at both union and non-union locations, made up of labor and management representatives, reached difficult but necessary decisions to help people make the transition as the closing date approached. This process—a temporary culture—is shown to draw upon a shadow organizational structure that has much influence over values, symbolism, and the modeling of behavior deemed necessary to manage such a transition.

The strength of the status quo, whether it comes from questionable projections of future success based on past victories or from those who think the organization is under too much stress to worry about "people issues" just now, remains as a major barrier to organizational revitalization, transformation, and the ability of people to influence decisions that affect their work lives.

Notes

1. Susan A. Mohrman and Allan M. Mohrman, Jr., examine this area in their article, "Employee Involvement in Declining Organizations," *Human Resource Management*, 22(4), 445–466 (1983). I was particularly impressed with their discussion of both the positive and the negative characteristics that emerge during times of organizational turbulence. I have borrowed some of their categories to show that Glacier, Inc., clearly demonstrated a number of positive characteristics in plants with employee involvement activities.

2. In his book, *Future Perfect* (Reading, MA: Addison-Wesley, 1987, pp. 30–31), Stanley M. Davis addressed this point. He states:

    People who identify problems generally identify themselves as problem solvers, yet the irony is that they then have a stake in the problem staying identified but unsolved.

How low does the crime rate have to get before it is a threat to law enforcement agencies?

3. Robert I. Sutton captured a number of the widely accepted and generally expected negative outcomes associated with what he terms "organizational death." He goes on, in his article titled "Managing Organizational Death," *Human Resource Management*, 22(4) (1983), to refute nearly all of them with actual research findings. The one area he leaves standing as equivocal regards the loss of the "best people." The closest work I have seen on this lately was reported in an article by Ann Howard, "Who Reaches for the Golden Handshake?," *Academy of Management Executive*, 2(2) (1988). She was able to show that there were no significant long-term job performance differences between those who took early retirement and those who elected to stay.

4. The concept of *culture* gained a great deal of exposure following the publication of *Corporate Cultures* (Reading, MA: Addison-Wesley, 1982) by Terrence E. Deal and Allen A. Kennedy. Debora Sholl Humphreys builds upon this work with her examination of a manufacturing plant scheduled to be closed. I have found her insights very helpful in framing much of the activity that occurred within Glacier's closing locations throughout its overall program. More details of her work can be found in "Decline as a Natural Resource for Development," a paper she presented to the forty-seventh annual meeting of the Academy of Management in New Orleans, Louisiana, in August 1987.

5. Several years ago, as I was gathering data pertaining to plant closings and other major changes affecting organizations, I was greatly impressed with a quote by Susan and Allan Mohrman in their article I have cited earlier (note 1). I have chosen to repeat it because it served as a helpful anchor for my thinking. Specifically, I had been struggling with the difficulties associated with bringing about significant change in an organization that had not experienced great pain. Glacier offered me additional insight into the resistance to innovation during its plant-closing program, and the two situations were identified in this article as both challenging the status quo. For me it opened the door to a whole different way of looking at what some see as the "negative research" associated with things like plant closings. As the quote suggests, lessons we can learn from such negative situations are applicable to others in which the status quo is being challenged, even though the organization itself is not undergoing decline or death.

Chapter 8

WE NEEDED THE EGGS

A guy goes to the psychiatrist and says his brother needs help because he thinks he's a chicken. The doctor asks how he knows this and the man says his brother clucks, flaps his arms, and has built a huge nest in the living room—now their friends won't come over. The doctor tells him this is very serious and asks how long this has gone on. The man replies, "Twenty years." The doctor is incredulous and asks why he has not sought help before now. The answer: "We needed the eggs."
—Woody Allen

THE EGGS?

A primary question in the minds of leaders and managers about to embark upon a major change is, "Will the organization survive, and is it worth the cost?" Years ago, as a production supervisor, I lived the daily challenge of mobilizing technical and human assets needed to sustain the vitality and production of my piece of the organization. The "normal" fluctuations were more than enough to contend with, and I shudder to consider what I would have had to do to manage even greater change. Yet this is often the crux of the issue of change within organizations—a Phoenix-like paradox, probing the riddle of rebirth after destruction. After all the philosophical debates have ended and the statistical models have been reviewed, there remains a lingering doubt as to whether life will actually parallel such tidy concepts when the impact of change is felt. We live in an age of skepticism, and employees have grown increasingly distrustful of what appear to be forms of organizational hypocrisy. Consider, for example, just one of the "new" ideas being currently promoted. At a time when quality is gaining prominence among management thinkers,[1] a legitimate question arises from those who have been asked to produce goods and services under very different circumstances: "If quality is so important, why haven't we stressed it before now?" Management's answer: "We needed the eggs." As grandma used to say, "Don't expect to talk your way out of something you behaved yourself into."

Given all the hyperbole over the years about the need for quality, employee involvement, concern for individual rights, the need to protect national markets, concern for the environment, and other lofty issues—all pitted against a seemingly endless array of contradictory organizational practices—it is not difficult to understand people's reticence to accept nearly any pronouncement by management at face value. Yet it is imperative that management be able to gain the trust and commitment of people when an organization faces major challenges. One of Glacier's general managers had great reservation about the long-term prospects of the closing plants after the closing announcement had been made:

> Frankly, I figured we would wind up shutting down most of the plants within six months after the closing announcement. Several people talked to me about the possibility of strikes, slowdowns, and that kind of stuff. I thought people would just get mad and take it out on the company. I really wasn't sure how, but if you had told me that we were going to not only keep these places running for a long time after the announcement—months turning into years in a few cases—and do it at record production and efficiency rates, I would never have believed it. But we did it and it's a tribute to the people.

As we look at the impact of one profound form of change—the closing of production facilities within Glacier, Inc.—we will see measures that reflect actual operational fluctuations at closing and receiving locations.

A PRODUCTIVITY PHENOMENON

There is a growing body of literature that suggests an unusual phenomenon occurs in organizations scheduled to be closed.[2] In short, overall productivity shows an increase above prior levels, sometimes a dramatic one. In at least one study,[3] a more detailed examination of the impact of a closing announcement on both productivity and quality within three separate production units was conducted. From this work emerged the hypothesized model shown in Figure 8.1. As the researchers examined their data, they found this pattern occurring across all locations. Each phase represents a distinct organizational event:

Phase I   This is a period of normal fluctuations that occurs prior to the actual closing announcement.

Phase II   This period is very short, often lasting just a few days, and occurs after the closing announcement. It is characterized by reduced operating efficiency. The researchers suggest it may be caused by an initial emotional reaction by employees.

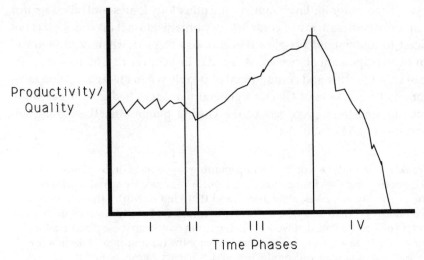

Figure 8.1   Hyphothesized Change Impact Model

Phase III   Productivity and quality rise above Phase I levels during this period. The researchers offer that employees may be going through a denial period. They may be unwilling to accept the decision, believing that increased effort can reverse it. A sense of pride may also be a factor.

Phase IV   This period is marked by a sharp performance decline. It begins when tangible evidence of the closing becomes imminent—when people or equipment are transferred, or when employees are told the exact date of their termination. The authors note that low morale, turnover, conflict, and occasional sabotage may occur during this period. At this point the organization could suffer a premature shutdown of the production unit.

Unfortunately, this work and others cited offer only sketchy information about the actual changes that occurred. Several questions remain to be answered:

1. Does this phenomenon occur generally, or are the past examples unusual cases?

2. Does this hypothesized model predict accurately such effects for other organizations?

3. Will this pattern hold up when a more sophisticated approach to data gathering and analysis is taken?

4. Do these changes only occur in closing plants? What about the closing announcement impact on other plants?

5. Can the debacle in the last phase be avoided or minimized?

GLACIER, INC., PRODUCTIVITY AND QUALITY

In Glacier, an opportunity to answer these and other questions presented itself. Eight locations scheduled to close and seven others that would receive equipment and people from those to be phased out were examined. Because of their long production measurement histories, each location was able to provide detailed quality and productivity data generated before and after the plant-closing announcement. For most locations, data were obtained at least four or five years prior to the announcement. Further, given that the actual closing process averaged more than a year, the impact of seasonality could be taken into account. What makes this analysis so unusual, in addition to the large quantity of high-quality measurement data, is the opportunity to compare closing facilities with receiving facilities—those that were to receive people and equipment from the closing plants.

Details of the analytic approach follow.[4]

MEASURES OF PRODUCTIVITY AND QUALITY

The most common measure of productivity within the Glacier plants was the number of units produced per hour by each employee. In a few locations, measures of direct labor efficiency were used; others were measured against historic engineering standards.

Most of the plants used material efficiency as their primary quality measure, although a few were beginning to use a more comprehensive assessment given by their quality control functions.

STATISTICAL METHOD

The basic design used was an interrupted time series to test the impact of the closing announcement on productivity and quality measures. This design involves periodic measurement of outcome variables (e.g., productivity, quality) both before and after a significant change is introduced. In Glacier, the "change" was the plant-closing announcement. If the closing decision and announcement had had an effect on performance, it would have been indicated by a change in the pattern of the productivity and quality time series.

After appropriate time-series modeling occurred, the data were subjected to least-squares regression analysis. The sensitivity of the time-series analysis was increased by:

- Using monthly versus quarterly data

- Using data over an extended number of years to account for seasonal fluctuations

- Performing the analysis after one full year had passed since the closing announcement to ensure that a full cycle of data was available

The analysis focused on the pre- and postclosing differences in productivity and quality. Specifically, the historic data allowed for a prediction of trend. Any deviations from the predicted trend were judged as to their statistical significance. Expressed in more technical terms, a statistically significant change in level (intercept) of the time series was interpreted as an abrupt change in productivity. A statistically significant change in drift (slope) would be evidence that the data had shifted to a new level over time, thus representing a different trend.

GRAPHIC ANALYSIS

In addition to the statistical analysis, a series of visual displays of the changes in measurement points were created. The displays chosen for discussion will be labeled as follows:

Closing Plant 1	Receiving Plant 1
Closing Plant 2	Receiving Plant 2
Closing Plant 3	

Quality measures at the closing plants did not show a significant statistical change, so the graphs for these measures are not shown. However, one quality graph from a receiving plant is shown, for reasons to be discussed later. In general, these visuals were chosen to represent the effects of the change found among all of the plants throughout the study. It should be noted that Glacier's actual productivity measurements are considered proprietary and the figures altered to protect confidentiality. The dark vertical line on the graphs represents the time of the plant-closing announcement. It should be noted that the closing period varied across locations. Therefore, some graphs for closing plants have more postannouncement data points than do others.

Closing Plant 1—Productivity

At this location, productivity showed a sharp and statistically significant increase since the closing announcement. This can be seen in Figure 8.2, which shows productivity unchanged immediately following the announcement and then rising very abruptly. This location was a sort of job-shop production facility, with literally hundreds of product lines. It should also be noted that this was a union-represented facility with a Scanlon-like incentive plan. The plan's production committees served as a particularly effective communication vehicle throughout the closing period. People at this location showed a willingness to train employees from the receiving location in the use of the equipment before it was dismantled and shipped.

Closing Plant 2—Productivity

Productivity at this plant (Figure 8.3) had been rising *prior* to the closing announcement. After that time, the trend continued to rise, though not at a statistically significant pace. This was the plant run by Bob Wilson, men-

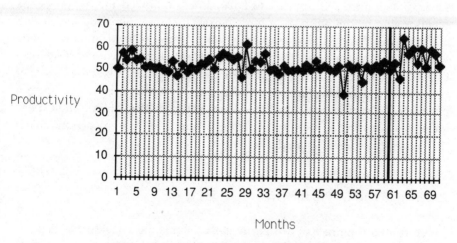

Figure 8.2   Closing Plant 1—Productivity

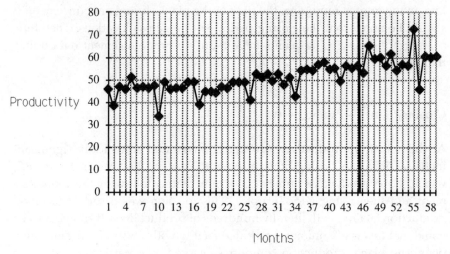

Months

Figure 8.3   Closing Plant 2—Productivity

tioned in Chapter 5. He had been brought in several years earlier to bring about a "turnaround." The graph depicts the trend under his leadership. It is quite impressive, and interviews with individual employees reflected their pride in his attention to the details necessary to produce such a record. This was a union-represented facility.

Closing Plant 3—Productivity

This plant (Figure 8.4) appears to have closely followed the hypothesized plant-closing model, with sharply rising productivity following the closing announcement. A declining productivity trend was reversed, and the change was statistically significant. While Closing Plants 1 and 2 were in rural locations, this one was in an urban center and was non-union. It had the benefit of being among the final locations to close and, therefore, benefited from a number of lessons learned by others. The combined effect of time and experience was seen in the quality of management and support actions taken throughout the closing period.

Receiving Plant 1—Productivity

These results (Figure 8.5) are particularly interesting considering that the productivity measure had risen prior to the closing announcement. It is likely

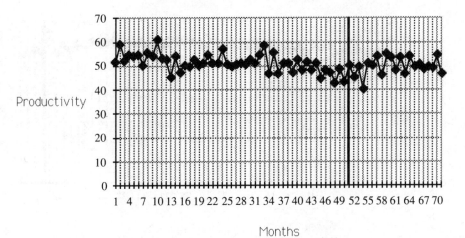

Months

Figure 8.4   Closing Plant 3—Productivity

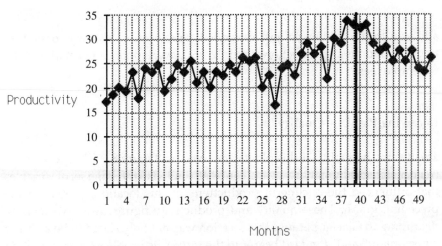

Months

Figure 8.5   Receiving Plant 1—Productivity

that new production requirements resulting from the planned movement of work from closing locations pulled this measure downward. This location also experienced some difficulty in starting up some new equipment. None of this should be considered unusual for a plant undergoing substantial transition. As Figure 8.5 shows, the measure of productivity is down sharply and this decline is statistically significant. This is a non-union facility, but there have been several attempts to organize the work force—all unsuccessful. In

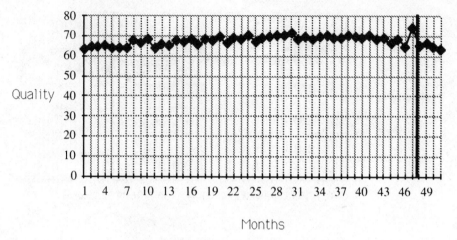

Figure 8.6   Receiving Plant 1—Quality

addition to the challenges just described, this location also was operating under a continuous production schedule, with overlapping and rotating shifts for employees.

Receiving Plant 1—Quality

The decline in quality at this plant can be seen in Figure 8.6. This downward trend is statistically significant and can be attributed to the same set of variables that influenced the decline in productivity at this location, shown on the preceding graph. These quality and productivity figures were particularly disturbing to Glacier because this location was not only slated to be a sort of "mega-plant" and standard bearer in the future, its problems were resulting in some additional unplanned issues. First, one of the closing plants had to be kept in operation far beyond its scheduled closing date. Second, the longer the closing plant was kept open, the more it showed improvement in its overall operation. This raised a sensitive issue for the general manager, who commented:

> If this were a straightforward business decision, I'd have to say that we are closing the wrong plant! The one with the lower production costs and higher quality measures is the one we are trying to close and the one with all the problems is the one we are betting on. Frankly, I can't afford to close the better

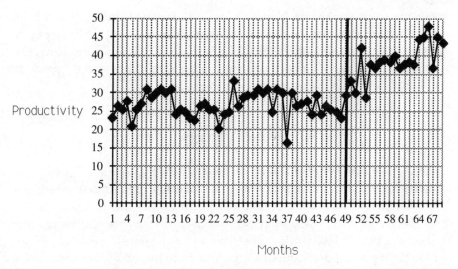

Figure 8.7   Receiving Plant 2—Productivity

plant because we couldn't meet our volume demand and would actually wind up buying production slack from competitors! This is a classic example of planning in a vacuum. I sure as hell never would have done this—but then I wasn't asked. . . .

Receiving Plant 2—Productivity

The results at this location were of particular interest. First, it can be seen in Figure 8.7 that the level of productivity at this location increased after the closing announcement. This increased level was statistically significant. Second, the trend increased sharply, and this change was also statistically significant. Two events occurred at this location that are likely to have affected these results. The plant manager was given responsibility for both this location *and* the closing location from which equipment was to be received. This allowed for a significant increase in coordination of activities compared to what occurred in other transitions. Second, the plant management group reported a significant increase in concern among their employees that they would be next in line to close. The plant manager assured them this was not the case but strongly indicated that job security would depend on how well the plant could absorb the new equipment and become productive. This pattern of results was somewhat unusual, as most receiving plants showed productivity or quality problems. Some of these were due to the lack of available inventory that the closing locations were supposed to have put in backlog prior to ceasing operations. In other cases, receiving plant managers complained that the inventory contained a backlog of low-quality product resulting in a higher-than-expected scrap rate.

CONCLUSIONS

Glacier's overall experience was consistent with the hypothesized model that showed the impact of such change on a manufacturing organization scheduled to close. However, it is disturbing to see the difficulties that receiving plants had. The overall results showed a clear pattern of performance across receiving and closing plants. Five closing plants showed an *increase* in productivity after the closing announcement. In a departure from the model, however, none of the closing plants experienced the sharp decline that was supposed to occur once people received firm evidence that the plant would be closing. The management practices and human resource assistance, coupled with historic working relationships at most of these locations, are likely sources of this ability to sustain production under such conditions. More will be said about this in Chapter 9.

Receiving plants experienced problems with productivity and, in some instances, quality. The reasons for this vary by type of plant. They include a shift in product mix, with added products associated with lower levels of material efficiency. Some locations had the added burden of introducing more complex equipment. The timing of some equipment movement could have been a factor, since some high-volume product lines were moved later than others. Although overall product volume did increase during the early stages of the plant-closing program, this explains only a portion of the problems found at the receiving location. Glacier headquarters managers, it should be recalled, restricted the involvement of all plant managers in the planning of the closing program. Many of the receiving plant managers complained that their difficulties could be traced back to this decision. In some situations, the transfer of people also affected operations at receiving plants. People moving from a non-union to a union location faced some major adjustments. Others moving from a moderately paced line to a faster paced line took time to adapt as well.

During the transition period, a number of plant staff managers indicated the movement of equipment appeared to result in improvement in product quality. Data gathered by Glacier headquarters managers in the quality area suggest that such improvements did occur and were likely due to "reengineering." This is a euphemistic way of saying that the woeful lack of blueprints or engineering drawings required the receiving plant engineers to make largely unplanned and undocumented modifications while reinstalling the equipment.

STEPPING BACK

There are a number of insights that can be gained from the Glacier example. To obtain a better perspective, let us revisit the questions raised earlier:

Does this phenomenon occur generally, or are the past examples unusual cases?

The Glacier results support the conclusion that the increase in productivity is not an isolated phenomenon and can be expected to occur under similar conditions.

Does this hypothesized model predict accurately such effects for other organizations?

The model appears to be fairly accurate, with one obvious exception. The final phase predicts a drastic decrease in both productivity and quality after the movement of people or equipment commences and after employees are given an exact date for the location to close. The ability of Glacier's managers to sustain productivity and quality levels throughout this final stage suggests that there is more leverage here than the model predicts.

Will this pattern hold up when a more sophisticated approach is taken to data gathering and analysis?

There are actually two elements involved in the present case that add much strength to the conclusions drawn. First, Glacier had a long history of close measurement, and this provided records dating back several years prior to the announcement, thus helping to identify changes associated with the closing program itself. Second, the analysis was statistically rigorous and therefore reduced the likelihood that these conclusions were spurious. These two elements add much support to the claim that the overall pattern—with the amendment cited earlier—is a close approximation to what can be expected to occur.

Do these changes occur only in the closing plants? What about the closing announcement impact on other plants?

Perhaps the most interesting part of the Glacier example is the opportunity to compare closing and receiving locations under these conditions. The closing locations fared quite well, all showing no drop in productivity or quality, and most showing an increase in productivity—sometimes significantly so.

For receiving locations, the picture is a darker one. In Glacier's example, the absence of plant manager involvement in planning the transition, the increase in product demands, the shifts in product mix, the introduction of new technology, and the influx of people unfamiliar with a new working culture served to deflate earlier measures of both productivity and quality at some locations. Clearly, it appears that much more concern was given to the management of the closing facilities than was given to those that would bear Glacier's production burden in the future.

Can the debacle in the last phase be avoided or minimized?

Apparently so. Glacier did not find a single example to support the negative predictions associated with the final phase of the hypothesized model.

The overall point from this examination is that the vitality and viability of organizations can indeed be influenced by the impact of organizational change. Even more important, we see what appears to be an emerging and predictable pattern. This pattern should offer hope to those who fear the aftermath of change will be unmanageable, a cure worse than the malady. In the following chapter we will look more deeply at the root causes underlying this pattern and related issues.

SUMMARY

This chapter examines the impact of an organizational change on hard data—actual productivity and quality numbers gathered before and during Glacier's plant-closing program. With regard to the change impact, these data allow us to examine the "what" but give only minimal insight into the "why"—a discussion picked up in the next chapter.

The phenomenon of increased productivity within closing locations is interesting, and this chapter offers several good examples from a variety of locations to show how pervasive it is. Further, the current data offer firm support of this prediction because of the way in which the analysis was done and the quality of data used. It was interesting to find that the four-phase hypothesized model of productivity changes was largely supported. I say "largely" because Glacier was able to sustain high levels of productivity well into the fourth phase without undergoing the predicted dramatic downturn. Also, the shifts in quality predicted by the model did not occur at the closing locations. It appears the model may be more accurate in describing changes in productivity.

A series of questions were raised regarding the impact of organization change on such measures and the answers provided by the data in this chapter help understand what actually occurs under such conditions. However, as we look at measures of employees' views and managers' practices in Chapter 9, we will gain additional insights into how an organization manages the impact of change.

Notes

1. The whole "quality" movement got a real shot in the arm when NBC broadcasted its White Paper titled "If Japan Can, Why Can't We?" in 1980. During the broadcast there were references to Dr. W. Edwards Deming and his work in Japan. A number of recent texts have either extended his message or created others in support of the need to compete more effectively through quality. Two examples: Phil B. Crosby, *Quality Is Free* (New York: McGraw-Hill, 1979), and Mary Walton, *The Deming Management Method* (New York: Dodd, Mead, 1986).

2. Jeanne P. Gordus, Paul Jarley, and Louis A. Ferman, in *Plant Closings and Economic Dislocation* (Kalamazoo, MI: W. E. Upjohn Institute, 1981), discuss how people in closing plants often deny the reality of what is happening. Alfred Slote's *Termination: The Closing at Baker Plant* (Indianapolis: Bobbs-Merrill, 1969) offers an in-depth case study that shows how such denial can lead to refocusing one's energy on preserving the status quo, even to the point of redoubling effort. Early work by W. R. Bion, *Experiences in Groups and Other Papers* (London: Tavistock, 1961), describes how groups will mobilize themselves when a clear external threat to the group is perceived. In a Conference Board report by Ronald E. Berenbeim, "Company Programs to Ease the Impact of Shutdowns," Report No. 878 (1986), six different businesses reported that productivity improvements occurred after the closure of the facility was announced.

3. An unpublished study (February 11, 1984) of effects found during the closing of three plants was conducted by E. Hordov, R. Maxa, E. Williams, and J. Zawistowski. This work, under the supervision of Dr. Michael Schuster at

Syracuse University, provided the earliest suggestion that a pattern of activity occurs over time, following the announcement of a facility's closing.

4. As I began to work with Glacier, Inc., to identify the plant-closing issues to be addressed, I asked Dr. Michael Schuster, head of Competitive Human Resources Strategies, Inc. (Syracuse, NY 13210) for his assistance. Mike was responsible for working with Glacier's managers to identify the sources for needed hard data, performing an appropriate level of analysis, and providing Glacier with an interpretation of the results. For a more complete description of the statistical techniques used, the reader is directed to a textbook by J. Cohen and P. Cohen titled *Applied Multiple Regression/Correlation Analysis for the Behavioral Sciences* (Hillsdale, N.J.: Lawrence Erlbaum Associates, 1983). For those who want a complete listing of the statistical tables generated, I will supply them upon request. The exclusion of detailed explanations of the *t*-values and probability levels is intentional so as to focus more attention on the results and their implications. I have drawn heavily on Mike's work throughout this chapter. Although I have done my best to represent his overall approach, I assume all responsibility for any whimsy that has gone astray. . . .

Chapter 9

WHO'S IN CHARGE HERE?

I strongly feel if we had better management in the past five years things might have been different.

I'm proud to work for a company that during the plant closing is offering their employees such good benefits. This will help people make the adjustment well.
—Employees in Closing Plant

I knew from the start that I would hate playing God.
—Upper-Level Executive

It isn't often that the inner workings of an organization that has undergone significant change can be held up to external scrutiny. The previous chapter examined some hard numbers representing the shift in productivity and product quality within Glacier's manufacturing plants affected by its plant-closing decision. This chapter goes yet another step by examining the management activity behind those numbers. The sources include input from people working within the plants as well as from the managers themselves. Given the ability of Glacier to withstand the impact of such a dramatic decision, the information from this analysis is crucial to understand the role their managers played in this outcome.

EXTERNAL THREATS—A DOUBLE-EDGED SWORD

On the surface, Glacier's results might be attributed largely to its management strength. Its past history of operating success certainly is not in dispute. However, these managers faced a challenge for which nothing in their past had prepared them. Indeed, there is irony in the way external threats to groups like these production operations affect both their internal relationships and their views of leadership. On the one hand, considerable research supports the hypothesis of increased group cohesiveness in the face of adversity.[1]

However, such threats to a group often result in "leader bashing"—particularly when the cause of the situation appears to be linked to the leader's past behavior. Since it is unlikely a group will achieve unanimity on the leader's culpability, it should be expected that those responsible for managing the impact of change will receive criticism from within the group. More pointedly, research has found that, under similar circumstances, people will scapegoat their leaders, resist change, exhibit reduced morale and organizational commitment, cast doubt on the credibility of the leader, and exhibit other forms of withdrawal.[2]

Managers are put under extraordinary stress because, in contrast to employees, who historically have accepted as givens their jobs, careers, and working conditions, managers are viewed (and, more important, view themselves) as being able to have more influence over such issues. Under these conditions, it has been shown that change can have a significantly greater impact on managers than it does on those at lower levels in the organization.[3] More specifically, managers who face changes such as plant closings must accept responsibility for at least three major areas: (1) operating a facility that will cease operations within a specified period of time, (2) providing the necessary support to people who will lose their jobs, and (3) serving as a liaison with a community likely to feel the impact of such a change.[4] On top of this, they also have to look out for their own best interests. All of this suggests that change presents daunting challenges to managers, and the management literature describes a wide variety of managerial responses—with decidedly mixed results.[5] What is needed is a clearer view of what actually occurs within such settings.

CHANGE MANAGEMENT: AN INSIDE LOOK

Glacier, Inc., offers an exceptional opportunity to examine the actions of management throughout the plant-closing process. The insights come from managers, plant staff members, and union representatives, as well as exempt, nonexempt, and hourly employees. The overall effort here will be to explore the impact of this change on them and to examine their views on management practices at their particular locations.

It is clear that Glacier is a measurement-driven organization. Chapter 8, for example, was able to draw on a rich and detailed source of historic production data. It should, therefore, not be surprising to find a similar approach in the gathering of employee input. In fact, Glacier has a long history of seeking employee views through surveys. One such instrument had been in use prior to the plant-closing decision, and a slightly modified version continued to be used throughout the closing process. Because of their quantitative nature, the survey results serve as a focal point in this discussion. These results, combined with information from interviews and small-group sessions, help form a grand mosaic depicting the management process and its impact within the closing and receiving plants.

Despite their past use of surveys and other measurement instruments, the occurrence of the plant closing raised questions in the minds of some executives about the appropriateness of surveying employees under such conditions. The decision to proceed was made in order to achieve two purposes. First, management believed that business as usual needed to be stressed throughout the program, as Glacier would continue to need a large quantity of high-quality products until the locations actually ceased production. In retrospect, this proved to be an understatement, because of an unexpected increase in consumer demand for its products during the first phase of the closings. Therefore, surveys were viewed as a means of gathering input on how the locations were being managed. It was assumed that operating managers would make efforts to improve the working environment, partly on the basis of survey data, regardless of the long-term fate of the plant.

The second purpose was to conduct research. Survey data would provide quantifiable answers to a number of questions. Specifically, they would identify particular areas of management practice that were significantly related to, or relatively unaffected by, the fate of the location and/or the passage of time following a closing announcement. This research effort was greatly benefited by the fact that such a survey process had been in place for several years to obtain information on employee attitudes as well as their views of management practices. This offered some unique opportunities:

- Several locations had been surveyed before the closing announcement, allowing a pre- versus postannouncement comparison of responses.

- Employees and managers at Glacier locations were familiar with this process and would view it as part of their normal activities.

The survey content covered the following eight categories:

Productivity.   This area focused on the availability of resources, how productivity was viewed by co-workers, and the overall working relationships among employees.

Work Management.   The emphasis here was on the setting of work priorities, the availability of qualified people, and the match between people and resources.

Supervision.   This category examined numerous facets of first-line supervision including providing performance feedback, resolving problems, involving people in decision making, encouraging teamwork, and so forth.

Pay and benefits.   This category covered the perceived competitiveness of Glacier's benefits as well as the perceived equity surrounding wage and salary administration. It also looked at the availability of information about employee benefits.

Communication.   This was a broad category that covered both interplant communication and activity that occurred at higher levels. It examined the level of assistance available from various internal functions, such as human resources, and gauged the perceived concern at higher management levels for issues and suggestions related to work done at lower levels.

Safety and health.   This was a mixture of items, some describing actual management activity and some assessing the manager's intention to maintain a safe and healthful environment for employees.

Personal development.   This category covered issues related to obtaining training as well as being able to access information pertaining to job opportunities.

Work climate.   This is another broad area that examined how well plant functions cooperated with each other, employee commitment to Glacier, and overall job satisfaction.

Most of the subsequent analysis centered on two critical variables: (1) whether the location surveyed was to close or was to receive people, processes, and equipment from a closing plant, and (2) the point in time at which the data were gathered. Specifically, measures were taken before and after the closing announcement was made. At both closing and receiving plants, the surveys were conducted approximately one year before the announcement and one year following it. In one plant, a third and final survey was conducted two years after the announcement—90 days prior to the cessations of its operations.

All locations had advance notice of the closing—most had two years.

Therefore, another year of operation followed all data collection except for the one plant mentioned. It is believed that this location provides insights into "final days" activities and views that had yet to emerge in the survey results from other plants. Further technical details surrounding this instrument, the sampling process, demographics, and related information are provided in Appendix 9A.

COMPARED TO WHAT?

Before examining the results, it should be noted that Glacier's employees historically held relatively positive views of management practices and had expressed a fair amount of satisfaction with their jobs. This is important to keep in mind because the changes in these views during the plant-closing process, though at times quite substantial, must be kept in context. In short, Glacier may have ended up being worse off than before in certain areas, but the views could still be taken as simply "less positive" than before. To underscore this point, Figure 9.1 shows a comparison of the closing and receiving plant responses across the survey areas described earlier.

These results were obtained approximately one year *after* the closing announcement had been made. The survey item responses ranged from "Not Applicable" (0) to "Strongly Agree" (5). Therefore, a higher number represents a more positive view. Based on this, it can be seen that the people at

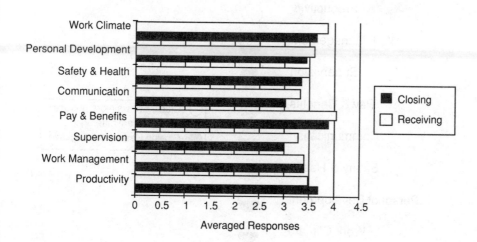

Figure 9.1   Closing versus Receiving Plants: An Analysis of Degree of Agreement Across Survey Areas

closing and receiving plants (approximately 2,500 in each group) shared relatively positive views across survey categories one year after the closing announcement.

WHO REALLY WON?

The first issue concerns the comparison between closing and receiving plants one year after the announcement. As Figure 9.2 indicates, the results for the closing plants were significantly different from those for the receiving plants with regard to employee views of productivity and supervision. In the first area, the closing plant employees perceived a significantly higher amount of resources being made available to get the work done. On the other hand, these same people were highly critical of first-line supervision. In particular, they saw:

- Fewer formal performance reviews were conducted.

- Less assistance was available to solve problems.

- Inadequate rationale was given for management decisions.

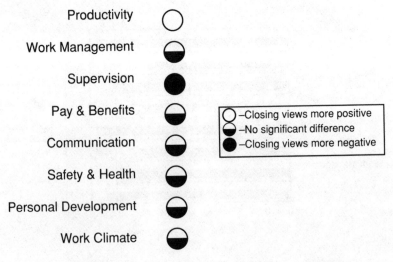

Figure 9.2   Closing versus Receiving Plant Survey Results

- There was reduced employee involvement in decisions affecting their work.

- There was less emphasis on explaining the big picture of the work assignments.

- There was less emphasis on teamwork.

The closing and receiving plants did not differ significantly across the survey areas of work management, pay and benefits, communication, safety and health, personal development, and work climate. Within these categories, however, some individual items showed significant differences.

Compared to the people in receiving plants, the employees in the closing plants indicated that:

- They received less assistance in job search.

- There was greater cross-functional cooperation.

- Layoffs were not being handled fairly.

- They had higher overall job satisfaction.

With regard to the job search assistance, it will be necessary to revisit this area later, as survey results are examined for the location that was 90 days away from shutting down. Recall that the current results were obtained at least a year before the locations actually ceased operations. There is some evidence that people will not take advantage of such job assistance until the eleventh hour.

THE IMPACT OF TIME

Narrowing the focus to only the closing plants, a question can be raised as to which survey areas showed the most change one year after the announcement. The results, shown in Figure 9.3, found the following categories to be most affected:

- Productivity
- Supervision
- Work management
- Pay and benefits

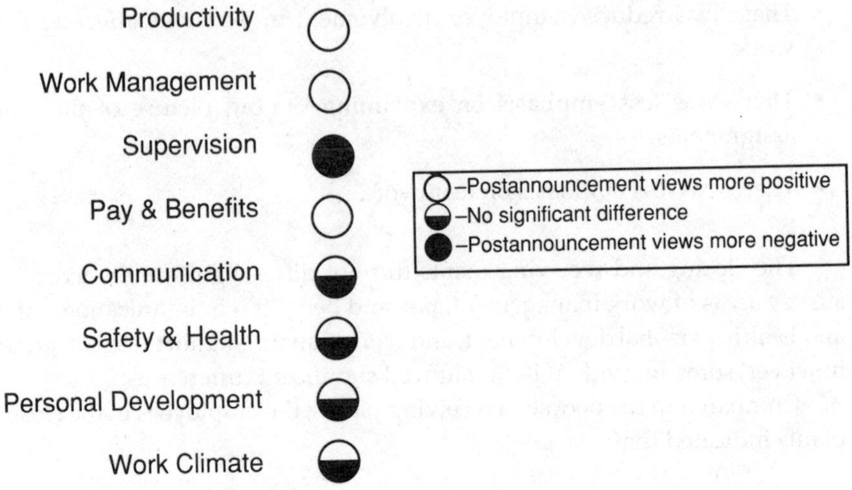

Productivity ○

Work Management ○

Supervision ●

Pay & Benefits ○

◐	–Postannouncement views more positive
◒	–No significant difference
●	–Postannouncement views more negative

Communication ◒

Safety & Health ◒

Personal Development ◒

Work Climate ◒

Figure 9.3   Pre- versus Postannouncement Survey Results for Closing Plants

Specifically, one year after the announcement, the closing plant employees expressed the following views:

Productivity

- More resources were made available to get the work done.

- There was a more cooperative atmosphere among co-workers.

A critical issue that has surfaced in a number of studies concerns the phenomenon of increased productivity at closing plants. Why does this happen? In the last chapter, we saw actual production figures that confirmed that this had occurred at several Glacier locations. The survey results confirm that people at closing locations had a stronger view of productivity than did those at receiving plants. Part of the explanation seems to be related to the availability of resources at closing plants. This was indeed true, for Glacier made certain that maintenance funds were not cut, capital appropriations for technical improvements were allocated, and so forth. However, another perspective emerged from interviews and small-group sessions to help explain this increase. Basically, four themes surfaced during these discussions:

- The idea that hard work will reverse the decision

I just tried to do more each day and thought that maybe it would show them what a mistake it was to close such a productive place.

- **An act of defiance to undercut the rationale for closing the plant**

These greedy bastards never really looked at just how good the place was. There were lots of things we could have done but they never asked or never let us. This was not an "ethical" decision. I decided to show them just what a stupid mistake it was by pouring on the steam. A lot of us feel this way.

- **Cleansing a work record**

I had missed some days over the past few years because I was sick and sometimes just to get my head straight. Well, it sorta caught up with me when this whole mess came about. I made damn sure I was at work on time and volunteered for extra work, even more overtime, so I could get a good evaluation before the place shut down.

- **Avoiding reality**

I just put it out of my mind, but it was real hard to do. Every day I came in and saw my friends and they would talk about it. I shut it out and worked harder than ever. It seemed the more I did, the less time I had to think. I guess it seems kinda dumb, but it helped me make it through the day.

Work Management

- There were more qualified people to get the work done.
- A more effective match existed between people and resources.

Supervision

- Fewer formal performance discussions were held.
- Less problem resolution assistance was available.
- There was inadequate explanation of management decisions.
- There was reduced involvement in decisions affecting the work.
- There was less emphasis on the big picture of the work.
- There was less encouragement of teamwork.

Pay and Benefits

- A reduced amount of benefits information was available.

- Glacier's benefits package was viewed as more competitive.

- Wage and salary administration was viewed as more equitable.

As these categories suggest, not only were the closing plants different from the receiving plants one year after the announcement, they were different from themselves as well. Although the remaining categories of communication, safety and health, personal development, and work climate did not show a significant change over time, a few items within some of these areas did. One year after the announcement, the closing plant employees indicated:

- They saw the problem-solving procedure as less useful.

- An increase in cross-functional cooperation had occurred.

- They perceived increased prestige gained from working for Glacier.

The results regarding benefits information must be interpreted with some caution. For example, under such conditions, the demand for such information increases dramatically, and it may be extremely difficult to meet such demand to everyone's satisfaction. This subject will be revisited later. The lack of change in personal development views may again reflect a delayed willingness to take steps in this direction until later in the closing process. It is interesting to note the lack of deterioration of views in the Safety and Health area, suggesting that management was viewed as continuing to support this area. During interviews with managers, they indicated that housekeeping, safety inspections, and even painting projects were carried out on a business-as-usual basis. They were keenly aware that these steps did not go unnoticed by employees.

In numerous interviews and small-group meetings at closing facilities, the managers expressed several common themes:

- Inadequate preparation for change impact

I couldn't believe how the whole benefits thing was handled, for example. The human resource people made a big deal about how we were going to help people. But after the announcement, they left us hanging out here. People wanted to know two things. When are we going to close? What benefits will I get?

Nobody at headquarters was prepared to help. What's worse, the first set of printouts we got were inaccurate and really scared the hell out of the people.

We have always tried to keep people informed, but now we have to both communicate and deal with all kinds of rumors on top of it. I bet I spend more time undoing nonsense than I do telling what little I actually have been told myself.

They think I know something that I'm not telling them, and I keep saying I don't but they don't believe it. The demand for information is incredible and I don't have any. Just trying to run this place is more than a full-time job and now this.

I'm really more of an individual contributor than a supervisor these days. And my employees seem to resent the lack of contact I have with them, but I just don't have the time. Now that some of the other supervisors have left, we are doubling up and the paperwork alone is a killer.

I'll tell you one thing. This whole thing has forced us into managing differently than ever before. We have to rely more on the hourly and hope they do things right.

- Impact of key staff turnover

The crazy part about this is that we used to complain about being locked into narrow jobs, but now we have to do everything. Frankly, I was disgusted by all the turnover. The worst of it was in the human resource area—the very group where continuity was needed desperately. Of course the other area was supervision on the line. But, what the hell can you expect from people who have given Glacier years of their lives and then are given no hope for a future job? I'd do the same thing if I could.

Actually, I kinda like the idea of doing different stuff and I just hope it will help me when I have to get another job. I just worry that I won't find a good job 'cause all these people with less service took off. I'm here 'cause of the money they got hangin' over my head. Otherwise, I'd be long gone.

They said they couldn't promise me a job and then came around the next day and told us to make sure to keep up the morale of the people on the line. Talk about a double standard! Really makes you wonder what the hell the last 15 years has been for.

While these and other issues were clearly visible to people below the supervisory level, the judgment by employees of their supervisors was unmistakable:

If they can't even help themselves, they sure as hell aren't going to be able to help me. Now I have to start looking out for myself and I'm not going to put up with any jive shit from someone who's just as bad off as I am.

NINETY DAYS AND COUNTING . . .

The location surveyed only 90 days before it closed offers an interesting opportunity to examine shifts in views at a later stage in the change process. The three measurement points for this location were:

Time 1 = One year before the closing announcement

Time 2 = One year after the closing announcement

Time 3 = Two years after the closing announcement (90 days before closing)

As Figure 9.4 indicates, areas showing a significant change impact were:

- Productivity
- Personal development
- Supervision
- Work climate
- Communication

Since there are three points in time being represented, the following approach will be used to explain the results. The symbols T1, T2, and T3 will

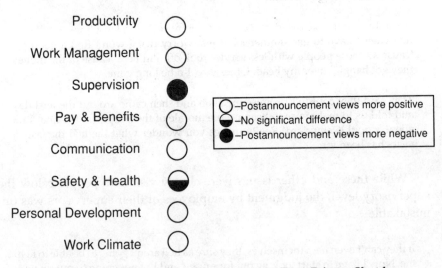

Productivity

Work Management

Supervision

Pay & Benefits

Communication

Safety & Health

Personal Development

Work Climate

○ –Postannouncement views more positive
◑ –No significant difference
● –Postannouncement views more negative

Figure 9.4   Survey Results for Closing Plant 90 Days Prior to Shutdown

be used to represent the average responses obtained for a given survey category at Time 1, Time 2, and Time 3, respectively. If the average response at one time period was significantly greater than another, the symbol ">" will be used. If the average response was significantly smaller, the symbol "<" will be used. No significant difference will be symbolized by the "=" symbol. For example, if the results for a given category showed that the averages did not change between Time 1 and Time 2, but a significant average increase occurred at Time 3, the result would be shown as follows: T1 = T2 < T3. Using this approach, let us examine the trends found within this closing plant:

Productivity

- More resources were made available to do   T1 < T2 < T3
  the job over time.

Supervision

- Less informal performance feedback given.   T1 > T2 > T3

- Less assistance in solving problems   T1 > T2 = T3

- Less involvement in work-related decisions   T1 > T2 < T3

- Less emphasis on the big picture of work   T1 > T2 < T3

- Less understanding of management's decisions   T1 > T2 = T3

Work Climate

- Improved cross-functional cooperation   T1 < T2 < T3

Communication

- Mixed upper-level management interest in

  work improvement ideas   T1 > T2 < T3

- More assistance from human resource department   T1 < T2 < T3

- Problem-solving process lost utility over time   T1 > T2 > T3

Personal Development

- Knowledge about whom to contact about job

  training   T1>T2>T3

- Improved assistance regarding job opportunities   T1=T2<T3

Two interesting differences stand out in the case of this location. First, people grew more aware of the assistance available to them in finding another job. Second, upper-level managers began to move toward a different management paradigm, one that was less control-oriented. Indeed, it appears that the circumstances can be characterized as moving reasonably close to what has been called a "commitment-oriented" approach.[6] The role of first-level supervision continued to deteriorate, while cooperation across functions continued to improve.

The Time 3 survey shows that upper-level management was viewed as being more in touch with views at lower levels. During discussions with the managers at this plant, a number of examples surfaced to substantiate the claim of a shift in their management paradigm. First, here is an excerpt from a letter the plant manager sent out to local business leaders in the community:

> Glacier's plant is closing as of December 31, 19XX. This closure is making available an immediate pool of above average and diverse employees with an excellent work ethic and good attendance. We would like to give you a first hand opportunity to take advantage of filling your job needs from a group of highly skilled employees. . . . Resumes of these employees are available upon request. Should you be interested in interviewing employees on site, you are welcome to do so. We will be pleased to cooperate with you in any way regarding this matter.

A second example comes in the form of how they orchestrated the final "exiting" of people from the plant. In their final in-house newsletter, the front cover led with the headline:

A CELEBRATION
THE BEGINNING OF SOMETHING NEW

An excerpt from subsequent text read:

> The last day of production for our plant has been set for Friday, November 22, 19XX. During the last week of operation, each unit will carry out its own planned events and activities including individual graffiti writing on supplied newsprint, a display of memorabilia and private home cooked lunches. The week of

activities will culminate in the lunchroom, when employees from both first and second shifts will gather for a celebration symbolizing the closing of our plant. {Name of General Manager} will be the special guest.

A plaque presented to the plant manager contained these words:

Your leadership has been honorable, unquestionable, in deed and shown us, your employees, tolerance and integrity. In the years that are ahead, no matter where your path will lead, remember we wish you success so deservedly.

Finally, a letter written from an ex-Glacier employee to the plant manager expressed the sentiments of many others:

It was very hard for me to leave our plant, it was a big part of my life for 14 of my 18 years of service.

I want to commend you and Glacier on the way you handled our plant closing, we as employees were very fortunate to have the transition team assistance that was provided. Without their help I might have had to leave feeling down and not knowing if I would find a job or not. With this help I left with confidence, knowing that if I worked at it I would find a job.

Thanks for helping me through this ordeal. Most of all for your honesty and openness with your employees, and the help you attained for us. I was in [a previous Glacier plant closing]. We didn't have any of the advantages we had here, and believe me, it makes a big difference.

Clearly, there was interest and participation in the outplacement activities, and the management activities underscored the need to take advantage of these services while helping to lead people through the final stages of transition. These results suggest that employees tend to delay their efforts to look for new jobs and that managers began to be more candid and opened the way for greater employee involvement in the last phase of the closing. Finally, the plant manager, reflecting on the changes that had occurred, added these observations:

Keeping my key technical people in place has been a major challenge, and using temporary people to fill in for people who have been able to find work was a winning strategy. We seem to have gone through several stages, and a major benefit has been to increase the involvement of people at all levels to help keep the communication flowing, encourage people to accept what was happening, and to get suggestions from people on how to handle this more effectively.

This plant manager was asked to come into this location with the intention of helping to close it. Upon completion of this assignment, Glacier was unable to find him a comparable position, and he was recruited away by a competitor. Others witnessing this event remarked, "They say that taking such assignments is good for your career, but look what happened here."

THE SURVIVORS

Glacier's planning for the plant closing was shaped almost exclusively around its concern for maintaining operations at closing locations. Within a relatively short period of time, it became clear that the receiving plants were running into unanticipated problems related to the closing activity. In the last chapter we saw some downturns in productivity that were attributed to having to adapt to the changes caused by the closing process. From the employees' standpoint, a number of survey areas showed the impact of change within the receiving locations one year after the closing program was announced. In particular, Figure 9.5 shows four areas that were affected significantly:

<table>
<tr><td>• Productivity</td><td>• Pay and benefits</td></tr>
<tr><td>• Supervision</td><td>• Work climate</td></tr>
</table>

The detailed item responses within these categories shed light on the type of management activities that were occurring at receiving locations.

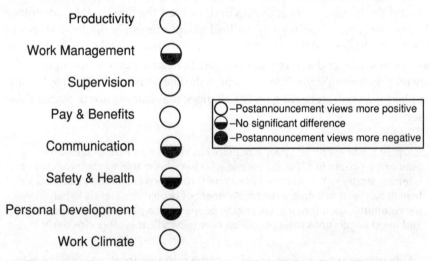

Figure 9.5   Pre- versus Postannouncement Survey Results for Receiving Plants

Productivity

- Greater cooperation among employees took place.

This apparent contradiction between improved employee views and actual productivity declines will be discussed later, when the impact of technology is examined.

Supervision

- More formal performance appraisals were held.
- More assistance by first-line supervision in problem-solving was offered.
- There was less understanding of management's decisions.
- There was more involvement in decisions offered by first-level supervisors.
- There was more stress placed on the big picture of the work.
- There was more encouragement of teamwork.

Pay and Benefits

- Glacier's benefits were viewed as more competitive.
- Wage and salary administration was viewed as more equitable.

Work Climate

- Layoffs were not viewed as being handled fairly.
- An increased amount of perceived prestige was associated with working for Glacier.
- There was an increased perception of product quality reflecting upon the people producing it.

The remaining survey categories did not show a significant change over time, but certain items within them did. For example:

- Fewer qualified people were viewed as being available to do the work.

- A better job was being done to allocate people and resources.

- The problem-solving process had less utility.

- Management did less consulting with employees before decisions were made.

- More assistance was forthcoming from various support functions.

- More business-related information was being made available.

- Management was more aware of employee views.

- Top management was showing more concern for problems at lower levels.

- Layoffs were not viewed as being handled fairly.

- Employees felt more prestige for working at Glacier and also felt the quality of the products they produced reflected on them more than before.

These views are helpful in understanding how managers at the receiving locations were trying to cope with the impact of the closing program and how they were beginning to shift their style of management in the process. Specifically, interviews with managers and others at the receiving plants surfaced these themes:

- Impact of technology

We are so busy trying to house-train this puppy that we are ignoring the core of our business. No one asked us questions like whether there would be sufficient space for raw inventory. Moving processes and product lines is not the same as moving machines. Sometimes we just moved "mistakes" from one place to another.

Our difficulties have largely arrived in the form of trying to integrate new types of products into an existing facility. Ironically, you might say we had a well-disguised quality program going because the equipment arrived with little or no technical documentation and our guys had to "reengineer" the stuff all over again. We are getting better results from the stuff we put in than they did in the last plant. You figure it out!

The people at headquarters were way too optimistic about how quickly we could put this new stuff in the plant. Why hell, some of the process hasn't even made it past the process-engineering guys! You just can't fight the war with a phantom army.

- Shift in management paradigm

We are having to do our jobs with a lot fewer people, and they are more expert in some of the process than we [supervisors] are. I can tell the mechanics like it when we ask their advice more. I heard one say, "We want to show that we are better than where this stuff came from." This [involvement] is even happening more with line people—we don't have a choice—there is just far less slack and you can't be everywhere at one time.

The crazy part is that us supervisors actually involve the people on the line more than the people above do with us! I still don't think they really buy into this stuff, but then they don't have to fight the battles we do every day down here either.

This is kind of a "good news–bad news" joke. On the one hand, we sure forced people to look hard at how competitive their pay and bennies are compared to the outside, and they know the score on that one. On the other hand, they don't trust Glacier anymore and are skeptical about the future.

I'm convinced our problems have come about because they underestimated the staffing needs at a plant going through this. They should have staffed the plant the same way you would during a startup. You simply can't continue to manage in the same way under these conditions.

The combined survey and qualitative results shed considerable light on the actual management activity that occurred during the plant-closing process. As we move beyond the "data," it is important to look at what lessons were learned from these managerial experiences. In the next chapter, we will examine these lessons and once again step back to view the broader aspects of leading organizations through change.

SUMMARY

The opportunity to examine closely the management activity that occurs during a major organizational change is uncommon. The analysis of Glacier's plant-closing activities is an exception. As we look at the challenges managers face when confronted by external events like these, it is important to understand the likely shifts in group dynamics that will occur. Most that occurred at Glacier are likely to happen elsewhere. Therefore, it is important to examine what actually took place.

The focal point of interest is a source of data from within the closing and receiving plants that was obtained by a combination of surveys, interviews, and small-group sessions. This blend of qualitative and quantitative information was very helpful in comparing the losers and winners as well as in examining the changes that occurred over time both in closing and receiving locations. A number of key insights are gained:

- Productivity views of employees increase at both types of plants.

- Supervision deteriorates at closing plants and improves at receiving plants.

- The fairness of benefits and layoffs begins to receive closer attention.

- Communication and overall work climate views did not deteriorate.

- Management was able to maintain the physical environment at previous levels.

- The lack of involvement of plant management in the planning of the closing continues to pay negative dividends.

- Some activities and views apparently shift only within the final days of the actual closing of the plant.

- The overall impact of this program pushed managers toward a new paradigm of management.

This information sets the stage for an examination of the lessons that can be learned from Glacier's managers' experiences . . .

Notes

1.   Some of the earliest work done in this area was Musafer Sherif and Carolyn Sherif, *Groups in Harmony and Tension: An Introduction to Studies in Intergroup Relations* (New York: Harper & Row, 1953), and Musafer Sherif, O. J. Harvey, B. Jack White, William R. Hood, and Carolyn W. Sherif, *Intergroup Cooperation and Competition: The Robbers Cave Experiment* (Norman, OK: University Book Exchange, 1961). For a more complete review, see Kenneth Dion's work, "Intergroup Conflict and Intragroup Cohesiveness," in William G. Austin and Stephen Worchel (Eds.), *The Social Psychology of Intergroup Relations* (Monterey, CA: Brooks/Cole, 1979), pp. 211–224. See also Barry M. Staw, Lance E. Sandelands, and Jane E. Dutton, *Threat-Rigidity Effects in Organizational Behavior: A Multilevel Analysis*, in Kim S. Cameron, Robert I. Sutton, and David A. Whetten (Eds.), *Readings in Or-*

ganizational Decline (Cambridge, MA: Ballinger, 1988), pp. 95–116, which looks closely at circumstances that can either enhance or threaten the leadership role under circumstances of external threat.

2. For a more complete overview of dysfunctional outcomes under these circumstances, the reader is directed to a chapter written by Kim S. Cameron, Kim U. Myung, and David A. Whetten, "Organizational Effects of Decline and Turbulence," in Kim S. Cameron, Robert I. Sutton, and David A. Whetten (Eds.), *Readings in Organizational Decline* (Cambridge, MA: Ballinger, 1988), pp. 207–224.

3. The increase in pressure on managers is discussed in several sources. One study examines this issue from a research perspective: J. P. Gordus, P. Jarley, and L. A. Ferman, *Plant Closings and Economic Dislocation* (Kalamazoo, MI: W. W. Upjohn Institute for Employment Research, 1981). Another source offers insights from a well-documented case study: A. Slote, *Termination: The Closing at Baker Plant* (New York: Bobbs-Merrill, 1969).

4. Ronald E. Berenbeim's report, *Company Programs to Ease the Impact of Shutdowns* (New York: Conference Board Report No. 878, 1986), examines the managerial responsibilities during a plant closing as well as some potential reasons for the upswing in productivity. In the latter instance, these reasons are cited:

    • The installation of employee involvement programs

    • Reduced pressure after the final decision was made

    • Goodwill resulting from a generous financial exit package

    • Trying to improve one's work record to secure future employment

5. In a recent book of readings edited by Ralph H. Kilmann, Teresa Joyce Covin, and Associates, *Corporate Transformation* (San Francisco: Jossey-Bass, 1988), there are some good examples of successful and unsuccessful management strategies that were used in businesses facing change. Specifically, see the chapter "Learning from an Unsuccessful Transformation: A 'Perfect Failure,' " by Peter Hess, William P. Ferris, Anthony F. Chelte, and Russell Fanelli (pp. 183–204) and the chapter, "Birthing a Factory of the Future: When Is 'All at Once' Too Much?" by David B. Roitman, Jeffrey K. Liker, and Ethel Roskies (pp. 205–246).

6. Richard E. Walton's *Harvard Business Review* article (March–April 1985) contains an in-depth look at the contrast between a control-oriented and a commitment-oriented management paradigm.

Appendix 9A

An Overview of Glacier's Management Practices Survey

The survey and the process surrounding it are covered in this appendix. The material will be presented in three sections. The first contains the survey items. The second provides information on the survey sample and the survey administration. The third discusses data analysis issues.

SURVEY CONTENT

The survey used by Glacier contained items grouped into eight categories. Respondents were asked to respond to items by using a response code as follows:

5 = Strongly agree

4 = Agree

3 = Neutral

2 = Disagree

1 = Strongly disagree

0 = Not applicable/no data

PRODUCTIVITY

1. I have the resources (e.g., equipment, tools,) required to do my job.

2. I think that productivity is important to my co-workers.

3. There is a cooperative and open working relationship among employees in my area.

WORK MANAGEMENT

1. Management establishes a clear priority of work to be done.

2. In general, there are enough qualified people where I work to do the job right.

3. There is an effective match between people and resources (e.g., equipment, tools) to do the job right.

SUPERVISION

1. I have received a formal performance appraisal within the last 12 months.
   1 = Yes
   2 = No

2. My supervisor and I have informal performance discussions during the year.

3. My supervisor can be counted on to help resolve problems I raise.

4. I usually understand why management decisions are made.

5. My supervisor tries to get the employees involved in decision making affecting their work.

6. My supervisor encourages employees to see the big picture of what our work is about.

7. Teamwork is encouraged by my supervisor.

PAY AND BENEFITS

1. I can get information I need about the Glacier benefits programs.

2. Overall, I consider the Glacier benefits to be competitive with those available elsewhere.

3. Employees are paid fairly for overtime work.

4. Overall, wage and salary administration is fair and equitable.

COMMUNICATION

1. People at higher levels are interested in ideas about how the work can be done better.

2. I can get help from human resources when I need it.

3. Other supporting functions/activities help me do my job.

4. Adequate information on company policies and practices is available to me.

5. The problem-solving procedure at my location works well.

6. I receive sufficient information about how the business is doing.

7. Management is aware of the opinions and attitudes of the employees here.

8. Top management is concerned with problems at my level of the organization.

9. Management consults employees before decisions affecting their work are made.

SAFETY AND HEALTH

1. Regular safety inspections are conducted to assure safe conditions within my work area.

2. Prompt action is taken to correct hazardous conditions/work procedures reported to my supervisor.

3. I think management tries to maintain a safe and healthy work environment.

PERSONAL DEVELOPMENT

1. I have had the training to do my job well.

2. I know whom to contact for information about available training.

3. I can get help in finding out what job opportunities are available to me.

WORK CLIMATE

1. The various functions in this organization (maintenance, human resources, quality control, production, distribution, sales, marketing, finance, etc.) work well together.

2. If layoffs must occur, they are handled fairly by management.

3. For me, working for Glacier has a certain amount of prestige attached to it.

4. I feel the quality of our Glacier products is a reflection on me.

5. I believe Glacier management is committed to producing quality products.

6. Which of the following statements best tells how well you like your job?

1 = I hate it.	4 = I like it.
2 = I don't like it.	5 = I love it.
3 = I am indifferent to it.	

The instrument used contained items drawn from a previous survey and was therefore backed up by a historic database of over 10,000 responses. The actual choice of items per category had been determined earlier by a technique known as factor analysis. In brief, this approach examines the mathematical relationship among all items and attempts to cluster those that appear to measure common underlying constructs. For present purposes, it should be assumed that each of the survey categories represents relatively independent constructs.

It was decided to represent each of the eight areas by a mathematical average of the responses to the items grouped in the area. For example, the three items under Productivity would have their responses averaged for each respondent, thus representing that person's "Productivity" response. Subsequent analysis of the individual items was also performed.

Several items pertaining to work force demographics were also included to gather information on areas such as pay classification, tenure with Glacier, sex, race, age, education, and shift assignment, if applicable.

SAMPLE AND ADMINISTRATION

The basic sampling process offered all employees the opportunity to complete the survey during business hours. The response rate using this approach ranged from 60 to 90 percent across the different locations. There were 2,753 responses from closing locations and 2,633 responses from receiving locations. Seven closing locations and five receiving locations were surveyed during the study.

Although the primary variables of interest were those pertaining to the fate of the plant (e.g., closing or receiving) and the time of data gathering (e.g., preannouncement or postannouncement), other variables were examined as well:

1. Labor (union versus non-union)

2. Geographic location (urban versus rural)

3. Type of plant (components versus assembly)

4. Size of plant (Less than 300 people versus 300 or more)

5. Demographic variables mentioned earlier (e.g., age, sex)

The demographic statistics on the sample of employees at the closing and receiving plants are shown in the following table:

Description	Closing (%) N = 2,753	Receiving (%) N = 2,633
Union/nonunion:		
Union employees	47	53
Nonunion employees	56	44
Plant type:		
Components	43	57
Assembly	52	48
Geography:		
Rural	23	77
Urban	63	37

Description	Closing (%) N = 2,753	Receiving (%) N = 2,633
Plant size:		
Small (less than 300)	38	62
Large (300+)	85	15
Company service:		
Less than 1 year	60	40
1–4 years	49	51
5–9 years	53	47
10–19 years	53	47
20+ years	50	50
Sex:		
Male	51	49
Female	52	48
Race:		
Minority	63	37
Nonminority	47	53
Age:		
Less than 20 years	70	30
21–30 years	48	52
31–40 years	49	51
41–50 years	52	48
51–55 years	50	50
56–60 years	57	43
60+ years	68	32

Description	Closing (%) N = 2,753	Receiving (%) N = 2,633
Education:		
High school graduate or less	50·	50
College—no degree	53	47
Two-year college degree	60	40
Bachelor's degree	64	36
Master's degree	50	50
Ph.D. degree or "other"	75	25

The selection of sites occurred naturally, suggesting that any within-category differences could be attributed to random error.

DATA ANALYSIS

The primary statistical technique used was multiple regression, chosen because of its capacity to allow simultaneous comparisons of several predictors, thereby demonstrating which were stronger than others. This is an important point because examining each predictor separately risks the possibility that individual effects could be overshadowed by another not being considered at the same time. The results discussed in the text are based on regression results that focused on the analyses of averaged survey results across the eight categories.

The regression of predictors on categories based on averaged items was followed by regressing these same predictors on individual items within each category. The regression procedure assigns a numerical weight to each of the predictors. The size of the weight is a measure of its predictive power, and the "sign" (positive or negative) of the weight indicates the direction of the relationship between the predictor value and the survey area value. For more details on the use of regression analysis, the reader is directed to J. Cohen and P. Cohen, *Applied Multiple Regression/Correlation Analysis for the Behavioral Sciences*, 2nd ed. (Hillsdale, N.J.: Lawrence Erlbaum Associates, 1983).

In addition to the regression technique described here, a different approach was also used in the case of the location that was subjected to three surveys. In addition to the regression results, a technique called an analysis of variance was used. Because there were three time periods to consider, the data were analyzed with this approach to determine first if significant averaged differences occurred across the three time periods and, if so, where these differences occurred. This latter was accomplished via post hoc tests. For more details on this procedure, the reader is directed to William L. Hays, *Statistics for the Social Sciences* (New York: Holt, Rinehart and Winston, 1973).

Chapter 10

STAND-UP CHAMELEONS

Innovators are inevitably controversial.
  —Eva Le Gallienne

Experience is a tough teacher. It tests you first, then offers the lesson.
  —Neil Springer, Chairman of Navistar

It is clear from the preceding chapter that the group that had the most diffi-culty in dealing with the impact of change was first-level managers. These "stand-up chameleons" often had to modify their management approach, quite literally, on their feet. More than nearly anyone else, they are in dire need of help.

As we review the experiences of Glacier, Inc., and other organizations that have undergone or are currently facing the uncertainties of change, it is useful to consider points of direction that come from leaders, managers, theorists, and practitioners who are caught up in this maelstrom. They are trying desperately to identify methods, models, rules of thumb, or even hints that could serve as guidance. One general manager said that trying to trans-form his organization was like trying to change a fanbelt at 80 miles per hour. Still, there are experiences of others to draw from, thoughts to consider, and well-intentioned criticisms to heed. As we move toward some lessons learned by Glacier, Inc., let us pause to consider a few of these points of view.[1]

A REFLECTIVE PAUSE

If, as some have said, our society is truly moving from a mechanistic to a more organic economy, where people are more apt to exchange knowledge than labor for organizational rewards, then there is plenty of work to do. All around us we see evidence that the status quo stands ready to go down fighting, taking in its death grip its surrounding economic and social symbi-otic partners. The problem has so many facets as to resemble a hall of mirrors, taunting the would-be innovators to guess where the true cause of intransi-gence lies.

It may be that the model in people's heads is just plain wrong for our times. We seem to keep referencing mechanical and industrial models that cannot reflect accurately the complexity of today's work environments. If you start with a flawed model, can you expect subsequent thinking and actions to be much better? Probably not. These old models assumed people would be willing to be paid off for plodding bureaucratic behavior when in reality they seem to hunger for more responsibility and not only want a piece of the action but are asking disturbing questions about ethics as well. Treating people as contractual adversaries will, at best, get you compliance. Some say it could turn to spiteful obedience. I think you simply wind up with cynical mercenaries.

Social activists often draw our attention to how language is unwittingly used to perpetuate stereotypes, even in such areas as children's literature. We tend to draw back, shocked, resentful, disbelieving, and yet—over time—we have come to accept that, indeed, we have for too long used seemingly innocuous forms as this to serve as a part of the status quo's infrastructure. Why, for example, do we still hear such overreliance on military metaphors to describe our work settings? Listen carefully to those who continue to insist on adversarial interpretations of the exchanges of differing views. Even descriptions of work as analogous to sports can only offer a level of simplicity incapable of capturing the whimsical and potentially devastating nature of the forces we face. We seem trapped within our own myopic pigeonholes.

Under such conditions it is not surprising that much effort is spent trying to shore up the fading authority of those who cannot fathom the newer paradigms aimed at gaining the commitment of people as opposed to their grudging compliance. It is also not surprising that most people are skeptical of the benefits to come from following the rules. In fact, following the rules may only be a refuge for those who choose less courageous ways of taking on the bigger issues of change. By simply obeying the rules and overrelying on formal, bloodless rationality, we avoid the terrifying thought that our situation is simply beyond our control. We don't feel comfortable openly acknowledging the political struggle for power that goes on around us. To do so would force us to confront another, even more unpleasant reality: Such situations nearly always leave facts and logic behind at the first turn. Finally, if one cannot make people believe what we believe, we take steps to distance ourselves from them, both physically and psychologically, so as to avoid the unpleasantness associated with conflicting paradigms and colliding destinies.

Under today's conditions of unparalleled turbulence, it is no longer possible to draw up rules and roadmaps to handle all contingencies. What is needed is something far more fundamental—a set of common beliefs that will keep people moving forward without the historic heavy hand of management or the use of technology as a surrogate boss—a form of automated intrusion. I am intrigued by the notion that each employee, to a remarkable extent, is a microcosmic replica of the organization. They are what we looked for during the recruiting interview, what we asked them to do on the job, what we rewarded them for accomplishing and for how they accomplished it. They are struggling to survive under the conditions and by the rules surrounding them—our own creations. We made them and they are us.

The place to start, then, is with a newer paradigm that uses as its base the notion that each person is the organization in miniature. Extending the metaphor into a biological analogy, each person carries the organizational equivalent of genetic memory, reflecting what the whole organization is intended to be and accomplish. With this as a beginning, the path at least becomes discernible, but only in faint outline. A critical missing ingredient in today's work settings is a guideline to help lead an organization through its challenges. Chapter 12 will pick up this theme of providing a framework for managing the impact of change.

Having a plan is not enough. There must be an environment that allows for—no, cries out for—new forms of leadership shaped by painful experiences of failure and threats to the future livelihood of nearly all its members, if not the very survival of the organization. Managers must feel rewarded for shedding the policeman's demeanor and for picking up the orchestrator's baton, facilitating the acquisition of needed resources, serving as a liaison for cross-organizational support, and personally knocking down barriers to productivity and effectiveness. Rather than hoarding information, using it as a form of "information float" to augment their power base, they must see the value in sharing this information with those who can use it to achieve work objectives.

What is the source of these lessons that can serve to transform the managerial models in the heads of today's leaders and managers? Glacier, Inc., discovered a substantial set during its plant-closing program. Their examination helps us see more clearly the turmoil of a business caught between two of Toffler's waves, trying to use historic models to guide its actions, sometimes succeeding, sometimes not. At times the lessons are painfully obvious and at other times subtle—yet they unmistakably highlight the issues encountered when attempting to manage the present on the basis of past successes rather than future needs.

GLACIER'S LESSONS LEARNED

It would be difficult to underestimate the personal anguish felt by most Glacier managers as they sought to stabilize their organizations and their own lives throughout the plant-closing program. The lessons they learned were important ones, and not all were easy to accept. The major lessons will be divided into two categories. The first set pertains to managers primarily responsible for running the operational side of the business. The second focuses on those who offered support to the operating managers.

OPERATING LESSONS

1. It is possible to operate manufacturing plants at historic levels of product quality and productivity for an extended period of time following a closing announcement if appropriate management practices are in effect. In short, the hypothesized fourth-phase debacle can be avoided.

One particularly useful strategy was the hiring of temporary people for positions requiring a minimum amount of training. This allowed for a smooth transition in cases where people found jobs prior to the closing, and created a positive and cooperative environment as well.

2. The lack of involvement of operating managers at closing and receiving locations in the planning of the closing program resulted in greater financial and psychological cost to the program than was anticipated—or necessary. The risks associated with possible information leaks were overstated and were dwarfed by the negative impact on those responsible for handling the effects at the plant level.

3. By focusing primarily on the closing plant challenges, Glacier overlooked a series of issues that seriously affected the receiving plant results. These included adhering too strictly to shutdown schedules despite a lack of adequate levels of quality inventory needed to bridge the transition of equipment and processes, the unavailability of local suppliers, lack of space for inventory, moving versus fixing production flow problems, introducing unproven technology, and increased demand for product volume, to name a few. For closing locations, the natural goal was to try to adhere to the stated closing schedule. In most instances, however, a firm date was not established for several months after the initial closing announcement. This became the prime issue for managers to contend with, and they indicate that selecting a date—even if it has to be changed at a later time—is imperative under these conditions.

4. Temporary structures in the form of program managers to help ease the transition of people, product, and equipment between closing and receiving plants proved beneficial. The exception occurred when such transitions were made across Glacier's major divisions. Under these conditions, a more

powerful adjustment is needed. Specifically, the receiving plant management should be given control of both operations.

5. People who are expected to operate production equipment at new locations need to begin skills training four to six months prior to the movement of the equipment. This may require sending them to the closing location for training. This was accomplished with the cooperation of people at the closing plants serving as trainers. In some instances, representatives from these plants traveled to the receiving plants to offer training on site following the equipment transfer.

6. The problems at several locations were attributed to a lack of people. However, two very different solutions were identified. One would increase staffing to levels commonly found during the startup of a plant. The other would change the perspective by relying more heavily on fewer people, but creating new work systems similar to self-directed work teams.

7. Additional costs were incurred as a result of long-term neglect in the area of updating engineering drawings and other process documentation. The major price appeared in the form of startup costs and an increase in purchasing activities of materials the receiving locations did not know were needed. If no preventive steps are taken before operations actually cease, production processes may have to be captured by means such as videotaping or hiring technical writers to develop operating documentation. It was found that user-friendly CAD-CAM software can help expedite the updating of the most critical engineering drawings over time.

Ironically, the lack of documentation often necessitated reengineering to bring transferred equipment on-line at receiving locations. This nearly always resulted in increases in productivity and product quality—a somewhat unexpected outcome.

8. Most managers credit their success at retaining credibility to their adoption of a business-as-usual operating stance throughout the closing period. This includes such things as routine maintenance, discipline, and quality control. However, one area that required extraordinary effort was communications. They learned that only intense, multiformat, sincere, and candid communication would be accepted by people. This was particularly true at receiving plants, because the "survivors" needed constant reassurance they weren't next in line to be closed down. Laxity in any of these areas was taken by employees as a sign that "the party's over."

9. The rapid and unexpected turnover of key staff positions caused added difficulties. This could have been reduced sharply by offering com-

mitment in the form of a safety net to people whose jobs were to be eliminated. It could take several forms:

- For employees the organization was certain it needed to retain, it could promise employment in a specific position after the location closed.

- For employees the organization wanted to keep but was unable to make a firm commitment to, offers of placement assistance within the organization could be made.

- For employees the organization would not be able to retain, offers of specific types of outplacement assistance could be made.

10.   It was found that productivity improvements occurred at nearly all closing plants following the announcement. For employees at the closing plants, their perceptions of productivity also increased significantly compared to employees at receiving plants and compared to their preannouncement views. Such a change was attributed to:

1. A belief that hard work could reverse the decision

2. An act of defiance to show the decision was wrong

3. A way to cleanse a spotty work record

4. A means of avoiding the realities of the closing

11. Various forms of employee involvement not only were found to survive the impact of the plant-closing announcement but were directly instrumental in reducing startup costs. This took the form of ideas and assistance surrounding the planning, dismantling, shipping, installation, and debugging stages of equipment moves. These involvement teams also aided in overall plant communication to help counter rumors or half-truths.

SUPPORT LESSONS

1. The period of time between the announcement and actual closing of a production location should not exceed one year. To accomplish this, it will be necessary to ensure that employee assistance programs are ready to be implemented at the time of the announcement. Input on these issues from the management of affected locations should be obtained prior to this event.

Such involvement will help plan the assistance so as to avoid disrupting operating schedules.

2. The lack of program managers in the support area—in contrast to their use in the operational area—proved detrimental. Turf battles erupted over such issues as who had responsibility for supplying accurate benefits information. Such a position should be given a temporary full-time assignment to oversee all support activity for the closing and/or receiving locations. These positions should be sanctioned as having the authority to cross functional lines to resolve support issue disputes.

3. The phrase *business as usual* had a positive connotation at the plant locations but came to have a very different meaning within the support areas, particularly at headquarters. There it described a lack of acknowledgment of how past policies were out of phase with the demands created by this change impact. Policies on hourly transfer allowances and on allowing nonexempt employees to bid on open jobs at nearby locations were debated by those fearful of setting precedents but ignoring the precedents being set around them.

4. The tendency toward lax performance evaluations for employees to be considered for transfers to receiving locations put pressure on managers to accept people they would not otherwise hire. Continued emphasis on candid performance assessment must be maintained. This will ensure the most appropriate selection and match of people and positions.

5. A high-quality communication plan to handle a closing announcement requires an extensive, highly interactive, well-structured planning process involving key operating and functional managers. Such a process should, at minimum, meet these criteria:

- Allows for input from affected managers and headquarters managers prior to the closing announcement.

- Encourages a free flow of ideas and suggestions across all participants. It should combine opportunities for creative ideas with a self-regulating capacity. Glacier found that the "storyboarding" technique worked well.

This process produced communication plans that were carried out in such a way as to inform broad categories of stakeholders of the rationale behind the change and plans to manage its impact. Interestingly, it also served as a reference point for criticism. Fundamentally, it was held up as an example of how a secret war room was created to plan events without the input of those who would have to manage their impact. Further, it became painfully obvious that planning for events to follow the announcement had not received as much effort or coordination. This was particularly true in terms of preparing operating managers to handle requests for benefits information.

6. Managers at affected plants needed a refresher course on employee benefits, with particular emphasis on those related to a plant closing. The delivery system in Glacier was found to be severely delayed and inadequate to meet the employee demand for information.

The content of the materials prepared did not take into account that the audiences were unaccustomed to the complicated language used to describe benefits. Further, although the literacy rate was quite high among the employees, this was often confused with their being able to read material with comprehension. Given the emotional environment, frequent and redundant communication was necessary. Its timing had to take into consideration employees' readiness to "hear" the message.

7. Significant adjustment issues resulted when employees changed work environments:

- Employees who had worked for an extended period of time in a non-union location joined a union at their new one almost immediately to avoid being perceived as outsiders.

- People used to a more participatory management climate at a non-union plant were regarded as difficult to control at a union plant. This was due, in part, to their past habits of unilaterally volunteering to help co-workers handle uneven production demands.

- Transferred employees often formed cliques among past acquaintances, thus delaying their acceptance into the new setting.

A realistic preview of the new work environment is needed for prospective transferees. This should include:

- A candid assessment of the similarities and differences between a union and a non-union location, urban versus rural settings, self-paced versus machine-paced operations, and other unwritten rules that define the culture at the new location.

- An on-site visit, including some hands-on activity for employees to try out the equipment they would be using. Such visits could include the use of a buddy system to pair up visiting employees with production employees who can give them behind-the-scenes information to help them make a better informed decision.

In addition, employees can be encouraged to accept a transfer if the organization is willing to offer:

- Financial assistance in the relocation of goods and family members.

- Personal counseling for family members facing emotional difficulties associated with relocation. This is recommended because there was a noted increase in divorces, runaway children, and delayed feelings of guilt on the part of employees who blamed themselves for the decision to close their former plants.

- A trial period at the new location with no loss of closing benefits if the person leaves within a specified period.

- Transfer of plant seniority rights with relocated employees. This would prevent the likelihood of people being the first ones laid off at the new location in the event of a downturn, despite having already worked for a substantial period of time at the previous plant.

8. There needs to be a serious reassessment of the potential harm that could come from announcement leaks due to involving affected managers in the planning process, compared to the damage caused by denying such opportunities for input. There is evidence to suggest that a stronger team effort results from taking the plant's operating managers into upper management's confidence.

9. The combination of personal insecurity and being prevented from seeking internal employment affected the managers' ability to handle day-to-day operations. More consideration should be given to providing managers at closing facilities an early safety net in terms of future employment.

10. Strong evidence indicates that first-level supervision is the main area where employees sense deterioration during a plant closing. This level of management should be monitored closely and steps need to be taken to ensure an acceptable level of continuity among this group as well.

11. An increase in productivity tends to occur at closing locations and is accompanied by a parallel improvement in employees' views toward productivity. An increase in similar employee views at receiving locations was also found, but the actual change in productivity was mixed.

12. The formation of a steering committee at closing locations, with representatives from all levels in the organization to oversee day-to-day issues arising throughout the transition period, was of great benefit. This was true at both union and non-union locations. At one particular plant with a long history of union–management confrontation, such a vehicle served to defuse numerous potentially disruptive disagreements.

13. Employee involvement programs can withstand the impact of a plant-closing process and were found to be instrumental in assisting in the movement of equipment, the training of employees, and the handling of communications.

14. Assistance given to people who will lose their jobs should be handled by a transition center staffed by people specially trained in this area. For Glacier, this meant having outside people in these roles. The reaction from employees was positive. They saw the outsiders as unbiased and—because their job was also eliminated after the plant closed—viewed these people as "in the same boat."

Assistance activity should include:

• Counseling	• Outplacement assistance
• Interviewing skills	• Testing
• Resume preparation	• Retraining
• Retirement counseling	• Job search skills
• Clerical assistance	• Job clubs
• Job availability information	• Liaison to external market

It was found that employees were deeply concerned about receiving lump sum payments of substantial amounts. For many, this was the largest amount of money they had ever received at one time. It was necessary to offer financial counseling to help them manage it.

The use of Title III funds to help pay for the employee assistance resulted in unplanned and substantial administrative costs. The size of these costs cast doubt on the usefulness of such government funds to a business wanting to provide transition assistance to its employees.

15. A large percentage of employees will delay a job search until three to six months prior to the closing of a plant. This is partially due to their perceptions of lump sum payments as a cushion that makes such a search un-

necessary until a later time. To counter this, a series of stepped-up communication efforts are necessary. They should focus on the benefits from finding a job in a marketplace that could become saturated.

It was also found that Glacier's people retained a strong loyalty after finding new jobs. The downside was that they often turned down offers or left jobs because they thought the employers offered substandard management practices compared to Glacier.

Close attention needs to be paid to how employees exit a closing plant. The use of carefully planned and well-orchestrated ending ceremonies was found to be beneficial in helping employees accept the change and turn their attention to life after Glacier.

16. Some data suggested that health and safety areas were adversely affected by the closing decision. The results are not conclusive, and careful monitoring of these areas should be conducted. This is a sensitive issue and could offer insight into the degree to which the stress of the transition shows up as problems related to health and safety.

APPLYING THE LESSONS

In the years following Glacier's plant-closing announcement, it closed several additional plants. The management decisions made during this time offer an interesting opportunity to see the degree to which Glacier was able or willing to apply its own lessons. Actually, Glacier's past history provides a clue to just how likely these lessons would be applied.

In the mid-1970s, long before such approaches were being touted in mainstream management literature, Glacier built and started up a plant with an innovative management approach. The work force was all salaried—no time clocks. No supervisors were used on the second shift and only a few on the first. The work rules were minimal. There were only a few job classifications, and people often rotated among them. When a new supervisor was to be hired, the plant manager asked line workers to interview candidates and submit their choice. There was a heavy emphasis on training, and people were encouraged to collectively decide how the work was to be done.

The results were dramatic. The plant met or exceeded its goals year after year and exported much of its product to customers with very exacting quality standards. Turnover was minimal, and the plant—located in an industrial park surrounded by manufacturing facilities that had all voted to become union-represented—remained non-union. Given this early and clearly innovative success, one might expect Glacier to diffuse its new-found approach throughout its existing manufacturing base. This never occurred, however, for several reasons:

- The plant concept was strongly opposed by a key HR manager who had a union avoidance background. He fought to stop the operating managers from introducing such a "radical" approach and, despite its clear success, refused to acknowledge it or help introduce its process to other plant management teams for several years.

- Many of the more traditional operating managers saw the new location as a "country club" that was too loosely governed. Since the plant did not produce a core product, they dismissed its successes as unique to the product line and predicted that it would not be able to sustain its record or management approach for long. This argument has continued for over a decade.

- The Glacier management style was clearly far from the "experimental" type at the new location. So many stakeholders would be threatened by diffusing its approach that it simply was left alone and treated as an oddity. To do otherwise would force Glacier to confront such issues as:
   –Why do we need so many levels of supervision?
   –Why are there so many work rules and job classifications?
   –Why aren't more locations able to produce more with fewer people?
   –Is our style of management as effective as it should be?
   –Do we rely on "shock absorbers" in the form of union relations and union avoidance managers instead of addressing the root cause of our disagreements?
   –Have we ignored the potentially disruptive styles of managers who "make their numbers"?
   –Is our overall measurement system actually promoting a less effective management approach?

The startup plant continues to be successful and is largely ignored or dismissed by Glacier insofar as diffusing its approach is concerned.[2] Given this tendency, what did Glacier do with the lessons learned from its own closing program?

The good news is that the overall approach taken to managing the impact of a plant closing was much improved. It was known what resources were needed and they were usually lined up in advance. The battles over policy interpretations and turf issues over who was supposed to support whom had largely subsided. In fact, it would not be inaccurate to say that Glacier had nearly mastered the mechanics of plant closing. There was, however, disturbing evidence that something fundamental was still missing. Consider this example.

Glacier had traditionally pursued a highly vertically integrated strategy. Therefore, it not only bought raw material, built its own components, and assembled them into final products; it also built its own equipment to accomplish all this. As the turbulence of the 1980s continued, Glacier was faced with some disturbing financial realities. Among them was the discovery that they were spending more than necessary to sustain this chain of vertically integrated links. An opportunity came to sell a plant that was part of this chain. A buyer was found and the plans for the sale were drawn up. An announcement was prepared for the employees and they were assembled to hear it. Their reaction was strong, immediate, and negative. It seems that, once again, a decision was made to plan this transition in secrecy, and a deliberate effort was made to deny input from those who would be affected. The net result was that the buyer backed off. It should be noted that the senior human resource manager who helped craft this effort was the same one who opposed the innovative plant started in the 1970s and refused to help diffuse its operating approach. When asked why he didn't take steps to try to involve the employees and managers to obtain suggestions or concerns before announcing this decision, he responded, "It would be too risky."

One is left with a mixed message. Managers will attempt to master the mechanics needed to address the impact of change. This can achieve a temporary respite but ignores what leaders know to be a larger challenge. Greater and more sustained success will only come about when some serious "head set" shifts occur among people who continue to operate based on antiquated modes of thinking. I have some doubts as to how much progress will be made with such individuals. As was pointed out in an earlier chapter, the strategic use of human assets has a number of leverage points, but a leader must have the wisdom to recognize their existence, the courage to use them, and the compassion to know when the timing is right. As for Glacier, one should consider that it continues to this day to stand out as a well-run and financially successful business. The issues it has faced and its reactions should not be considered unique. In fact, I believe it has handled most of its challenges as well as or better than is usually the case. It is precisely because of this assessment that I lament. If a business this strong, with managers of such talent, with challenges this dramatic, in such troubled times, has such difficulty taking more full advantage of its own lessons—what can be expected of the lesser organizations that clearly make up the majority?

Let us assume that Glacier will eventually evolve or die. Someone said to me, "You will always reap what you sow—but not necessarily where you sow it." Such should be the case with these lessons. If Glacier cannot or will not benefit from its lessons, let us examine our own circumstances, review these lessons, and avoid the potholes we might otherwise have hit. If there is a final lesson for all of us, it should be to ask why organizations have such difficulty learning from their own lessons. Who, inside our own organizations, is currently trying to bring similar information to our attention? It should be remembered that philosophers are revered in all lands but their own.

SUMMARY

There are strong forces to contend with as organizations face the impact of change. Too often these forces are assumed to be external and able to be addressed by a rational plan. Actually, there are also strong forces within the organization, and rationality takes a back seat to the emotional and value-laden infrastructure that exists to support the status quo. Leaders may face the unenviable task of convincing their organization not to commit suicide. This will require that people begin to look within themselves, to examine their unquestioned assumptions about how people should be managed, what measures truly reflect organizational success, and the realities of the power struggles around them.

As new managerial paradigms continue to emerge, we must become involved in crafting them. A potential starting point could hold that each person is the organization in miniature. How the person is managed and will ultimately perform will reflect the broader success or failure to be expected of the organization. Having a roadmap to help plan for the impact of change will be necessary, but having an environment ready to accept the dramatic steps needed to prepare is critical. This readiness often can come from the organization's own lessons—often painful ones.

Glacier's lessons learned from its plant-closing program show that both its operating and support managers identified numerous areas where future actions need to be taken to avoid problems they encountered or to duplicate their successes. A critical issue that was woven throughout these lessons was how much harm was caused by not involving operating managers in the plans for closing plants and transferring people, processes, and equipment. Also, it became clear that denying dedicated and talented long-term managers any hope for future employment was both unnecessary and harmful.

As rich as these lessons are, the question can be raised: Were they ever applied? The answer is, to some degree, yes. Glacier improved its mechanical process for handling the day-to-day activities surrounding the actual logistics needed to manage this type of event. Unfortunately, there is still evidence that Glacier is unable or unwilling to accept some of the more fundamental lessons that stem from its philosophical positions regarding the value to be gained from involving employees in decisions affecting them. Some of Glacier's managers' support of involvement increases in direct relation to how distant it is from them. The closer it comes, the more risk they see.

This leaves the lessons to be reviewed by those who face the impact of change. They stand out as unvarnished insights gained by managers who struggled to keep their organizations on track. Their value will ultimately be judged by those who attempt to weave their insights into plans for managing the impact of change.

Notes

1. I have deliberately sought out thinking by my "old friends," who represent some of the finest thinkers in the area of management and, in some cases, managing the impact of change. As I have cited them in earlier chapters, I will only list their names and the titles of their work here. Over the years, I have found it very helpful to sit down in a quiet spot, and engage in some "conversation" with these friends. I find from my marginal notes that we still do not agree on certain things, but I enjoy being reminded of our debates and would encourage the reader to join in:

Ames, B. Charles. "Corporate Strategies for a Shrinking Market." *Wall Street Journal*, January 13, 1986.

Bennis, W., and Nanus, B. *Leaders.*

Block, P. *The Empowered Manager.*

Davis, S. M. *Future Perfect.*

Drucker, P. *The Effective Executive .*

Grove, A. S. *High Output Management.*

Kanter, R. M. *The Change Masters.*

Kilmann, R. H. *Beyond the Quick Fix.*

Lawler, E. E. *High Involvement Management.*

Naisbett, J., and Aberdeen, P. *Reinventing the Corporation.*

Naisbett, J. *Megatrends.*

Peters, T., and Austin, N. *A Passion for Excellence.*

Peters, T., and Waterman, R. H. *In Search of Excellence.*

Peters, T. *Thriving on Chaos.*

Sutton, R. I. "Managing Organizational Death." *Human Resource Management* (1983).

Tichy, N. M., and Devanna, M. *The Transformational Leader.*

Toffler, A. *The Third Wave.*

Walton, R. E. "From Control to Commitment in the Workplace." *Harvard Business Review* (1985).

Yankelovich, D. *New Rules.*

Zuboff, S. *In the Age of the Smart Machine.*

2. For a fuller treatment of the problems organizations face in trying to diffuse these types of new work systems throughout an existing structure, the reader is directed to an outstanding article by Richard E. Walton, "The Diffusion of New Work Structures: Explaining Why Success Didn't Take," *Organization Dynamics*, 3(3), 3–22 (1975).

Chapter 11

PSYCHOCERAMICS

Insanity in individuals is rare—but in groups, parties, nations, and epochs it is the rule.
—Nietzsche

A man needs a little madness or else he will never dare to cut the rope and be free.
—Zorba the Greek

It's hard to fight an enemy who has outposts in your head.
—Anonymous

Leaders will be confronted by many paradoxes as they attempt to manage the impact of change. Few, however, will be as perplexing as having to distinguish between allies who can successfully champion change and others who are driven by zealotry, who are mentally shackled to their past, or whose persistence and linear thinking outweigh their common sense.

I call this latter group the "psychoceramics" (less charitably known as crackpots. . . .). In their never-ending quest to master their fate and not look stupid in the process, they inevitably fail at both. Still, they serve as excellent examples to show how their unchecked influence manifests itself. The Glacier plant-closing program offers up several of these examples.

I suppose this chapter can be viewed as a form of Shakespearean comic relief, but keep in mind that, although the episodes may strike us as odd and amusing, the truly disturbing side is that each vignette was created by people who actually believed they were acting in a rational manner.

TWISTED LOGIC

THE CHESHIRE NET

As we have seen in the preceding chapters, Glacier found itself facing numerous dilemmas because of its insistence on applying antiquated solutions that were out of phase with its contemporary turbulence. It seems, looking back, as though it should have been obvious that people who had invested decades of their professional lives in support of Glacier, and on whom Glacier would need to depend in the future, deserved better treatment than they received. Instead, a sort of perverted "fairness doctrine" was put into play. Specifically, so as to not be seen as giving unequal treatment to people in closing locations, no employment assurances were given to even the most critically needed people. In short, to use Glacier's own terminology, the overriding concern was for "optics." They wanted it to appear to the news media and others as though everyone was facing the same level of job uncertainty.

Second only to the destruction of employee belief in Glacier's commitment to providing employment, the deliberate withholding of security from those who needed to be retained appears uncommonly shortsighted. This particular "brainstorm" was created, endorsed, and strongly enforced by—of all functions—the human resource group—despite objections from other support and line functions.

Of course, withholding information from its employees had been a part of Glacier's past practices for some time. For example, few people actually knew any financial details about Glacier's productivity, because such information was considered too sensitive to be shared with lower level employees. This persisted even as Glacier was trying to promote employee involvement programs calling for employees to consider themselves "business partners" with management. In reality, Glacier's policies and practices continued to support the management's treatment of adults as children, once they began their day of work.

HELP 'TIL IT HURTS

It has been mentioned that the union avoidance activities were often carried out as though in the heat of battle, and that local management was often swept aside until the war was won. With a similar sense of righteous fervor, Glacier's assistance programs for employees in closing plants were planned and introduced with minimal concern for the operating schedules at these locations—or the readiness of people to take advantage of the help! Plant managers were confused and angry to find such insensitivity taking place in the name of "assistance." On the one hand, the motives couldn't be challenged. On the other, managers knew their plants' output was in great demand and that people needed the continuity in their lives that working provides, at least as much as the "help" being thrust upon them.

THE SHELL GAME

The union avoidance and union relations representatives agreed that locations with unions deserved them because of lousy management practices. Yet they became united behind a contradictory assumption. Transferring people from a union to a non-union location was deemed dangerous because "it might spread." It would have been easier to understand their indignation if the *management* of the union location was to be transplanted into a non-union plant. Somehow the direction of the causal arrow got confused. Looking at the situation from another angle, the difficulty in managing people from non-union locations certainly became an issue in union plants. Among their transgressions were these:

- Scheduling their own overtime, deciding what work needed to be done and how best to allocate the time needed to accomplish it.

- Voluntarily helping out when people nearby appeared to be having difficulty keeping up with the production flow or whenever their own work pace lessened.

- Rather than asking permission to leave their work areas, these people actually made such decisions themselves.

Given the current messages being delivered in the management literature about innovative work systems and the shifting roles of managers and supervisors, one can see that there is a price to be paid for being ahead of your time.

SECRET ANNOUNCEMENT

In a final look at the logic used at Glacier, consider the work that went into its widely acclaimed communication plan to announce the plant closing itself. All the trappings of past practices were in evidence. A "war room" was constructed, complete with special locks on the doors so the participants could deliberate without the intrusion of nonessential people. The participants met in secrecy so they could decide what was best for those who would be losing their jobs, having to manage under closing conditions, or both. The primary concerns were to ensure that no leaks occurred, to consider carefully the messages and media needed to contact a wide range of stakeholders, and to prepare for several worst-case scenarios in the event that things didn't go exactly to plan.

The outcome was magnificent. Where announcements of smaller events of this type had generated outrage within the financial, business, labor, and political communities for other businesses, Glacier's message was met with barely a ripple. The job had been done quite well. With all this practice in how to plan things, one might have expected the next step to focus on how to handle the closing itself—particularly areas the group had been so careful to outline, such as dislocation benefits. Instead, the tangle of internal politics, together with the realities of not adequately ensuring that people had the necessary information or skills, caught up with these planners. While they were busy taking a second bow for their communication achievements, the rest of Glacier awaited their second act—delivering what was communicated. This proved to be one of the most difficult things for Glacier to do. Why? Quite possibly because the outcomes that could occur because of poor communication were viewed as potentially more severe than those related to marginal follow-through.

AN UPLIFTING EXPERIENCE

As I walked into the "transition center" at one of Glacier's locations, I was struck by the carnival atmosphere created by the use of streamers, colored paper, and mobile-like objects hanging from the ceiling. I wasn't the only one so impressed. It seemed that the salaried employees were convinced that this was not intended for "professionals" and therefore avoided it. Unfortunately, the situation took a bizarre twist as the actual date of closing approached.

The manager of the center brought in a huge quantity of balloons, strips of paper, and a tank of helium gas. Next, she asked people losing their jobs to write down the kind of work they were seeking, sign their names, and insert this information inside the balloons. (You can see where this is headed—to the parking lot.) There she assembled a crowd of job seekers, and had them inflate their balloons with helium, and—at her signal—release them into the air.

One can only speculate on the kind of thought process used under these circumstances. I can report the reaction of the general manager who was responsible for this and other plants when he heard the news. The color left his face and he was unable to finish his lunch. He wondered aloud if the prevailing air currents might possibly carry such a balloon as far as the backyard of the vice-president above him.

THE CURE IS WORSE THAN . . .

For anyone who has spent time in a production setting, it becomes clear that people there are hard to fool. Most have experienced more than their share of life's surprises and have developed substantial resilience as a result. Imagine their astonishment when, after being told they would be losing their jobs, the following events took place:

- Groups of these grizzled veterans were herded into sessions run by counselors spouting psychobabble about the terribleness of this blow and how they needed to "get in touch with their grief" so they could get on with their lives. A common reaction among participants was, "Hell, I felt better *before* the meeting. All I want to know is what my benefits are gonna be."

- A sleek Cadillac convertible pulled up to the plant. The driver, dressed in designer clothes, pulled out her plant-closing slides and materials. Inside the meeting room, she gazed out at a group of production employees facing unemployment and the prospect of a sharply reduced standard of living for their families, and intoned, "Now, I know just how you must feel."

While reflecting on these incidents, I was reminded of a comment made by an executive who had responsibility for hiring external consultants. He had grown disillusioned by those who came to him with their own singular solution for all problems. He likened their approach to that of the little boy with a new toy hammer who finds the whole world has suddenly turned into a nail.

ORGANIZATIONAL ARTERIOSCLEROSIS

THE TIP OF THE ICE CUBE

Glacier long had a policy that restricted its clerical employees from bidding on jobs at neighboring plants or locations. The primary reason was concern that such "bumping" could cause unrest and be exploited by union organizers. When the plant closing began in earnest, a clerical employee's request for a transfer from a closing plant was denied. I took the liberty of looking into this issue because the reaction seemed a bit callous. I was shown Glacier's policy and informed of the rationale behind it. I asked, "How many requests of this type had been made prior to the policy being put into place?" The answer: Two. This has led me to conclude that one of the best sources for modern-day organizational archaeologists is the so-called personnel policy manual to gain insight into both the mind set of the organization and efforts to paper over past foul-ups.

A MOVING EXPERIENCE

The on-again/off-again decisions pertaining to production line employee transfers proved to be an example of political power games played between Glacier and the corporate structure above it. This was one of those issues that never got decided until its negative impact had already occurred. It seems incredible that so little consideration was given to such a fundamental area as the physical transfer of key talent to receiving locations. Several employees agreed to such transfers, assuming that the cost of moving their families and household goods would be born by Glacier. This payment was agreed to and later denied. A few people tried to move their goods themselves, incurring property damage in the process—only to be told that the decision was yet again reversed. Had they used a professional mover, the employees were told, the damage likely wouldn't have occurred. And, of course, it would have been covered by insurance.

THE RETRAINING CZAR

As part of the assistance package offered to people at closing plants, financial help for retraining was made available. This was an interesting situation. Most of the people affected by the closing could take advantage of testing to help them determine what fields they might want to consider preparing themselves for in the future. However, the amount of retraining funds allocated were well below what was required by most technical schools. Further, the decision as to whether the person's choice of education or training was appropriate was left up to one headquarters person. The irony was that the funds for such courses were obtained from the operating managers' budgets at these locations, but they were not allowed to approve the courses themselves. This is made all the more ludicrous when one considers what an infinitesimally small number of people even *consider* applying for retraining. Apparently Glacier believed that one cannot be too careful about such things. Someone might actually end up learning things that aren't particularly helpful.

(A precedent worth avoiding, to be sure, as graduates of most public school systems can attest.)

THE SOUP LINE

This is one of my favorite stories. On the day of the plant-closing announcement, Glacier's headquarters managers were nervous and concerned about the reaction they would receive once the enormity of their decision became known to those outside of the business. Months of secret planning had finally been made public to a select few, who were about to announce the decision simultaneously across several states and to a very broad spectrum of powerful people.

On the morning of the announcement, a guard at the front gate called the communications department. It seems that a large can of soup was being driven into the headquarters area, and he wondered if anyone knew why. The answer was an incredibly ill-timed public relations gesture. The food company was on a promotional tour that offered employees free lunchtime soup at any major business location willing to allow the giant soup can to be located on their premises. As word of the situation spread, near-panic ensued. Visions of the local TV networks having a field day with the simultaneous announcement of the plant closing *and* the offer of a free soup line was just too much to bear. Needless to say, the offer of free soup was politely—and quickly—declined. The soup can was last seen lumbering away.

THE VICE-PRESIDENT'S HAMMER

Unpredictable things—like the arrival of giant soup cans—unfortunately can and do occur, leaving the best laid plans in the dust. But at least one can live with the knowledge that these events were serendipitous and beyond the reach of rational thought. No vice-president, for example, would ever dream up something so stupid. Well, nearly so, anyway. As it turned out, there was a vice-president with a toy hammer. . . .

The "hammer" came in the form of a giveaway program that focused on cost savings identified by employees. If you could identify costs to be saved and document this to management's satisfaction, you could earn bonus points exchanged for various gifts. Unfortunately, some of these saved "costs" were in the form of salaries paid to one's co-workers. This insidious side of the giveaway program was lost on the vice-president, who had used it successfully at a previous business. Not to be deterred by present circumstances, he had colorful hardbound gift catalogs mailed to each employee's home—about the same time many of them learned that their jobs were being eliminated. One human resource manager quipped, "If we time this whole thing right, we could give each person a pink slip, a cup of soup, and a free toaster."

ORGANIZATIONAL LIPOSUCTION

I suppose it should have been anticipated. An organization that referred to the occasional explosion of one of its consumer products as a "nonpassive failure" should not be expected to do much better at naming a plant-closing program. Still, referring to it as a "leadership" program was a real stretch. Once past this barrier, however, it was easy to make the next leap into explaining what had happened to past promises of job security.

It was simple—they had been replaced with "career security." What's this? Yes, *career* security was the operative phrase—surely one to be placed in the organizational pantheon of non sequiturs and euphemisms, alongside such gems as delayering, deskilling, outplacement, redundant positions, natural wastage, and rightsizing. In this case the message was, on the surface, almost convincing. It seemed that people's jobs, according to Glacier, could not be guaranteed anymore because the marketplace could not be controlled. Therefore, since we are all in this big uncontrollable spiral, the best that one can expect is to hang onto one's personal skills, roll with the punch, and hope to end up in another—albeit temporary—assignment. If this sounds a little "punchy" to you, imagine how it sounds when you are one of the walking wounded?

These examples help bring back memories of meetings when Glacier executives would pound the table and decry the "fat" in their organization, vowing to remove it. They may, however, have merely chosen a form of organizational liposuction. On the one hand, there is a removal of unsightly excess—at least temporarily. On the other, it is possible that this is just a cosmetic procedure, and one that runs the risk of seriously damaging the body while sucking out the brains in the process.

SUMMARY

Leaders seeking allies in the management of change turbulence are confronted with a difficult selection process. While some people will be of vital assistance, others offer more problems than help. There are more horse's asses than there are horses. That may be the back end of the psychoceramic problem, but the front end is created by well-meaning people who simply cannot imagine a context beyond the one they are in. The discovery of water was most certainly not made by a fish.

Several examples of questionable logic applied during Glacier's plant closing program include:

- Withholding job security from people critical to Glacier's future

- Claiming that mismanaged employees cause unions to be organized

- Fearing leaked information more than marginal follow-through

- Subjecting adults to childlike treatment

These and other examples are provided to show that, in the midst of a large program with several positive and well-managed outcomes, often the right hand did not know what the left was doing—or that there even was another hand. Finally, the whole issue comes into focus around what is called "organizational liposuction." Rather than manage its human assets in a better planned and more flexible way, organizations decide on radical approaches to "suck out the fat." As past chapters have shown, there is reason to believe that more than this is being removed. Long-term commitment, organizational memory, and "muscle" are likely to be lost as well.

In the final chapter, we examine how organizations can establish a framework for thinking about and planning for the impact of change. Glacier has provided several useful pieces of information to consider, along with their lessons learned. The next step is to consider how to create a more effective roadmap to guide managers as they attempt to maneuver through changes affecting their organizations.

Note

Note: The material for this chapter was obtained from a fairly large number of people, in addition to my own observations. To respect their privacy, I will not attribute some of these "gems" to them, but they certainly will recognize their input. As I attempted to sort through all of the potential stories that could have been related, I had a difficult time trying to strike a balance between the content and the message. On the one hand, the content is fairly entertaining and—at times—distractingly bizarre. On the other hand, there are some powerful lessons to be gained.

As so many of these incidents were occurring, managers were struggling to maintain a productive work environment, and people's lives and their family's future hung in the balance. From a distance, we can take a dispassionate view, even finding some of the events bordering on the hilarious. Up close, the impact was much more sobering.

Chapter 12

BLUEPRINTS AND ROADMAPS

For every action, there is an equal and opposite criticism.
   —Harrison's Postulate

To those critical of our lack of progress, we are pleased to announce a major breakthrough. The executive team has had numerous heated agreements over the beauty of the problem.
   —Vice-Chairman, Proactive Change Management Committee

PARTIAL SUCCESS

It's well known that even a stopped clock is correct twice a day. Unfortunately, organizations attempting to traverse the turbulence of change often hold up equally meager evidence of their "success." Why do over 50 percent of mergers and acquisitions fail? Why can't organizations absorb new technology without major internal disruptions? Why aren't so-called downsizing efforts managed more efficiently, effectively, and with both a humane and a longer term view of the reallocation of human assets? Why does it take otherwise stellar management teams so incredibly long to recognize they are in trouble and even longer to mobilize their resources to do something about it? In short, what is keeping leaders and managers from doing a better job of managing the impact of change?

Throughout this book we have examined the efforts of Glacier, Inc., to address their plant closing and resource reallocation challenges. Clearly, they were successful in some areas and less successful in others. Why couldn't they do better? What is it about organizations like Glacier that results in only partial success?

Some believe the situation is nearly hopeless because most organizations are in the final stages of death.[1] Others cite management's clinging to outmoded notions, such as chasing cheaper labor costs abroad and not addressing fundamental issues such as antiquated work rules, excessive job classifications, and other internal distractions that keep managers preoccupied. This leads them to ignore even more key issues, such as process technology requirements and knowing one's market and customers.[2] Still others think some cultures, such as that of the United States, simply cannot bring themselves to behave in less destructive ways because to do so would require too great a shift in their underlying philosophies.[3] Put simply, the Lone Ranger mythology of the U.S. entrepreneurial mind set keeps organizations from exploiting the benefits from cross-organizational cooperation—even when their competitors are eating their lunch.

Of course, all of these shortfalls—and many others—are certainly evident. However, there appears to be an even more fundamental area that dooms organizational efforts either to fail or to fall far short of what could have been accomplished. The leaders and managers start off without two key tools: a blueprint and a roadmap.

ORGANIZATIONAL BLUEPRINTS

THE BASICS

For quite some time researchers and management experts have expounded on the need to address the numerous and interdependent systems within an organization in order to be more effective.[4] Unfortunately, relatively little attention has been paid to this issue, and this has resulted in management actions based on inadequate and fragmented models that lead inexorably down the path to—at best—partial success.[5] Some conclude that this yields management decisions that result in decentralized multidivisional structures, increased emphasis on a detached analysis of business, and overly tight financial controls in the face of risk-averse capital markets.[6] This ultimately leads to a serious decline in competitiveness.

Numerous examples can be found where the lack of attention to an organization's fundamental structure and the interconnections across key areas have resulted in decidedly negative outcomes. Of course, some will read these words and believe that such a problem must be occurring elsewhere because *their* business or *their* markets or *their* economic segments are *different*. The malaise that results from having an inadequate organizational blueprint in mind has affected a wide spectrum of organizations. Here are just a few examples:

- An unsuccessful attempt at factory automation focused primarily on the technological issues, without sufficient regard to the transformations required within the social system.[7]

- A CEO of a health care system decried the lack of a more systematic look at the interventions used to transform the organization into a more competitive and effective organization.[8]

- The partial success at transforming a major public-sector bureaucracy is traced to never having put an all-inclusive plan on paper that adequately captured political subtleties that would later hinder the process.[9]

HISTORIC BLUEPRINTS

The good news is that many organizational models exist. The bad news is that—despite considerable overlap among them—they are often substantially different from each other. As we examine several of them, keep in mind that a good model should not be merely descriptive. It should serve as a guide for both diagnosing and managing organizational change.

Figure 12.1 shows a relatively early model depicting a complex industrial organization having four interacting variables: task, people, technology, and structure.[10] In this example, *task* refers to the actual products or goods and services as well as the smaller tasks leading up to the final production. *People (actors)* focuses primarily on people but allows for actions set in motion by people as well. *Technology* combines both process and tools into a single category. *Structure* means systems of communication, authority, and work flow.

This model deliberately positions the organizational elements in such a way as to highlight their interdependence. Though modest in detail, it clearly draws our attention to the fact that organizations can be viewed as having multiple facets. Further, it sends a clear signal that changes in one area cannot be viewed as occurring in a vacuum. Almost certainly, a ripple effect will occur throughout some or all other parts of this model.

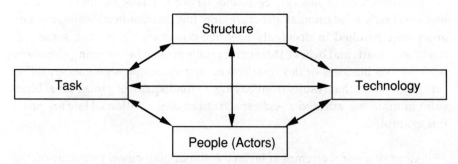

Figure 12.1   Leavitt's Organizational Model

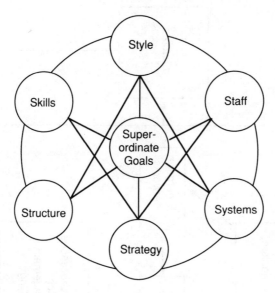

Figure 12.2   The 7-S Model

A model that extends the concept of complexity is shown in Figure 12.2. Its developers have redrawn a hypothetical organization in an imaginative way.[11] First, the list of key attributes has been expanded to include some from our earlier example (staff, structure, systems) as well as several others (strategy, skills, style, superordinate goals). This last category has also been called "shared values."[12] Second, the clustering helps focus on the core of beliefs that influence all remaining areas. Third, the new areas open up interesting issues for review. *Style* suggests that "how" something gets done deserves attention. *Strategy* points to the need for planful activity and begins to highlight areas that may go beyond the organization's direct control. *Skills* describes that assembled package of potential actions that can be channeled to achieve organizational goals. *Superordinate goals* (or shared *values*) is directly related to earlier discussions concerning the "culture" of organizations.[13] The seven items, termed *levers*, point to the need for more careful orchestration of change activity. In short, the balance achieved among these elements is more critical than the pulling of any single lever.

Figure 12.3 shows an organization model that moves in a somewhat different direction.[14] It takes a network perspective to show differing degrees of strength in the interdependent relationships among the key organizational variables. For example, the organizational processes, such as communication

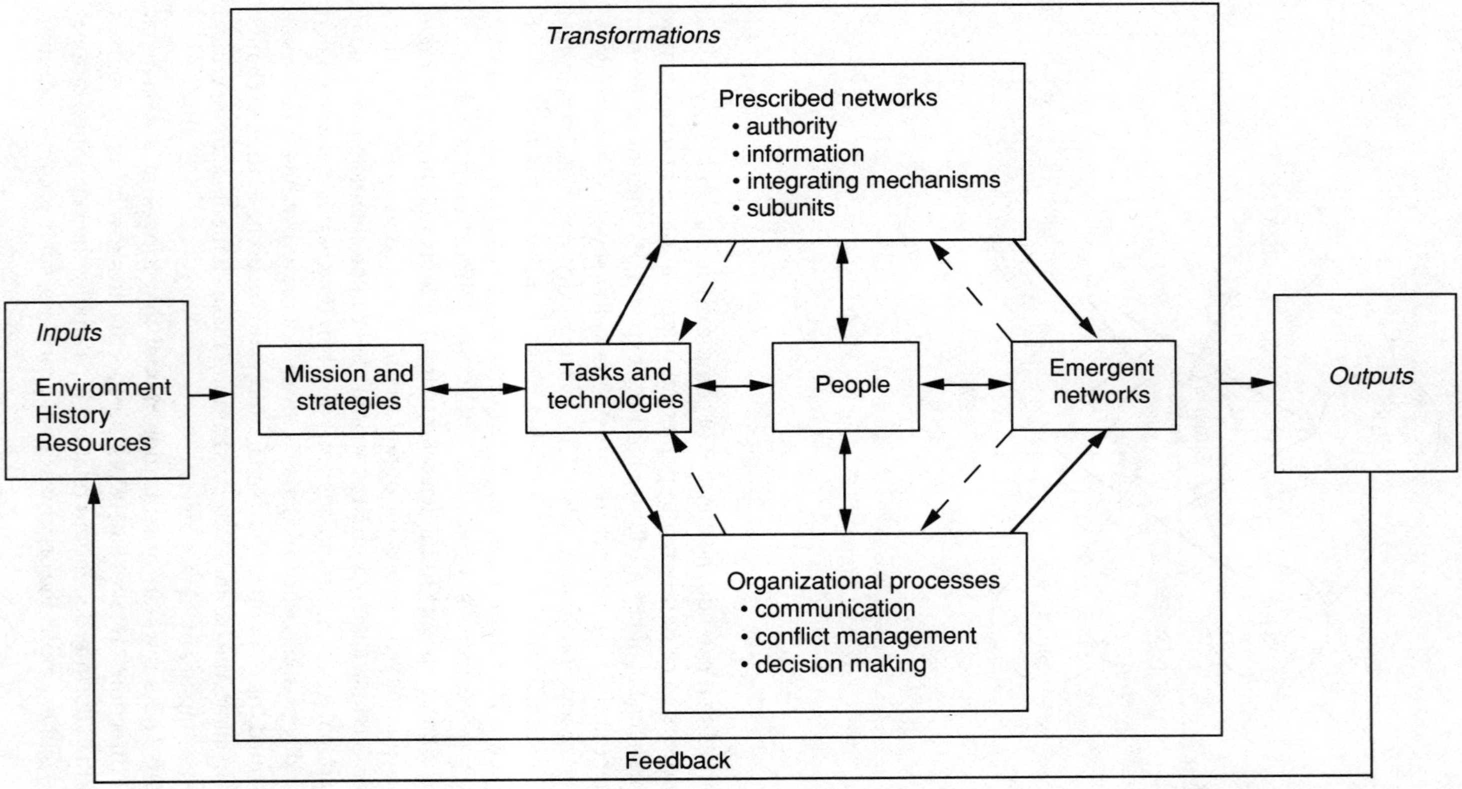

Figure 12.3 Tichy's Organizational Network Model

and conflict management, are shown by a dotted-line arrow as having a weaker impact on tasks and technologies than the reverse situation, shown by a solid-line arrow. As we have seen, some of the earlier organizational areas (e.g., people, outputs, tasks, and technologies) are present. In this model, however, several additional interesting points are represented.

A clearer point is made regarding the existence of a somewhat less-sanctioned infrastructure, labeled here as "Emergent Networks." This has also been called a "shadow organization," and it begins to differentiate between power that can be readily identified and that which can be determined only by observing the interplay among several variables. A second point regarding "Organizational Processes" introduces us to the need for a safety valve in the form of conflict management. Up to now, the models have highlighted interdependence. This model goes a step further by drawing our attention to what many of us experience daily: Finite resources lead to conflict over who gets them. A third point has to do with the box drawn around several variables. Although the preceding models have mentioned the importance of such areas as "strategy," this model explicitly draws a boundary around several areas that appear to be apart from what might be called the "outside world." Therefore, the "Transformations" label pertains to actions that focus on the internal workings of the organization itself. The final point is the model's explicit recognition of the importance of forces outside the organization in the form of its environment, its history, and available resources.

The model shown in Figure 12.4 adds two interesting insights worth examining as we look at organizational characteristics for leaders to consider.[15] This model has less detail than some previous ones but does offer two key points. First, the internal organizational leverage point of "Human Resource Management" is highlighted. This is a very important development because it points to the need for considering how human assets fit into the strategic picture. In an earlier chapter, we looked in some detail at a strategic human assets model showing the interplay of leverage points in this area. The second major point concerns how the external environment is depicted. As can be seen, it is divided into three categories: economic, political, and cultural. This delineation is helpful because it forces us to consider an organization's environment as something less than monolithic. An even more important interpretation is that perhaps the environment is not totally beyond the influence of the organization itself—a key issue few leaders or managers pursue.

Up to this point, the models presented have described organizations in terms of two dimensions. Figure 12.5 takes us into a third dimension. In fact, the developer specifically refers to the "holographic" aspects of this model.[16] The figure shows what are termed "Barriers to Success," a warning to pay

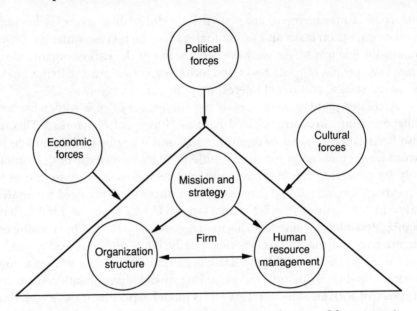

Figure 12.4   A Framework for Strategic Human Resource Management

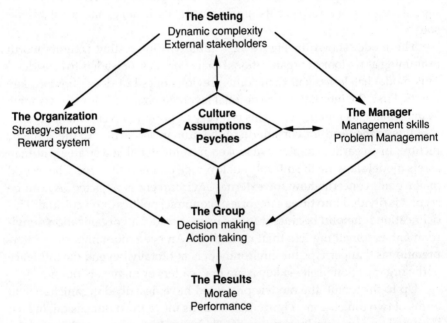

Figure 12.5   Barriers to Success

close attention to how failure to adapt to one's surroundings can lead to unmet goals or worse. This model helps us see several critical linkages among the key organizational categories: organization, setting, manager, and group. Its most intriguing point, however, is the deliberate positioning of a "holographic diamond" beneath these categories.

This diamond contains the organization's culture, assumptions, and psyches. Considered separately, these take on interesting definitions. *Culture* refers to an invisible force that unifies an organization—the equivalent of an individual's personality—a set of shared values, beliefs, and assumptions. *Assumptions* are highlighted as operating at a deeper level than culture because these are basically untested beliefs about how things are. While clearly helpful in providing continuity, they can also become a burdensome weight that keeps organizations from acknowledging changing conditions requiring a reexamination of these assumptions. Finally, *psyches* draws us into relatively unchartered and the deepest waters—human nature as it applies to making assumptions about how the world operates and, more important, about the basic beliefs held regarding people. As I examined this model, it occurred to me that it was the first time I found someone actually taking into account the *possibility* that people are not entirely rational. I realize that for many of us this does not come as a blinding revelation, but I continue to be surprised at how often organizational change is planned without regard to this . . . possibility.

The *setting* refers to the rapid and interdependent changes affecting organizations as well as the need to expand our horizons as we consider those who are affected by the organization's fate—the stakeholders. The *organization* includes such aspects as its strategy, structure, and reward system. Of these, I have found the reward system the most impregnable and, ironically, the most likely to get people's attention. The *manager* category contains both management skills (e.g., technical, conceptual, analytical, administrative, social, interpersonal, and motor), as well as how managers manage the solution of problems. The *group* focuses on the most powerful force in dealing with complex issues: teams of people who operate in a highly interactive and cohesive manner. Their methods of making decisions and their abilities to deal with bureaucratic constraints are key issues here.

The final element of this model, *results*, offers for the first time an explicit recognition that an organization's output is both tangible and intangible. Its more tangible side can be seen in terms of goods and services produced. The less tangible side has to do with creating a work environment that is valued by its members. Although this model clearly does not attempt to surface all interrelationships, it has much to offer in its perspective of an organization as being something other than a simple machine.

In a deceptively simple model, depicted in Figure 12.6, three major organizational variables (behavior, structure, and processes) are shown as being interdependent and surrounded by environmental forces. The authors of this model use it as a core of an excellent textbook examining many of the nuances of organizations.[17] Looking more specifically at this model, its elements contain several important subelements within them. *Behavior* looks at individual differences, motivation theories, the impact of stress, the rewards and punishments process, how power is used, group dynamics, and leadership. *Structure* pertains to the design both of organizations and of jobs within them. *Processes* includes communications, decision making, performance evaluation, and how careers are managed, in addition to a broader look at an organization's socialization process.

Of particular interest here is the model's emphasis on the critical element of behavior within organizations. It introduces the major differences between how individual behavior is managed and how group behavior is managed.

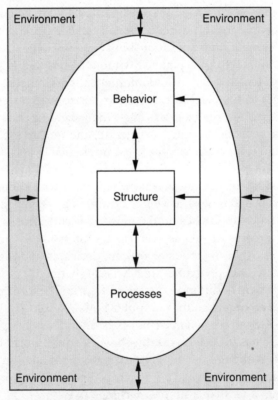

Figure 12.6   The Gibson, Ivancevich, & Donnelly Organizational Model

This is a crucial distinction because today's work environments are placing a greater demand on leaders and managers to focus on the dynamics of groups whose expectations of their employers, managers, and overall organizations is significantly changed from just a few years earlier. This model, and its supporting literature, addresses this issue directly.

An earlier model emphasized the importance of balancing its elements. A further step in this direction was taken in the model shown in Figure 12.7.[18] As can be seen, several familiar elements emerge to make up its key components. However, there are some interesting points of emphasis that add to our understanding of both the complexities and the dynamics of the area of organizational change. Let us begin by examining the model's components.

On the left side is the *input*, which consists of environment (competitors, regulators, and possibly another larger organizational component), resources (capital, raw materials, technologies, people, intangibles such as "good will," etc.), and history (past practices, policies, decision-making processes). On the right side is *output*, described in terms of nonbehavioral and behavioral outcomes. Nonbehavioral outcomes include an examination of how well the organization is doing in meeting its goals, the effective use of resources, and its ability to sustain itself in a changing environment. Behavioral outcomes focus on how well groups or units perform, the degree to which communication is carried out effectively, how differences are resolved, and the like.

The key internal organizational components are relatively straightforward, and we have seen them before. However, of the four components (people, work, formal structure, and informal structure), the one describing the informal structure deserves further discussion. The developers of this model have highlighted an area of growing importance to those who desire to effect change within an organization. An informal structure includes such issues as power gained by access to knowledge versus positional power. It looks at informal channels of communication (the "grapevine") and uncovers existing parallel structures, shadow organizations, and other informal processes that have been developed to subvert formal structures, policies, and practices. Incidentally, their existence should not be taken as prima facie evidence of malicious intent. Rather, this may simply be a rational approach to an irrational environment.

Two important points should be taken from this model. First, it shows us an explicit set of linkages. The first one demonstrates a relationship between the organization's output and its input. In short, the organization is shown as having the capability of influencing its environment, its resources, and—obviously—its upcoming history. The second link is between output and strategy. This is something that has not been stated as directly before. The second important point is the authors' description of the need for the

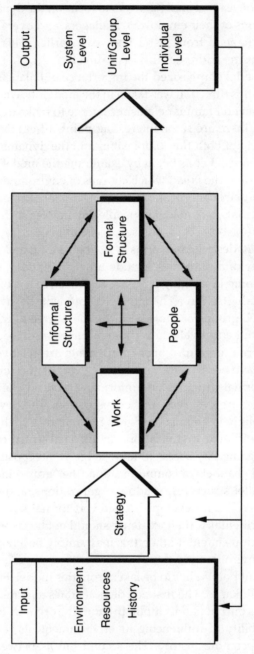

Figure 12.7 The Congruency Organization Model

components within the organization to both fit together and be congruent with the overall strategy of the organization itself. In short, poorly synchronized internal elements, or even well-synchronized internal elements that operate in opposition to an organization's strategy, result in less efficiency. However, achieving efficiency also sets up powerful barriers to change—a paradox to be managed very carefully.

All of the preceding models have helped identify key organizational elements and stress the importance of the connections between them. The next model, in my view, is the most interesting. Figure 12.8 shows an approach that goes beyond description and also beyond a call for congruence.[19] Although drawing from general systems theory insofar as input, throughput, and output are concerned,[20] it takes a bold step into the area of diagnosis and planning for change. It is the most complex model shown thus far, but it is also the most ambitious effort to examine important distinctions. Let's examine a few.

The authors deliberately positioned the model so as to highlight the relative weight of influence various elements have on each other. The clear implication is that organizational change is driven more by environmental impact than by any other source. (Recall the discussion of Philosopher Kings in Chapter 3.) The relative positioning of the remaining variables also indicates that organizational change is more directly affected by strategy, leadership, and culture than by structure, management practices, and systems (e.g., policies and procedures). Before turning to the distinction drawn between variables that affect transformational versus transactional change, a review of the individual model elements is offered.

- *External environment:*   Includes external political, financial, and marketplace forces.

- *Mission and strategy:*   A collective understanding of the overall purpose and direction of the organization by its people.

- *Leadership:*   Executive behavior and values that serve to energize others to act.

- *Culture:*   Collective beliefs, visible and sometimes hidden rules and practices that have been shaped by the organization's history and past momentum.

- *Structure:*   The placement of people into positions that allows for an optimal alignment of authority and responsibility needed to achieve the organization's strategic objectives.

- *Management practices:*   The management activity that draws upon technical, financial, and human assets to carry out the organization's strategy.

- *Systems:* The procedures, written guidelines, and other mechanisms that constitute predetermined answers to help guide people in decision making. The budgeting process, the reward system, and the human resource flow process are examples.

- *Climate:* The collective current impressions, expectations, and feelings of the members of local work units. These serve to influence relationships in multiple directions throughout the organization.

- *Task requirements and individual skills/abilities:* The skills and knowledge required to be successful in a specific assignment. This can be considered a job–person match.

- *Individual needs and values:* The internal psychological factors that both provide attraction to, and assign value to, specific outcomes. These can be tangible or intangible.

- *Motivation:* The force that propels humans toward desired objectives. This energy comes from such basic motives as achievement, power, affection, discovery, security, and freedom.

- *Individual and organizational performance:* Organizational outcomes such as productivity, profit, service level, and the satisfaction of both internal and external stakeholders.

Returning to the issues of transformation and transaction, it is necessary to examine specific pieces of the model as being primary players in each of these categories. According to the authors, the distinctions are as follows:

Transformational Factors	Transactional Factors
• External environment	• Management practices
• Leadership	• Structure
• Mission and strategy	• Systems (policies and procedures)
• Organization culture	• Work unit climate
• Individual and organizational performance	• Task requirements and individual skills/abilities
	• Motivation
	• Individual needs and values
	• Individual and organizational performance

As indicated earlier, Figure 12.8 shows the relative weight each of these has to the others in each category. The model is intended to demonstrate that a change in an organization's culture is transformational and requires changes among the transformational factors. A change in the organization's climate is basically transactional and focuses on the transactional factors.[21]

All of the models presented have attempted to portray the complexity of organizations in terms of their major factors. This review is useful because it

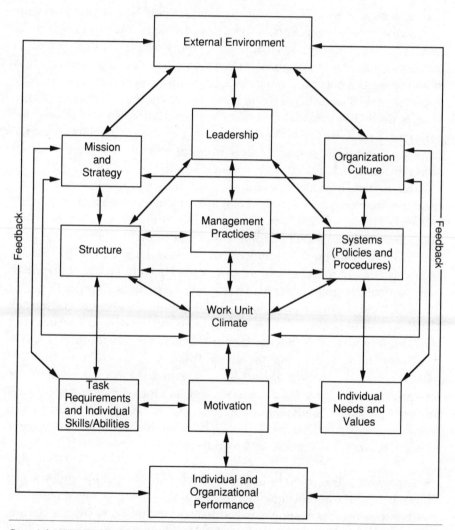

Figure 12.8 The Burke-Litwin Model of Individual and Organizational Performance

helps us discover interrelationships and examine points of debate among experts who have derived these models from their research, experience, and work that has preceded them. In a similar spirit, a final model is presented that draws upon earlier models, extensive field research and experience, and contemporary shifts in societal and organizational directions.

A BLUEPRINT FOR CHANGE

The fundamental issue facing leaders and managers is how best to capture the essence of their organizations when considering how to position them for coming change. This suggests that, whereas the description and alignment of primary segments is important, it is even more important to understand how to anticipate the potential impact of change and assess the organization's readiness to deal with it. In a world that appears chaotic and uncontrollable, what is needed is a model that takes a dramatic step forward—one that portrays the organization in the rich detail that exists in fact, while setting the stage for subsequent paths to follow in order to minimize the turbulence caused by change. Figure 12.9 shows such a model.

This particular model draws upon a rich legacy of research and experience from many people in the field of management and organizational study and application. Its primary architect, however, is my colleague at Andersen Consulting, Robert Laud. In addition to orchestrating the inclusion of good ideas from relevant literature throughout numerous iterations of this model, he has also drawn from his own past work to help craft this final blueprint.[22] I am particularly grateful for his efforts and suggestions in preparing both the model and the descriptive material that follows. I have only taken small liberties so as to retain the overall direction of his work, and I assume full responsibility for any misinterpretations that may thereby result.

To set the stage for this discussion, it is important to know that this particular model has three distinct levels within it. At its broadest level are four primary organizational dimensions. Beneath each dimension are several influence systems. Finally, all of the foregoing draws upon the third level, numerous change techniques. To begin, let us define the major dimensions: leadership, structure, process, and workforce.

- *Leadership.* The primary ingredients here are the people and systems propelling the organization into the future. It should be noted that these four dimensions are shown embedded within the organization's culture. It would be difficult to create a singular definition of culture without reference to them.

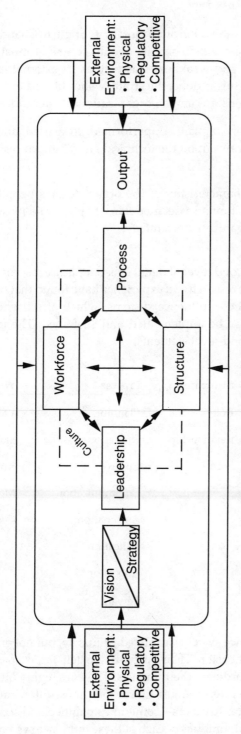

Figure 12.9 Change Management Organization Model

- *Structure.*   This combination owes most of its origin to Chandler's original work.[23] As the organization sets its overall course, it must examine its internal strengths and weaknesses as well as its external opportunities and threats. Once this is done, the strategy should lead to the formation of roles and relationships among organizational units and individuals.

- *Process.*   How work is planned, performed, measured, and controlled. This dimension draws upon the technical and financial resources of the organization.

- *Workforce.*   The characteristics of the organization's people. Recall the use of the strategic human asset model in Chapter 6 and its demonstrated linkages to the organization's strategy.

As indicated, a second level of detail called *influence systems* lies beneath these dimensions. Past research and experience have found that organizations comprise several of these influence systems, which affect whether and to what extent change can be implemented and sustained. The following list shows 22 of these second-level elements:

Leadership	Structure	Process	Workforce
Vision	Role	Planning	Values
Image	Relationship	Operations	Skills
Power	Form	Control	Knowledge
Innovation		Communication	Motivation
Style		Automation	Commitment
Risking		Education	
		Allocation	
		Rewards	

Each of the influence systems is related primarily, but not exclusively, to one organizational dimension. Their purpose is to help target specific changes and systematically coordinate their impacts. They are highly interactive and interdependent. Therefore, changes to any one most often cause, or have been caused by, changes to others—sometimes planned and sometimes not.

This model offers definitions of each of these influence systems, describes them in terms of their unique characteristics, shows their relationships to other organizational dimensions, and offers advice about special conditions pertaining to their role in organization change. Although the breadth of this material is clearly beyond the scope of our present discussion, a definition of each of the influence systems is provided:

Leadership Influence Systems

- *Vision.* This is what the organization imagines or wants to achieve in the future. It provides a reason for existence and helps assure stability and continuity of direction. It embodies the goals, values, and characteristics the organization strives to attain. Visions are long term and should transcend temporary changes.

- *Image.* This represents the perceptions that individuals or groups have of the organization. It is considered a long-term phenomenon, stable and resistant to change. A goal of any organization's change effort is to determine and align existing images with the organization's vision of itself in the future—and then reinforce these images throughout the transformation process.

- *Power.* The ability or capacity to influence the behaviors of others. Power can be vested in individuals or in groups, and can be real or perceived. Power is evidenced by an individual's ability to influence the organization's direction.

- *Innovation.* The process of bringing new problem-solving or value-adding ideas into use. It can involve trying new business strategies or developing new products or processes. Innovation is not limited to new technology; organizational innovation is equally important. Many productivity improvements are due to innovations regarding job design or other social issues.

- *Style.* The pattern of behaviors throughout the organization, often reflective of its management or leadership.

- *Risking.* The tendency to take chances when the conditions are uncertain. Since change involves a confrontation with the uncertain or the unknown, the propensity of organizations and individuals to risk is an indicator of their ability to change.[24]

Structure Influence Systems

- *Role.* The "expected-perceived-enacted behavior patterns attributed to a particular job or position." Each person's or group's role is to add, protect, enhance, or expand value to the organization.

- *Relationship.*   Relationships shape the interaction among organizational units and their members. They are the interpersonal component of a job. They can be based on expressed policies, procedures, and roles, and they can also be assumed through custom, personality, or indirect association. They may be formal, as with reporting relationships from subordinates to supervisors, or informal, as with networks of members with common interests and shared goals or values.

- *Form.*   This is the configuration or shape of an organization. Structural form is typically depicted on organization charts. "Forms are the strategies of organizations to (1) increase their ability to preplan, (2) increase their flexibility to adapt to their inability to preplan, or (3) decrease the level of performance required for continued viability. Which strategy is chosen depends on their relative costs to the organization. The function of the framework is to identify these strategies and their costs."[25]

Process Influence Systems

- *Planning.*   Determining what factors are required to achieve goals before an activity takes place. It involves the choice of achievements, as well as decisions among strategic, operational, and production alternatives and preparation for action. Planning takes place at many levels and for many purposes. Ideally, all plans are consistent, are synchronized, and contribute to the attainment of collective goals.

- *Operations.*   The primary prescribed processes conducted by any organization. Operations are those activities directly contributing to service, production, and creation of wealth. Although other processes may be crucial, their value lies only in their contribution to operations. A critical aspect of operations is the thorough understanding of the actual work flow. In addition to helping in the assessment of the impact of technology, this sets the stage for examining issues related to changes in roles, needed skills, and optional organization redesigns such as innovative work systems (e.g., self-directed work teams.)

- *Control.*   This assumes adherence to plans and standards to achieve objectives. Controls exist at all levels (strategic, operational, or production) and apply to all organizational units (corporate, division, department, project, or work team). These are the mechanisms by which deviations from plans and standards are prevented, detected, and corrected. Controls are enforcing and regulating. They may be positive (inspection to detect production irregularities) or negative (contractual terms requiring cost penalties for late delivery by vendors).

- *Communication.* The exchange of data, information, or meaning. Communication can occur between people, between people and information systems or automated processes, and among information systems or automated processes. It can be transmitted through print, verbally, by demonstration or nonverbal signaling, electronically, or visually.

- *Automation.* The use of technology to enhance the work of people. Processes are automated when there is a conversion to the use of automatic machines or devices designed to control various processes. Automation attempts to improve the conduct and outcome of processes by changing the way they work.

- *Education.* The development of abilities into specific, required, or desired skills, knowledge, or attitudes. The object of education is to increase an individual's performance and potential. When skills are taught, performance should increase, and when knowledge is advanced, potential advances as well. Training is often associated with skill development (e.g., how to use a computer system), while education is associated with knowledge advancement (e.g., learning the fundamentals of information system design). Motivation and commitment within a workforce can be directly affected by education.

- *Allocation.* The distribution of resources within an organization. Resources include money, time, information, people, authority, material, equipment, and attention. Ideally, managers will attempt to predict changes in operating conditions, revise the exchange of inputs and outputs, and continually evolve mutual agreement with resource contributors.

- *Rewards.* These may take a variety of forms, including salary, bonus, stock, benefits, perquisites, promotions, transfers, training, security, opportunity, and autonomy. Rewards and the systems that provide them provide positive reinforcement in shaping the work behavior of individuals. When examining reward systems, we seek to identify those which promote or retard the planned organization change and those which affect the sustainability of change.[26]

Workforce Influence Systems

- *Values.* The principles, enduring beliefs, and customs held dear by individuals and groups in an organization. They are what individuals consider to be good, important, and right. They may be moral, ethical, or social in nature, and commonly reflect cultural norms, belief systems, or personal codes of behavior.

- *Skills.*   Abilities that contribute to performance. Skills may be multiplied or leveraged through equipment, computers, or other people, but they reside in individuals. A primary objective of training and experience is to exercise and improve individual skills.

- *Knowledge.*   Familiarity with facts, conditions, or principles. Knowledge pertaining to the conduct of certain processes or work tasks is termed *skill* for our purposes. The term *knowledge* is reserved for processes or work tasks not specifically related to the particular work at hand. Skill is what one must do or know at any given time: knowledge is what one does know, regardless of whether it is put to use.

- *Motivation.*   A state of mind that causes one to behave in certain ways. Motivation is process-oriented. Whatever process an individual goes through (choices, goals, directions), motivation is concerned with how the behavior begins, proceeds, or ends. It also refers to the type of subjective feelings one has during a certain behavior.

- *Commitment.*   The desire to persist. It refers to the degree of connection one feels to a certain position. Commitment is a very strong perception. It affects resistance to change (commitment to the past or present), propensity to change (commitment to the vision or to the new organization) and leadership (commitment to others).[27]

The third level of this model's change framework focuses on "change techniques" that are applied locally or across an organization to effect change in the influence systems and hence in the organization as a whole. Although they are too numerous to list here, an example of several techniques can be found among the elements of the strategic human asset model presented in Chapter 6. Past experience—some cited at the beginning of this chapter—has shown that this is a critical area and that the selection and application of appropriate techniques demands careful diagnosis and planning as well as finding someone capable of handling the "how to's," "what if's," and "Oh no's!"

This model calls our attention to some familiar variables we've seen earlier, such as workforce, leadership, strategy, structure, and output. In addition, it highlights the vision needed to set the stage for managing various types of organization transformation. This is a key addition because it underscores an issue that continues to be debated—whether such activity is needed and, if attempted, can actually show benefits to an organization. Clearly, this model sees the relationship between an organization's vision of its future state and its subsequent transformation as critical. The close relationship between the formation of a future state and the development of a supporting strategy is highlighted in this model. Further, it is deliberately set within a boundary surrounding the organization as a whole. Thus, beginning with a vision and ending with actual output, the model has established a clear area of demarcation between the organization and external variables.

The remaining variables pertain to external forces. While the formation of a vision and strategy are shown as being directly influenced by the organization's environmental forces, these same forces are shown acting on several other areas as well. Finally, the model is based on the assumption that the organization is not powerless over the entire spectrum of its external environmental forces. This is a key assumption that has been too long overlooked.

As we now consider the insights gained from these models, it becomes clear that managing the impact of change demands that leaders and managers begin with a rigorous examination of their organizations in terms of their major dimensions, underlying systems, and techniques that could be used to effect change. As stated earlier, this is an area that has received insufficient attention by those responsible for positioning for the impact of change. However, knowing the terrain and plotting a path are very different challenges. Having set the stage with an adequate blueprint, we now turn our attention to the problem of drawing up an effective roadmap.

ORGANIZATIONAL ROADMAPS

THE ORIGINAL PATH

The path taken to navigate through change is one of discovery. It can trace its origin back to the earliest forms of experimentation, including work done by scientists trying to unlock nature's secrets through carefully controlled investigations. To guide them and to provide useful points for future reference, a methodology was developed and used broadly so as to allow for replication. This approach, called the scientific method, is shown in Figure 12.10.[28] As can be seen, the activity flows from awareness to educated guesses to calculated steps to understanding to continued study. This basic approach has served science well over the centuries and forms the basic backdrop for many students of organizational change as well. For, as will be seen in the following review of methodologies, the fundamental steps shown in this figure, though varying somewhat across methods, are returned to in each case.

HISTORIC PATHS

Just as physical scientists recognized the need to follow the steps of the scientific method, social scientists also recognized the wisdom of taking a similar approach. Figure 12.11 shows a relatively early example of an approach taken to bring about organization change.[29] As can be seen, three major steps are involved. The *Unfreezing* step occurs when the problem of needing to change behavior is both perceived and identified by groups. *Movement* occurs when behavioral options are chosen and tested out to determine if the hoped-for outcomes begin to occur. Finally, *Refreezing* is the "locking in" of new behaviors, now becoming the status quo. By continuing to behave in the new way, the organization both verifies the results of its preferred choices for change and supports them with its overall infrastructure of rewards and sanctions.

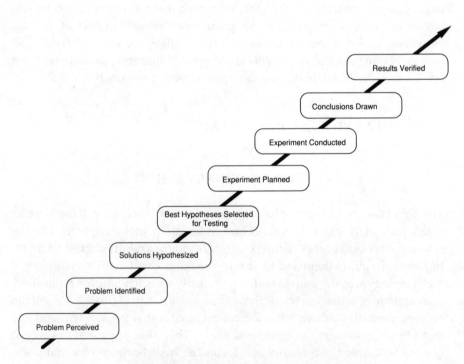

Figure 12.10   The Scientific Method

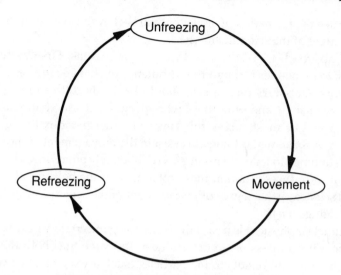

Figure 12.11   Three-Step Change Process

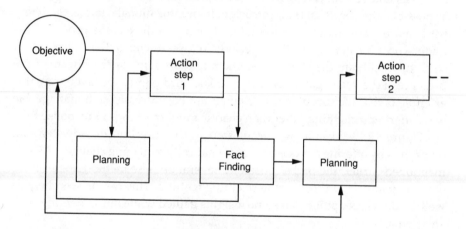

Figure 12.12   Action Research Model

This process is important because it shows the linkage to the scientific method and demonstrates that students of organizational change need to recognize the importance of sequencing the steps of change. It is also important because, as the circular nature of the figure suggests, organizational change is a continuous process, despite its often deceptive appearance of being a discrete event, not to be encountered again—a sort of Halley's comet experience. A direct descendant of this approach is shown in Figure 12.12.[30]

Here we see the formation of steps that parallel even closer both the format and the intent of the scientific method.

This approach is held up for three major reasons. First, as the image suggests, to maneuver through the turbulence of change requires a recognition of how temporary one's plans should be. In short, this process itself is affected by change, and only those who recognize it and continually adjust their path will be most successful. This is another paradox that goes often unnoticed. A fixed methodology to assist in the management of the impact of change is doomed to failure. This method deliberately builds in such flexibility. Second, it introduces a notion more often true in the behavioral versus the physical sciences—the degree of involvement of the scientist in the phenomenon of change itself.

The nuclear physicist learns of the Heisenberg uncertainty principle, which asserts that it is impossible to determine at the same time both the position and the momentum of subatomic particles (such as electrons) because subatomic events are altered or destroyed by the act of observing them. However, scientists take special care to avoid such contamination by controlling, as far as possible, the degree of their intrusion. In organizational change, the scientist is more often than not an actual participant in the change process. This underscores further the need for periodic reassessments of the process itself so as to recalibrate the steps to be taken and account for the effects of the presence of the investigator/participant. The third point to be taken from this example is that the turbulence of change can be addressed in a manageable way, offering something other than chaotic random swings in response to it.

Figure 12.13 takes a significant step in the direction of side-stepping quick fixes by offering a process for systematically managing change.[31] As was mentioned earlier, the paths chosen by several of these methodologies have obvious parallels to those of the scientific method. This can be seen here as well. Its developer points out some insights gained while implementing such an approach:

- In the *Initiating the Program* stage, it has been found that most programs are started during times of trouble, often as a last resort. This requires that the organization confront its own readiness to accept the consequences of its future options, a point we will return to later.

- The *Diagnosing the Problems* stage requires the organization to use what we have been calling a "blueprint" or organizational model that captures both the complexity of its components and the interplay among them. Too often this step is shortchanged, particularly in the area of failing to recognize the interests of parties not represented in the deliberations. Such a diagnosis requires multiple sources of information so as not to

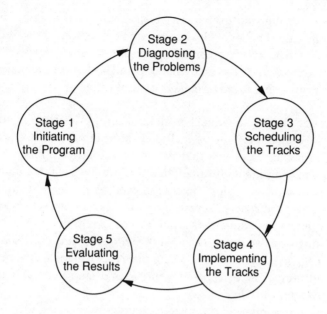

Figure 12.13   The Five Stages of Planned Change

overuse one single tool or approach that, by design, ignores important data.

- The *Scheduling the Tracks* phase refers to the five tracks the author views as necessary to bring about change (culture, management skills, team building, strategy-structure, and reward system). A key finding here is that organizations too often believe that they can introduce change in a "pilot" approach, only to discover that the portion of the organization selected is never accepted as real by other parts of the organization. Unless a significant mainstream segment is represented, it has been found that even dramatic positive changes are often summarily dismissed. Recall the discussion of how Glacier's innovative plant results were explained away.

- *Implementing the Tracks* offers this advice: Consider creating a temporary organizational structure with members having the clout both to oversee the change effort *and* to deal with major resource and power issues that are likely to come up. This structure has been called a steering committee and will be discussed in more detail later.

- The final step, *Evaluating the Results,* has been found to work well when it is recognized that such results must include both short-term and long-term outcomes. In the latter case, organizations often have to admit that the cycle of change more often must be measured in terms of years versus days or months. I believe this is quite often the reason that well-designed approaches with much potential are disabled and discarded. The next wave of management has no ownership and seeks ways to make its own mark, versus being mere caretakers of established approaches.

In the next example, shown in Figure 12.14, an approach is offered to show three "states" of change.[32] I have included this method because it offers an interesting sequence of events that is not often followed. First, it asks the organization to examine its future. Often this involves gaining some collective agreement on the "vision" to be followed as the organization moves forward. But here the goal is to create a reasonably detailed representation of what the organization's members want it to be like in the future. I find this step interesting because it suggests that the *unfreezing* process discussed earlier can be triggered by looking into the future as well as by examining the present condition. This, of course, is the second step in this method, one called *Diagnose Present State*.

By using this sequence, the insights gained by peering into the future serve as anchor points when examining the present situation. This has much to recommend it because a diagnostic approach nearly always runs the risk of operating with an inadequate scope and breadth. By deciding early on what elements in the future are going to be different, this approach helps to focus on key present issues leading to that transition. Of course, the next logical step in this method is to fill in the gap between what is desired and what is currently in place.

The final step, then, is to *Determine What's Needed to Get to Future State*. Again, an effort is made to acknowledge the need to focus valuable resources on key areas that require attention versus a broader and potentially less useful barrage of activities that will chew up valuable time, effort, and money. Recall the steps in the scientific method. This approach can trace its roots to this methodology and yet demonstrates once again that there are planful ways of positioning an organization so as to benefit from, if not minimize, the impact of change.

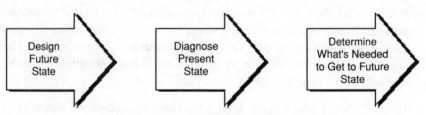

Figure 12.14   Three "States" of Change

A ROADMAP FOR CHANGE

This final approach is clearly the most detailed.[33] Figure 12.15 and Figures 12.16a through 12.16d provide visual representation of the overall framework. Before describing this particular example, it is worth pointing out that its origins can be found throughout several of the examples already presented. Clearly it draws on the scientific method. It also parallels much of what has been learned from organizational researchers and practitioners throughout the years, as shown in previous approaches. It does, however, take an aggressive approach in making explicit several nuances that have proved to be fatal flaws when organizations have proceeded without attending to them. Further, it positions its process in several stages to show the importance of temporal sequence.

Let us begin with definitions of each of the four major phases to this framework:

Diagnostic Review.   This phase involves initial scanning and assessment of the organization. It requires the establishment of a change action group and a project team. It includes reviews of the four major organizational dimensions, leadership, workforce, structure, and process, as well as an assessment of the gaps between present conditions and future needs within each.

Change Strategy Development.   This phase provides planning for the changes to be implemented. It includes the creation of a vision and communication strategy, the design of new organizational features, the selection of areas for change, an assessment of the impact of the proposed changes, and a risk analysis. The end result is a formal change plan approved by the organization's representatives.

Organization Transformation.   This is the implementation phase of the change project, when the existing organization is converted to a new one. It requires change action teams, a transformation approach, and the design and deployment of change techniques. It often involves the design, development, and implementation of new processes and procedures, including modification of manual and automated systems and related user education and training necessary to operate in the new organizational form. This phase includes organizational adjustments in reaction to the information concerning their effectiveness and impact that becomes available as changes are implemented and evaluated. It also contains the alternative of one or more pilot transformation efforts.

Continuous Improvement.   Continuous improvement ensures that changes made are sustained over time. This phase includes periodic reviews and adjustments. It promotes institutionalization of the organizational changes and the continuous adaptability of the organization to future conditions.

As shown in Figure 12.15, the four phases depict and guide the process of significant organizational change efforts and are to be considered parts of a continuing process. Of course, the uniqueness of each situation where this has been applied has required the framework to be tailored or modified to meet specific needs, objectives, and environments of various organizations. Further, some situations require only a partial application of this approach. However, the importance of its detail should not be overlooked. As can readily be seen, scaling back is far less difficult than developing a process from scratch.

Figures 12.16a through 12.16d provide additional detailed views of the contents within each of the four phases. Although beyond the scope of the present discussion, I would like to point out some important points that can be drawn from examining this detail:

- There is a clear emphasis on creating teams of people responsible both for overseeing the effort and for actually participating in it. In fact, a hallmark of this approach is its deliberate involvement of various stakeholders both within and outside the organization. Further, this approach is only a first step in what ultimately becomes a fairly rigorous project management effort throughout the entire framework—a seldom understood and even less frequently applied area of infrastructure that can make or break an organization's ability to sustain its change efforts over time.

- The organizational review segment uses a broad array of instruments to tap into sources of input so as to not overrely on any one tool or approach. Further, it employs a multidisciplinary team so as to avoid becoming too parochial in its day-to-day operating philosophy as it examines the organization's current state.

- Some crucial pieces of this framework can be seen targeting the future state in terms of vision, the organization's readiness for change, and the need to plan a formal communication strategy to support the change efforts. As was mentioned earlier, change readiness is a critical issue here and has received attention elsewhere.[34]

- The framework deliberately builds in both a quality review by the change team itself and reviews by management. These checkpoints have proved to be critical because of the dynamic nature of the type of work being done. This goes back to earlier statements about how the impact of change demands a more flexible approach. In addition, it requires fairly frequent reality checks to assure all players that the rules haven't changed as well.

- The underlying assumption at work here is not obvious in the figures shown. A fundamental going-in position is that it is usually necessary for teams to be taught how to work together on this type of assignment. This is not going to be like other temporary assignments where one can "wing it" and get by. Rather, the political issues and the potential for organizational turbulence are of such magnitude that careful attention is paid to both the selection and the preparation of the teams who will ultimately shoulder the burden of this work.

- Finally, the framework, despite its detail shown here, masks the massive amount of additional material that is drawn upon when actual transformations are in progress. To begin to understand this depth, one should return to the discussion of the blueprint shown at the end of the previous section. In it, each of the influence systems is connected to literally hundreds of actual techniques that must be chosen carefully in response to the needs of any given organizational situation. Taken together, this combination of an effective organizational model and change framework makes for a powerful platform from which the impact of change can be managed.

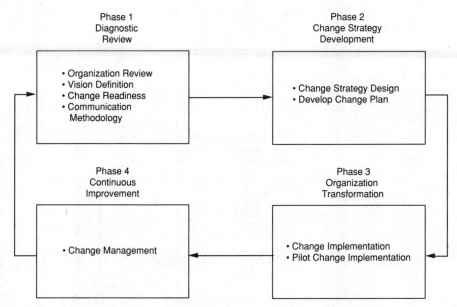

Figure 12.15   Organization Change Framework Overview

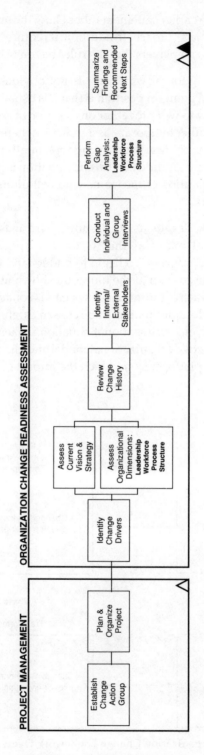

Figure 12.16a. Organization Change Framework
Phase 1: Diagnostic Review

△ - Quality Assurance Review

▲ - Management Approval Review

Figure 12.16b. Organization Change Framework
Phase 2: Change Strategy Development

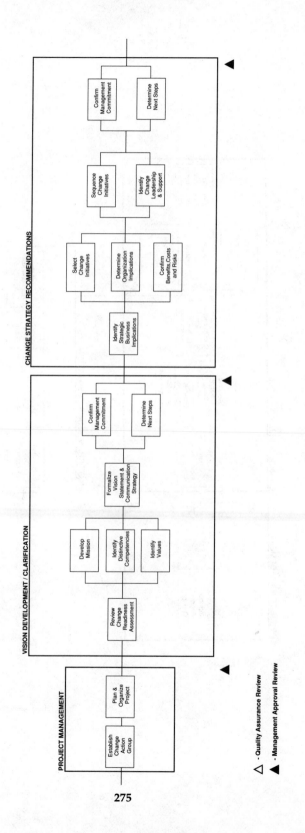

275

Figure 12.16c.   Organization Change Framework
Phase 3: Organization Transformation

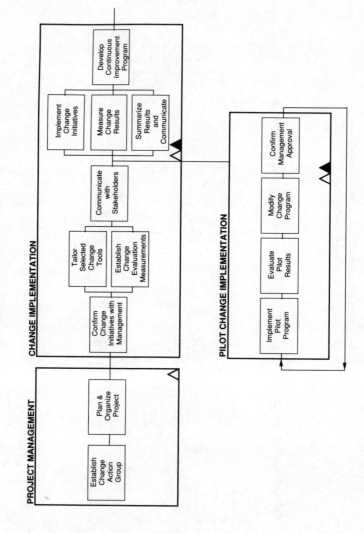

△ - Quality Assurance Review

◤ - Management Approval Review

**Figure 12.16d. Organization Change Framework
Phase 4: Continuous Improvement**

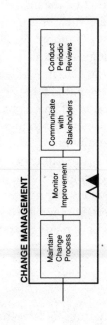

CHANGE MANAGEMENT

| Maintain Change Process | Monitor Improvement | Communicate with Stakeholders | Conduct Periodic Reviews |

△ - Quality Assurance Review

▲ - Management Approval Review

NO MORE GOOD EXCUSES

We come to a point where the cynic taunts us with the age-old line, "So what's new?" It is perhaps too bad that so many people actually are waiting for the magic potion, the silver bullet, or some amazing technological break-through that will make all of this bothersome business go away. Further, the more we examine the successes and failures of organizational change, the more chagrined we become when it dawns on us that a lot of it is pretty obvious stuff that was simply overlooked. Or was it?

We continue to run the risk of assuming that arming people with better tools and rational arguments will somehow make the difference. This chapter certainly loads up any willing Change Riders with an ample supply of ratio-nal ammunition. The good news is that the material presented helps remove some of the confusion and mystery surrounding the management of change impact. Just avoiding an expensive "random walk" is reason enough to look over these models and methodologies. But, as has been pointed out through-out this book, rationality alone won't cut it. A balance between the emotional and rational aspects of change is essential for success.

As we approach the conclusion of this book, it seems to me that the reader should take away at least two major thoughts from this chapter. First, there are a lot of people who actually know something about this area who could help organizations avoid wasting time and taking useless and poten-tially destructive paths. Second, enough material has been alluded to so as to make it possible to learn some lessons vicariously without having to experi-ence the same pains as have others. Somewhere out there among the readers is a potential Philosopher King who is ready to "ride" before being forced to.

SUMMARY

This chapter looks at some heavy-duty tools needed to guide organizations in their quest to manage the impact of change. It begins by examining some examples of organizations that have encountered only partial success and shows some ways that this could have been avoided. Two major categories of tools are provided to improve this past track record.

The first tool is called a blueprint or organizational model, showing the major variables that need to be considered when the need to address change arises. A historic review of past models precedes a presentation of one that helps to capture the richness of detail and the complex interactions possible when organizations look at themselves both as closed systems and as open systems subject to the forces external to them. Special emphasis is placed on discussing the major insights offered by various experts in terms of the models they use to describe organizations.

The second tool is a roadmap or framework for planning out the steps to be taken to manage the impact of change. The absence of a logical sequence of events was highlighted as a major flaw in many organizational changes. Several methodologies, beginning with the earliest use of the scientific model, are presented to show how students of organizational change have adhered to the rigor needed to understand the subtleties involved and pass along their knowledge gained in the process. A final framework is presented that embraces the rigor of project management, the dynamic qualities found essential by past researchers, and the logical sequencing that has proved successful in many change efforts.

The availability of good models and methodologies can no longer be used as an excuse for poor management practices in the face of change. These tools can indeed help address rational problems associated with inexperience or ignorance, but they will never be able to overcome additional emotional barriers to managing the impact of change. An open mind must absorb both the vicarious lessons that have been presented and the prospect of having to reexamine personal values, beliefs, and motivations that are based on motives far from the realm of rationality.

Notes

1.   In his book *Barbarians to Bureaucrats* (New York: Clarkson N. Potter, 1989), Lawrence M. Miller indicates that by the 1980s, most large U.S. corporations had entered into their declining stages. Even efforts to ward off demise through mergers are in doubt, as studies have found that merged companies lose about 40 percent of the market share the premerged companies had. Stanley M. Davis, in *Future Perfect* (Reading, MA: Addison-Wesley, 1987), also expresses serious doubt about the longevity of even today's organizational giants.

2.   This point was made by Peter F. Drucker in a *Wall Street Journal* article titled "Low Wages No Longer Give Competitive Edge," March 16, 1988.

3.   Philip Elmer-DeWitt's *Time* magazine article, "Battle for the Future" (January 16, 1989), discusses the difficulties many U.S. organizations have in trying to overcome their historic competitiveness in the face of new global competitors.

4.   For readers interested in more detail, I would recommend the following references:

Galbraith, J. *Designing Complex Organizations*. Reading, MA: Addison-Wesley, 1973.
Katz, D., and Kahn, R. L. *The Social Psychology of Organizations*. New York: Wiley, 1966.
Lawler, E. E. "Transformation from Control to Involvement." In Ralph H. Kilmann, Teresa Joyce Covin, and Associates (Eds.), *Corporate Transformation*. San Francisco: Jossey-Bass, 1988.
Nadler, D. A. "The Effective Management of Organizational Change." In J. Lorsch (Ed.), *Handbook of Organizational Behavior*. Englewood Cliffs, NJ: Prentice-Hall, 1987.

5.   Bill Veltrop and Karin Harrington "Proven Technologies for Transformation," in Ralph H. Kilmann, Teresa Joyce Covin, and Associates (Eds.), *Corporate Transformation* (San Francisco: Jossey-Bass, 1988).

6.   For more details, see Charles W. L. Hill, Michael A. Hitt, and Robert E. Hoskisson, "Declining U.S. Competitiveness: Reflections on a Crisis." *Academy of Management Executive* 2(1), 51–58 (February 1988).

7.   David B. Roitman, Jeffrey K. Liker, and Ethel Roskies. "Birthing a Factory of the Future: When is 'All at Once' 'Too Much'?," in Ralph H. Kilmann, Teresa Joyce Covin, and Associates (Eds.), *Corporate Transformation* (San Francisco: Jossey-Bass, 1988).

8.   Michael O. Bice, "The Transformation of Lutheran Health Systems," in Ralph H. Kilmann, Teresa Joyce Covin, and Associates (Eds.), *Corporate Transformation* (San Francisco: Jossey-Bass, 1988).

9.   David O. Renz, "The Transformation of a Public Sector Bureaucracy," in Ralph H. Kilmann, Teresa Joyce Covin, and Associates (Eds.), *Corporate Transformation* (San Francisco: Jossey-Bass, 1988).

10.   Harold J. Leavitt, "Applied Organizational Change in Industry: Structural, Technological and Humanistic Approaches," in James G. March (Ed.), *Handbook of Organizations* (Chap. 27, pp. 1144–1170) (Chicago: Rand McNally, 1965).

11.   Richard T. Pascale and Anthony G. Athos, *The Art of Japanese Management* (New York: Simon and Schuster, 1981).

12.   T. J. Peters and R. H. Waterman, Jr., *In Search of Excellence: Lessons from America's Best-Run Companies* (New York: Harper & Row, 1982).

13.   T. E. Deal and A. A. Kennedy, *Corporate Cultures: The Rites and Rituals of Corporate Life* (Reading, MA: Addison-Wesley, 1982).

14.   Noel M. Tichy, "Networks in Organizations," in Paul C. Nystrom and William H. Starbuck (Eds.), *Handbook of Organizational Design, Vol. 2: Remodeling Organiza-

tions and Their Environments (London: Oxford University Press, 1981), pp. 225–249.

15. Noel M. Tichy and Mary Anne Devanna, *The Transformational Leader* (New York: Wiley, 1986).

16. Ralph H. Kilmann, *Beyond the Quick Fix: Managing Five Tracks to Organizational Success* (San Francisco, Jossey-Bass, 1984); Ralph H. Kilmann, Teresa Joyce Covin, and Associates (Eds.), *Corporate Transformation* (San Francisco: Jossey-Bass, 1988).

17. James L. Gibson, John M. Ivancevich, and James H. Donnelly, Jr., *Organizations: Behavior Structure Processes* (Homewood, IL: BPI Irwin, 1988).

18. Over the years I have read several pieces by David Nadler and his colleagues related to organizational change and have found them very useful. Specific references include:

   Nadler, David A. "Organizational Frame Bending: Types of Change in the Complex Organization." In Ralph H. Kilmann, Teresa Joyce Covin, and Associates (Eds.), *Corporate Transformation*. San Francisco: Jossey-Bass, 1988.
   Nadler, David A., and Tushman, Michael L. "A Diagnostic Model for Organization Behavior." In E. E. Lawler and L. W. Porter (Eds.), *Perspectives on Behavior in Organizations*. New York: McGraw-Hill, 1977.
   Nadler, David A., and Tushman, Michael L. "Organizational Frame Bending: Principles for Managing Reorientation." *Academy of Management Executive*, 3(3), 194–204 (August 1989).

19. W. Warner Burke, *Organization Development: A Normative View* (Reading, MA: Addison-Wesley, 1987).

20. D. Katz and R. L. Kahn, *The Social Psychology of Organizations*, 2nd ed. (New York: Wiley, 1978).

21. As much as I appreciate this particular model, I still have difficulty accepting the distinctions between *climate* and *culture* insofar as the impact of leadership is concerned. Several researchers emphasize how much influence a leader's behavior can have on the day-to-day environment of a business. This might be considered a "climate" change. However, the difference between climate and culture may only be a function of time. If behavior change precedes any meaningful shift in beliefs and values, can it not be said that the leader affects both climate *and* culture? Further, if this is true, does culture exist? According to many writers, culture is very difficult to change, but a well-placed leader armed with knowledge about leverage might be able to bring about dramatic changes within a short period of time. Is this only a shift in "climate"? From personal experience in more than one large organization, I can say that it sure *felt* like more than that. Something tells me that we may be kidding ourselves about the durable and permanent nature of culture, assuming it exists as defined in the literature.

22. Bob's work in this area draws on his past research. For example, see Charles J. Fombrun and Robert L. Laud, "Strategic Issues in Performance Appraisal: Theory and Practice," *Personnel*, November–December 1983, pp. 23–31, and Robert L.

Laud, "Performance Appraisal and Its Link to Strategic Management Development," *Journal of Management Development*, 3(4) 3–11 (1984).

23. See A. Chandler, *Strategy and Structure: Chapters in the History of American Industrial Enterprise* (Cambridge, MA: MIT Press, 1962).

24. References pertinent to vision, image, power, innovation, style, and risking follow:

Conger, J. A., Rabindra, N. Kanungo, and Associates. *Charismatic Leadership*. San Francisco: Jossey-Bass, 1988.
Davis, Keith. *Human Behavior at Work*. New York: McGraw-Hill, 1977.
Fombrun, Charles, Tichy, Noel M., and Devanna, Mary Anne. *Strategic Human Resource Management*. New York: Wiley, 1984.
Kanter, Rosabeth Moss. *The Change Masters*. New York: Simon and Schuster, 1983.
Szilagyi, Andrew D., Jr., and Wallace, Marc J., Jr. *Organizational Behavior and Practice*. Glenview, IL: Scott, Foresman, 1983.
Williams, Clifton J. *Human Behavior in Organizations*. Cincinnati: South-Western, 1978.

25. References pertinent to role, relationship, and form follow:

Galbraith, J. R. *Organization Design: An Information Processing View*. Reading, MA: Addison-Wesley, 1977.
Kilmann, Ralph H., *Beyond the Quick Fix: Managing Five Tracks to Organizational Success*. San Francisco, Jossey-Bass, 1984.
Szilagyi, Andrew D., Jr., and Wallace, Marc J., Jr. *Organizational Behavior and Practice*. Glenview, IL: Scott, Foresman, 1983.

26. References pertinent to planning, operations, controls, communications, automation, education, allocation, and rewards follow:

Fombrun, Charles J., and Laud, Robert L. "Strategic Issues in Performance Appraisal: Theory and Practice," *Personnel*, November–December 1983, pp. 23–31.
Jewell, L. N. *Contemporary Industrial/Organizational Psychology*. St. Paul: West, 1985.
Newman, William H., and Logan, James P. *Strategy, Policy and Central Management*. Cincinnati: South-Western, 1976.
Pasmore, William A. *Designing Effective Organizations: The Sociotechnical Systems Approach*. New York: Wiley, 1988.
Rosenberg, Jerry M. *Dictionary of Business and Management*. New York: Wiley, 1987.
Szilagyi, Andrew D., Jr., and Wallace, Marc J., Jr. *Organizational Behavior and Practice*. Glenview, IL: Scott, Foresman, 1983.
Tosi, H. L., and Carroll, S. J. *Management: Contingencies, Structure, and Process*. Chicago: St. Clair Press, 1976.

27. References pertinent to values, skills, knowledge, motivation, and commitment follow:

Feuer, D. "The Skill Gap—America's Crisis of Competence," *Training Magazine*, December 1987, pp. 27–35.

Jewell, L. N. *Contemporary Industrial/Organizational Psychology*. St. Paul: West, 1985.
Szilagyi, Andrew D., Jr., and Wallace, Marc J., Jr. *Organizational Behavior and Practice*. Glenview, IL: Scott, Foresman, 1983.
Tosi, H. L., and Carroll, S. J. *Management: Contingencies, Structure, and Process*. Chicago: St. Clair Press, 1976.

28. Barry F. Andersen, *The Psychology Experiment: An Introduction to the Scientific Method*. Belmont, CA: Wadsworth, 1966.

29. K. Lewin, "Group Decision and Social Change," in E. E. Maccoby, T. M. Newcomb, and E. L. Hartley (Eds.), *Readings in Social Psychology* (New York: Holt, Rinehart and Winston, 1958).

30. H. A. Shepard, "An Action Research Model," in *An Action Research Program for Organization Improvement* (Ann Arbor, MI: Foundation for Research on Human Behavior, 1960).

31. Ralph H. Kilmann, *Beyond the Quick Fix: Managing Five Tracks to Organizational Success* (San Francisco: Jossey-Bass, 1984).

32. R. Beckhard and R. T. Harris, *Organizational Transitions: Managing Complex Change*. Reading, MA: Addison-Wesley, 1977; R. Beckhard, "The Executive Management of Transformational Change," in Ralph H. Kilmann, Teresa Joyce Covin, and Associates (Eds.), *Corporate Transformation* (San Francisco: Jossey-Bass, 1988).

33. This framework is drawn from my own consulting work and material developed by several of my colleagues within the Change Management Services practice of Andersen Consulting. It continues to be an evolving framework, which seems appropriate, given the subject it covers. I believe the framework presented here, while admittedly an amalgamation of several strands of thought, offers a reasonably accurate view of the major phases to be considered when managing the impact of change.

34. The notion of assessing an organization's readiness for change is certainly not a new one. In fact, practitioners—a few of whom have probably been "burned" by not doing it—stress the importance of making sure the organization isn't going to devour those with the temerity to suggest that change is needed. A few references in this area follow:

   The last three references can be found among the collection of works found in a book edited by Ralph H. Kilmann, Teresa Joyce Covin, and Associates (Eds.), titled *Corporate Transformation* (San Francisco: Jossey-Bass, 1988).

   Burke, W. Warner, *Organization Development: A Normative View*. Reading, MA: Addison-Wesley, 1987.
   Hess, Peter, Ferris, William P., Chelte, Anthony F., and Fanelli, Russell. "Learning from an Unsuccessful Transformation: A 'Perfect Failure.'"
   Kilmann, Ralph H. "Toward a Complete Program for Corporate Transformation."
   Moore, Maggie, and Gergen, Paul. "Turning the Pain of Change into Creativity and Structure for the New Order."

CONCLUDING THOUGHTS FROM WITHIN THE CHUTE

One should never underestimate the stimulation of eccentricity.
—Neil Simon, *Biloxi Blues*

"This is your captain. We have just merged with Alta Vista Airline and will land at a different airport."

WHAT DOES ALL THIS MEAN?!

It should be fairly obvious that if all this change stuff was easy, no one would be talking about it—it would have already been done. Trying to put the best face on it, we hope that someone else will take care of it so that we don't have to confront the fact that managing the impact of change requires much of our attention. Of course, that's not the case.

If I had all the answers, I'd probably have my name on airplanes, casinos, board games, and high-tech commodes. Nonetheless, I think I am in a pretty good position to say this whole area of study and application is not just a passing fad. Rather, I believe we are witnessing the emergence of a new discipline that leaders and managers and nearly everyone else will have to master to some degree in order to succeed, or even to survive amid the organizational turmoil that will continue well into this decade. The point is that having all the answers isn't the issue. Most of the answers have been around for quite some time. Getting people to recognize the need to ask questions is the first step. I suspect many will wind up thinking that the answers aren't all that new. Most are not, but it doesn't bother me that much. I'm comfortable just knowing that there *are* some answers, regardless of their commonplace appearance and lack of table manners. No, the answers, for the most part, have been waiting patiently for us to rediscover them after we decide to stop bumping around in the dark.

But the material we have seen also sends out a clear signal: People aren't necessarily ready to accept the truth about what lies ahead or what they must do about it. Too often I find that irrationality has enough sense to wear the mask of rationality, although it takes a lot of psychic energy to do this and the pretense doesn't last long. Unfortunately, the attention span of many senior executives is about the same as that of a charging rhinoceros—about 30 seconds. Therefore, wearing the mask of rationality can lead to some pretty bizarre top-level decisions based on short, punchy, and vacuous presentations by people who appear to have their heads on straight—but actually it's just their masks.

Assuming that one understands, in the intellectual sense, what is going on in the face of change impact, it doesn't make it any easier to take when it becomes one's own personal life experience. The old line about the difference between a recession and a depression is appropriate here. A recession is when your neighbor is put out of work. A depression is when it happens to you. Expecting people to act rationally in the face of overpowering emotional events is a bit much. Glacier expected its managers to keep everyone focused on their jobs despite the fact that the managers' own lives were being turned upside down.

Overall, I think we have had a good close look at both positive and not-so-positive examples and some material to consider as we move forward to prepare for the impact of change on our own organizations. We certainly have not heard the last word on the subject, and we should be wary of anyone who claims to have produced the "definitive" work on it. At most, this is another checkpoint that should allow us to recalibrate our thinking, look within ourselves to see if we're being reasonably honest about why we are acting so strangely, and give it our best shot. At a minimum, we should try to avoid hitting the same potholes others have hit.

SOME ADMONITIONS

Briefly, here are some things to watch out for:

- It is imperative that leaders and managers do a better job of respecting the value of ambiguity. Change and ambiguity are very close relatives, and the latter stubbornly withholds vital information from the impatient who value expediency over effectiveness won through this struggle.

- A related issue: Begin at the beginning, not in the middle. Beware of those who say this is impossible because we are already in the middle of something. Everything is simply at another point in an endless cycle, and such arguments play into the hands of the anal-compulsives around us who want to develop matrices to eradicate ambiguity. The methodologies offered clearly point out the need to follow a path that minimizes turbulence. This requires starting at the beginning, no matter where you are.

- Heed the lessons offered in this book. Beware of those who see only the differences between the organizations discussed and their own. The wise person will be able to identify and profit from seeing the similarities that lead to insights. I get weary of listening to people who refuse to accept anything but home-grown homilies. Such an approach not only is parochial, it can lead to ignoring critical information that can make the difference between successful and unsuccessful positioning for change.

- Beware of the siren song sung by those with more words than experience. Recently I witnessed the impact of such an individual on an organization. He convinced upper management he knew a great deal about how to manage within change, but in reality he was only able to make speeches and write articles. When it came to actually offering the benefits of his personal experience and skills, the game was over. He had never done this type of work before. As incredible as it sounds, he actually believed that writing and speaking about change was the same as knowing how to manage its impact. Before he was discovered, he had not only managed to delay the organization's progress, but had hurt management's credibility as well.

NOW WHAT?

I have been interested in the fact that some people deliberately avoid thinking about the nasty side of change impact, preferring instead to focus on only the bright and cheery stuff. But, as Eastern philosophers have so often reminded us, life is a constant struggle between yin and yang, harmony and strife, good and evil, and—of course—the death and rebirth associated with change. A few days ago I received a circular from a leading think tank with the announcement, "The Focus Isn't Downsizing Anymore." Well, maybe it's just me, but look at the headlines that have crossed my desk just within the last couple of months:

- *Kodak Plans to Cut Work Force by About 4,500 and to Sell Units*

- *Campbell Soup Plans to Cut 2,800 Jobs in Restructuring to Boost Efficiency*

- *Digital Offers Severance Plan to 700 Workers*

- *Digital Equipment Will Boost Prices, Reassign Workers*

- *GM Will Shut Lakewood, Ga., Assembly Plant*

- *Bell Atlantic Hopes to Cut 1,200 Jobs, Will Consolidate Several Phone Lines*

- *Cullinet Ex-Aides Say Buyer Has Cut About 900 Jobs*

- *Cray Research Says It Plans to Lay Off 400*

- *Barclays to cut costs by £200m—Bank jobs under threat as Britain's biggest clearer follows Midland's lead*

- *Prime Cuts 20% of Work Force, or 2,500 People*

- *Quotron Plans to Dismiss 16% of Work Force*

- *White-Collar Layoffs Open 1990, and May Close It Too*

- *GM Plans to Cut Its White-Collar Work Force 25%*

- *AT&T Plans to Trim Staff by 8,500 in 1990 . . .*

Further, outplacement consultants are finding that the average salary of their clients is dropping as the cuts into organizations begin to go deeper. Even the heady predictions for Europe in 1992 have been tempered by Sir John Harvey Jones, former chairman of Britain's ICI conglomerate. He cautions that the next decade could see half of western Europe's factories closed.

This is just part of the continuing loss of commitment by organizations to their people and vice versa.[1]

Where this will ultimately lead few are willing to speculate, but there are some likely scenarios. Peter Drucker, in a recent article, states:

> Businesses tomorrow will follow two new rules. One: to move work where the people are, rather than people to where the work is. Two: to farm out activities that do not offer opportunities for advancement into fairly senior management and professional positions (e.g., clerical work, maintenance, the "back office" in the brokerage house, the drafting room in the large architectural firm, the medical lab in the hospital) to an outside contractor. The corporation, in stockmarket jargon, will be unbundled.[2]

This approach has been described as part of a "shamrock organization."[3] The three leaves consist of a professional core, a contractual fringe, and a group of part-time and temporary workers. Such a split has enormous implications for managers who have come to rely on employees with a predominantly single-organization identity. This could be the compromise between jettisoning fully capable people prematurely and retaining costly and unproductive overhead. It is important that organizations focus on both the growth and the decline associated with change. Ignoring this cycle can lead to having one's past become enemy to one's future.[4] The past, as we know, is indeed prologue to the future, and this has been particularly true with regard to how the impact of change has been managed.[5] As we continue our journey, let us remember to keep this balance in mind.

As Change Riders, we have come a long distance together. Now our conversation draws to a close. What is left is to act. I am confident you can approach your challenges with more wisdom, workable alternatives, and the inner strength and courage that only needed the right opportunity to surface. Remember that you cannot learn anything from experiences you are not having, and that ignorance is a powerful anesthetic. The time is now—Let's ride.

Notes

1. For an excellent overview in this area, see Janice Castro, "Where Did the Gung-Ho Go?," *Time* (September 18, 1989). Recently I uncovered a letter written by a union representative to the head of the corporation responsible for shutting down the plant where the representative worked. In response, the representative had this to say:

    > We need a program with people who understand us. We are the people who left schools in the 9th–11th grades in the 1950s with little formal skill in reading, writing, languages, math, or science. We are the people, largely southerners, who came north to work at this plant in 1950–1954 because we could go to no better place way back then. Yet that was a time when even we had some advantages: We were young. We were energetic. We lived in an age where life moved slowly enough to allow almost anyone a chance to learn enough on his own to get by or even get ahead. That was not a rosy time either, but it did offer people like us hope. Our company was our hope back then. We trusted that relationship; we gave our best years only to find that we confront another time, a harsher era with little room for hope or help . . .

2. I have never been disappointed by an article written by Peter Drucker. The quote cited is taken from a recent one, "The Futures That Have Already Happened," published in *The Economist*, October 21, 1989, pp. 27–30. The quote takes aim at what could very well be the issue of the 1990s—namely, who is permanent and who is not. The article also raises a second issue that intrigues me. The absence of the small investor and the furor over program trading has served to highlight the fact that the majority of stock of many major organizations is now held by relatively few large institutions. Drucker says this is tantamount to "going private" in the sense that the self-interests of these large holders lie primarily in building long-term value. This would serve as a dampening effect on the dramatic economic swings driven by short-term trading strategies. This could help form a backdrop for revised management strategies that are not held hostage to quarterly results. I would hope that the emphasis given to the development of long-term financial assets will be placed on the human assets as well.

3. Recently I came across an interesting book by Charles Handy, *The Age of Unreason* (London: Business Books Unlimited, 1989). His description of several "unreasonable" circumstances surrounding businesses today reminded me of much of what Tom Peters has brought to our attention. However, there was one aspect I found intriguing: the "shamrock organization." His description goes beyond Drucker and delves into several of the management challenges associated with such a three-way split. The critical points he makes are that such an approach forces managers to regard organization structure as made up of people—not boxes—and that each of these new subgroups will have different expectations, must be managed differently, and will have their own organizations. If ever there was a bellwether statement about what the new skills of future managers will have to be, it was made in this book.

4. Jack Falvey has written a very insightful piece on how DEC will have to confront its overall management paradigm now that it has to confront its changing position in a shifting technology marketplace. Its title is "A Winning Philosophy Becomes an Albatross," *Wall Street Journal*, September 25, 1989.

5. The theme of renewal and rebirth has received some attention in the management literature. Some examples include Noel Tichy's use of a three-act-play metaphor to show the path leaders take when transforming organizations. The final act is followed by a statement that the past just keeps repeating itself. See Noel M. Tichy and Mary Anne Devanna, *The Transformational Leader* (New York: Wiley, 1986). Ralph Kilmann's most recent book, *Managing Beyond the Quick Fix* (San Francisco: Jossey-Bass,1989), picks up on this same theme when discussing the need for organizations not only to learn how to restructure themselves but also to know it will have to be done several times throughout the cycles of the organization. The change management methodology followed by Andersen Consulting's Change Management Services practice specifically targets the need to address continuous improvement as well.

BIBLIOGRAPHY

Abegglen, James, & Stalk, George. *Kaisha: The Japanese Corporation*. New York: Basic Books, 1985.

Abernathy, W. J., Clark, K. B., & Kantrow, A. M. *Industrial Renaissance*. New York: Basic Books, 1983.

Aiken, M., Ferman, L. A., & Sheppard, H. F. *Economic Failure, Alienation and Extremism*. Ann Arbor: University of Michigan Press, 1968.

Andersen, Barry F. *The Psychology Experiment: An Introduction to the Scientific Method*. Belmont, CA: Wadsworth, 1966.

Argyris, Chris. "Organizational Defensive Routines: An Unintended Human Resources Activity." *Human Resource Management*, 25(4), Winter 1986, pp. 541–556.

Barnette, C. K., Kent, T. E., & Ernst, T. F. "Organizational Decline: The Challenge of Institutional and Individual Renewal at Navistar International Corporation." Paper presented to the Forty-seventh Annual Meeting of the Academy of Management, New Orleans, Louisiana, August 1987.

Barrett, Gerald V., & Kernan, Mary C. "Performance Appraisal and Terminations: A Review of Court Decisions since Brito v. Zia with Implications for Personnel Practice." *Personnel Psychology*, 1987, pp. 489–503.

Beckhard, R. "The Executive Management of Transformational Change." In Ralph H. Kilmann, Teresa Joyce Covin and Associates, *Corporate Transformation*. San Francisco: Jossey-Bass, 1988, pp. 89–101.

Beckhard, R., & Harris, R. T. *Organizational Transitions: Managing Complex Change*. Reading, MA: Addison-Wesley, 1977.

Beer, M., Spector, B., Lawrence, P. R., Quinn Mills, D., & Walton, R. E. *Managing Human Assets.* New York: Free Press, 1984.

Bennis, Warren. *Why Leaders Can't Lead.* San Francisco: Jossey-Bass, 1989.

Bennis, Warren, & Nanus, Burt. *Leaders.* New York: Harper & Row, 1985.

Berenbeim, Ronald E. "Company Programs to Ease the Impact of Shutdowns." *The Conference Board Report No. 878,* New York: The Conference Board, 1986.

Berk, Ronald A. *Performance Assessment: Methods and Applications.* Baltimore, MD: Johns Hopkins University Press, 1986.

Bernstein, Aaron. "Where the Jobs Are Is Where the Skills Aren't." *Business Week,* September 19, 1988.

Bice, Michael O. "The Transformation of Lutheran Health Systems." In Ralph H. Kilmann, Teresa Joyce Covin and Associates, *Corporate Transformation.* San Francisco: Jossey-Bass, 1988, pp. 435–450.

Bion, W. R. *Experiences in Groups and Other Papers.* London: Tavistock, 1961.

Block, Peter. *The Empowered Manager.* San Francisco: Jossey-Bass, 1987.

Blumenthal, Karen. "Manager's Journal." *Wall Street Journal,* February 9, 1987.

Bowen, D. E., & Greiner, L. E. "Moving from Production to Service in Human Resources Management." *Organization Dynamics,* Summer 1986, pp. 34–45.

Bowsher, Jack E. *Educating America.* New York: Wiley, 1989.

Brady, J. V. "Ulcers in 'Executive' Monkeys." *Scientific American,* 199, 1958, pp. 95–100.

Brenner, M. *Mental Illness and the Economy.* Cambridge, MA: Harvard University Press, 1973.

Bureau of National Affairs. *Layoffs, Plant Closings and Concession Bargaining,* Washington, DC: BNA, 1983.

Burke, W. Warner. *Organization Development: A Normative View.* Reading, MA: Addison-Wesley, 1987.

Cameron, K. S., Myung, K. U., & Whetten, D. A. "Organizational Effects of Decline and Turbulence." In Kim S. Cameron, Robert I. Sutton, & David A. Whetten, eds., *Readings in Organizational Decline.* Cambridge, MA: Ballinger, 1988, pp. 207–224.

Castro, Janice. "Where Did the Gung-Ho Go?" *Time,* September 18, 1989.

Catalano, R., & Dooley, D. "Does Economic Change Provoke or Uncover Behavior Disorder? A Preliminary Test." In L. Ferman & J. Gordus, eds., *Mental Health and the Economy.* Kalamazoo, MI: Upjohn Foundation, 1979, pp. 321–346.

Challenger, James E. "When Outplacement Is a Sham." *Personnel Journal,* February 1989.

Chandler, A. *Strategy and Structure: Chapters in the History of American Industrial Enterprise.* Cambridge, MA: MIT Press, 1962.

Cleland, David I. *Matrix Management Systems Handbook*. New York: Van Nostrand Reinhold, 1984.

Cohen, J., & Cohen, P. *Applied Multiple Regression/Correlation Analysis for the Behavioral Sciences*. Hillsdale, NJ: Lawrence Erlbaum Associates, 1983.

Conger, J. A., Rabindra, N. Kanungo, & Associates. *Charismatic Leadership*. San Francisco: Jossey-Bass, 1988.

Congressional Office of Technology Assessment. *Plant Closing: Advance Notice and Rapid Response*. Washington, DC, 1986.

Crosby, Philip B. *Quality Is Free*. New York: McGraw-Hill, 1979.

Davis, Keith. *Human Behavior at Work*. New York: McGraw-Hill, 1977.

Davis, Stanley M. *Future Perfect*. Reading, MA: Addison-Wesley, 1987.

Deal, Terrence E., & Kennedy, Allen A. *Corporate Cultures*. Reading, MA: Addison-Wesley, 1982.

Dick, Walter, & Carey, Lou. *The Systematic Design of Instruction*. Glenview, IL: Scott Foresman, 1985.

Dion, Kenneth. "Intergroup Conflict and Intragroup Cohesiveness." In William G. Austin and Stephen Worchel, eds., *The Social Psychology of Intergroup Relations*. Monterey, CA: Brooks/Cole, 1979, pp. 211–224.

Dooley, D., & Catalano, R. "Economic Change as a Cause of Behavior Disorder." *Psychological Bulletin*, 87, 1980, pp. 450–468.

Dorsey, J. W. "The Mack Case: A Study in Unemployment." In Otto Eckstein, ed., *Studies in the Economics of Income Maintenance*. Washington, DC: Brookings Institution, 1967.

Drucker, Peter. "Goodbye to the Old Personnel Department." *Wall Street Journal*, May 22, 1986.

——— . "The Coming of the New Organization." *Harvard Business Review*, January–February 1988.

——— . "Low Wages No Longer Give Competitive Edge." *Wall Street Journal*, March 16, 1988.

——— . "The Futures That Have Already Happened." *The Economist*, October 21, 1989, pp. 27–30.

Dublin, L., & Bunzel, B. *To Be or Not to Be: A Study of Suicide*. New York: Smith and Haas, 1933.

Dunnette, Marvin. "The Hawthorne Effect: Its Societal Meaning." In Cass and Zimmer, eds., *Man and Work in Society*. New York: Van Nostrand-Reinhold, 1974.

Elmer-DeWitt, Philip. "Battle for the Future." *Time*, January 16, 1989.

Falvey, Jack. "A Winning Philosophy Becomes an Albatross." *Wall Street Journal*, September 25, 1989.

Farran, D. C., & Margolis, L. H. "The Impact of Paternal Job Loss on the Family. The Economic Context: Consequences for Children." Detroit: Society for Research: Child Development, April 1983.

Fear, Richard A. *The Evaluation Interview*. New York: McGraw-Hill, 1984.

Feinstein, Selwyn. "Views of Younger Managers Suggest New Way for U.S. Business to Compete." *Wall Street Journal*, October 10, 1988, page 85.

Ferman, L. *Death of a Newspaper: The Story of the Detroit Times*. Kalamazoo, MI: W. E. Upjohn Institute for Employment Research, 1963.

Ferman, Louis A. & Gardner, John. "Economic Deprivation, Social Mobility and Mental Health." In Louis A. Ferman and Jeanne P. Gordus, eds., *Metal Health and the Economy*. Kalamazoo, MI: W. E. Upjohn Institute for Employment Research, 1979, pp. 193–224.

Feuer, D. "The Skill Gap—America's Crisis of Competence," *Training Magazine*, December 1987, pp. 27–35.

Flaim, Paul O. & Sehgal, Ellen. "Displaced Workers of 1987–88: How Well Have They Fared?" *Monthly Labor Review*, June 1985.

Foltman, F. F. *White and Blue Collars in a Mill Shutdown*. Ithaca: New York State School of Industrial and Labor Relations, 1968.

Fombrun, Charles J. & Laud, Robert L. "Strategic Issues in Performance Appraisal: Theory and Practice." *Personnel* November–December 1983, 23–31.

Fombrun, Charles, Tichy, Noel M., & Devanna, Mary Anne. *Strategic Human Resource Management*. New York: Wiley, 1984.

Franzem, Joseph J. "Easing the Pain." *Personnel Administrator*, February 1987.

Gagne, R. M. & Briggs, L. J. *Principles of Instructional Design*. New York: Holt, Rinehart and Winston, 1979.

Galbraith, J. *Designing Complex Organizations*. Reading, MA: Addison-Wesley, 1973.

———. *Organization Design: An Information Processing View*. Reading, MA: Addison-Wesley, 1977.

Gibson, James L., Ivancevich, John M., & Donnelly, James H., Jr. *Organizations: Behavior Structure Processes*. Homewood, IL: BPI Irwin, 1988.

Gilbreath, Robert D. *Forward Thinking*. New York: McGraw-Hill, 1987.

Goddard, Robert W. "Workforce 2000." *Personnel Journal*, February 1989.

Gordus, J. P., Jarley, P., & Ferman, L. A. *Plant Closings and Economic Dislocation*. Kalamazoo, MI: W. E. Upjohn Institute for Employment Research, 1981.

Gore, S. "The Effect of Social Support in Moderating the Health Consequences of Unemployment." *Journal of Health and Social Behavior, 19,* 1978, pp. 157–165.

Guyon, Janet. "Combative Chief: GE Chairman Welch, Though Much Praised, Starts to Draw Critics." *Wall Street Journal,* 1988, pages 1 & 7.

Hall, Douglas T. *Careers in Organizations.* Pacific Palisades, CA: Goodyear, 1976.

Handy, Charles. *The Age of Unreason.* London: Business Books Unlimited, 1989.

Harris, Stanley G. & Sutton, Robert I. "Functions for Parting Ceremonies in Dying Organizations." *Academy of Management Journal, 29,* 1986, pp. 5–30.

Hass Philbrick, Jane & Hass, Marsha E. *The Academy of Management Executive,* November 1988, pp. 325–330.

Hays, William L. *Statistics for the Social Sciences.* New York: Holt Rinehart and Winston, 1973.

Hess, P., Ferris, W. P., Chelte, A. F. & Fanelli, R. "Learning from an Unsuccessful Transformation: A Perfect Failure." In Ralph H. Kilmann, Teresa Joyce Covin and Associates, *Corporate Transformation.* San Francisco: Jossey-Bass, 1988, pp. 183–204.

Hill, Charles W. L., Hitt, Michael A. & Hoskisson, Robert E. "Declining U.S. Competitiveness: Reflections on a Crisis." *The Academy of Management Executive, 2* (1), February 1988, pp. 51–58.

House, James S. "Effects of Occupational Stress on Physical Health." In *Work and the Quality of Life.* Cambridge MA: MIT Press, 1974, page 161.

House, Karen Elliott. "The '90s & Beyond." Wall Street *Journal,* February 13 and 21, 1989.

Howard, Ann, "Who Reaches for the Golden Handshake?" *The Academy of Management Executive,* May 1988.

Humphreys, Debora Sholl. "Decline as a Natural Resource for Development." Paper presented to the 47th Annual Meeting of the Academy of Management in New Orleans, Louisiana, August 1987.

Jewell, L. N. *Contemporary Industrial/Organizational Psychology.* St. Paul: West, 1985.

Kanter, Rosabeth Moss. *The Change Masters.* New York: Simon and Schuster, 1983.

Kasl, S. V., Gore, S., & Cobb, S. "The Experience of Losing a Job: Reported Changes in Health, Symptoms and Illness Behavior." *Psychosomatic Medicine, 37,* 1975, pp. 106–122.

Katz, D. & Kahn, R. L. *The Social Psychology of Organizations,* 2nd ed. New York: Wiley, 1978.

Kaufman, H. G. *Professionals in Search of Work: Coping with the Stress of Job Loss and Unemployment.* New York: Wiley, 1982.

Kaye, Beverly L. *Up is Not the Only Way*. Englewood Cliffs, NJ: Prentice Hall, 1982.

Kaye, David. *Gamechange*. Oxford: Heinemann Professional Publishing, 1989.

Kerr, Steven, Hill, Kenneth D., & Broedling, Laurie. "The First-Line Supervisor: Phasing Out or Here to Stay?" *Academy of Management Review*, 11 (1), 1986, pp. 103–117.

Kiam, Victor K. "Fortress Europe 1992? Don't Hold Your Breath." *Wall Street Journal*, September 11, 1989.

Kilmann, Ralph H. *Beyond the Quick Fix: Managing Five Tracks to Organizational Success*. San Francisco: Jossey-Bass, 1984.

———. "Toward a Complete Program for Corporate Transformation." In Ralph H. Kilmann, Teresa Joyce Covin & Associates, *Corporate Transformation*. San Francisco: Jossey-Bass, 1988, pp. 302–329.

Kilmann, Ralph H., Covin, Teresa Joyce, & Associates. *Corporate Transformation*. San Francisco: Jossey-Bass, 1988.

Klein, Janice A. "Why Supervisors Resist Employee Involvement." *Harvard Business Review*, September–October 1984, pp. 87–95.

Kuhn, Thomas. *The Structure of Scientific Revolutions*. Chicago: University of Chicago Press, 1962.

Kupfer, Andrew. "Managing Now for the 1990s." *Fortune*, September 26, 1988, pp. 44–47.

Laud, Robert L. "Performance Appraisal and Its Link to Strategic Management Development," *Journal of Management Development*, 3 (4), 1984, pp. 3–11.

———. "Performance Appraisal Practices in the Fortune 1300." In C. Fombrun, N. M. Tichy, M. A. Devanna eds., *Strategic Human Resource Management*. New York: Wiley, 1984, 111–126.

Lawler, Edward, E. III. *Pay and Organization Development*. Reading, MA: Addison-Wesley, 1981.

———. *High-Involvement Management*. San Francisco: Jossey-Bass, 1986.

———. "Transformation from Control to Involvement." In Ralph H. Kilmann, Teresa Joyce Covin & Associates, *Corporate Transformation*. San Francisco: Jossey-Bass, 1988, pp. 46–65.

———. *Strategic Pay*. San Francisco: Jossey-Bass, 1990.

Leavitt, Harold J. "Applied Organizational Change in Industry: Structural, Technological and Humanistic Approaches." In James G. March, ed., *Handbook of Organizations*. Chicago: Rand McNally, 1965, Chapter 27, 1144–1170.

Lewin, K. "Group Decision and Social Change." In E. E. Maccoby, T. M. Newcomb, & E. L. Hartley, eds., *Readings in Social Psychology*. New York: Holt, Rinehart and Winston, 1958.

Lopata, R. "Failure Can Be Hazardous to Health." *Iron Age*, August 1981, pp. 59,63, 65.

Mahler, Walter R. & Gaines, Frank, Jr. *Succession Planning in Leading Companies*. Midland, NJ: Mahler, 1983.

Majchrzak, Ann. *The Human Side of Factory Automation*. San Francisco: Jossey-Bass, 1988.

Marshall, J., & Funch, D. "Mental Illness and the Economy: A Critique and Partial Replication." *Journal of Health and Social Behavior, 20*, 1979, 282–289.

Maslow, Abraham. *Motivation and Personality*. New York: Harper and Brothers, 1954.

Miller, Lawrence M. *Barbarians to Bureaucrats*. New York: Clarkson N. Potter, 1989.

Mohrman, Susan A. & Mohrman, Allan M. "Employee Involvement in Declining Organizations." *Human Resource Management, 22*(4), 1983, pp. 445–466.

Moore, Maggie, & Gergen, Paul. "Turning the Pain of Change into Creativity and Structure for the New Order." In Ralph H. Kilmann, Teresa Joyce Covin & Associates, *Corporate Transformation*. San Francisco: Jossey-Bass, 1988, pp. 368–392.

Nadler, David A. "The Effective Management of Organizational Change." In J. Lorsch, ed.,*Handbook of Organization Behavior*. Englewood Cliffs, NJ: Prentice Hall, 1987.

———. "Organizational Frame Bending: Types of Change in the Complex Organization." In Ralph H. Kilmann, Teresa Joyce Covin and Associates, *Corporate Transformation*. San Francisco: Jossey-Bass, 1988, pp. 66–84.

Nadler, David A. & Tushman, Michael L. "A Diagnostic Model for Organization Behavior." In E. E. Lawler & L. W. Porter eds., *Perspectives on Behavior in Organizations*, New York: McGraw-Hill, 1977.

———. "Organizational Frame Bending: Principles for Managing Reorientation." *Academy of Management Executive, 3* (3), August 1989, pp. 194–204.

Naisbitt, John. *Megatrends*. New York: Warner Books, 1982.

Naisbitt, John, & Aburdene, Patricia. *Reinventing the Corporation*. New York: Warner Books, 1985.

Newman, William H., & Logan, James P. *Strategy, Policy and Central Management*. New York: South-Western, 1976.

Nussbaum, Andrew. "Needed: Human Capital." *Business Week*, September 19, 1988.

Osipow, S. H. *Theories of Career Development*. Englwood Cliffs, New Jersey: Prentice Hall, 1983.

Pascale, Richard. *Managing on the Edge*. New York: Simon and Schuster, 1990.

Pascale, Richard T., & Athos, Anthony G. *The Art of Japanese Management*. New York: Simon and Schuster, 1981.

Pasmore, William A. *Designing Effective Organizations: The Sociotechnical Systems Approach*. New York: Wiley, 1988.

Pearce II, John A. & David, Fred. "Corporate Mission Statements: The Bottom Line." *The Academy of Management Executive*, May 1987, pp. 109–116.

Peters, Tom. *Thriving on Chaos*. New York: Knopf, 1987.

Peters, Tom, & Waterman, Robert H., Jr. *In Search of Excellence: Lessons from America's Best-Run Companies*. New York: Harper & Row, 1982.

Peters, Tom, & Austin, Nancy. *A Passion for Excellence*. New York: Random House, 1985.

Porter, Michael E., & Millar, Victor E. "Five Forces Model." *Harvard Business Review*, July–August, 1985, pp. 149–160.

Reibstein, Larry. "Survivors of Layoffs Receive Help to List Morale and Reinstill Trust." *Wall Street Journal*, December 5, 1985.

Renz, David O. "The Transformation of a Public Sector Bureaucracy." In Ralph H. Kilmann, Teresa Joyce Covin and Associates, *Corporate Transformation*. San Francisco: Jossey-Bass, 1988, pp. 470–496.

Riesman, David, et al. *The Lonely Crowd: A Study of the Changing American Character*. New Haven: Yale University Press, 1969, (21st printing), pp. xvi, xviii.

Roethlisberger, Fritz J. "The Foreman: Master and Victim of Double Talk." *Harvard Business Review*, 23(3), 1945.

Roitman, D.B., Liker, J. K., & Roskies E. "Birthing a Factory of the Future: When Is 'All at Once' Too Much?" In Ralph H. Kilmann, Teresa Joyce Covin, & Associates, *Corporate Transformation*. San Francisco: Jossey-Bass, 1988, pp. 183–204.

Rosenberg, Jerry M. *Dictionary of Business and Management*. New York: Wiley, 1987.

Schuster, Michael H., & Miller, Christopher S. "Employee Involvement: Making Supervisors Believers." *Personnel*, February 1985, pp. 24–28.

Shepard, H. A. "An Action Research Model." In *An Action Research Program for Organization Improvement*. Ann Arbor, MI: Foundation for Research on Human Behavior, 1960.

Sherif, Musafer, & Sherif, Carolyn. *Groups in Harmony and Tension: An Introduction to Studies in Intergroup Relations*. New York: Harper & Row, 1953.

Sherif, M., Harvey O. J., White, B. J., Hood, W.R., & Sherif, C. W. *Intergroup Cooperation and Competition: The Robbers Cave Experiment*. Norman, OK: University Book Exchange, 1961.

Shultz, George P., & Weber, Arnold B. *Strategies for the Displaced Worker*. New York: Harper & Row, 1969.

Simms, Clifford M. "1992: A Brave, New Europe?" *Strategic Services Insights*. Andersen Consulting, December 1988, pp. 1–3.

Slote, A. *Termination: The Closing of Baker Plant*. New York: Bobbs-Merrill, 1969.

Staudohar, Paul D. "New Plant Closing Law Aids Workers in Transitions." *Personnel Journal*, January 1989.

Staw, B. M., Sandelands, L. E. & Dutton J. E. "Threat–Rigidity Effects in Organizational Behavior: A Multilevel Analysis." In Kim S. Cameron, Robert I. Sutton, & David A. Whetten, eds., *Readings in Organizational Decline.* Cambridge, MA: Ballinger, 1988, pp. 95–116.

Stern, J., Root, K., & Mills, S. "The Influence of Social Psychological Traits and Job Search Patterns on the Earnings of Workers Affected by Plant Closure." *Industrial and Labor Relations Review, 28,* 1974., pp. 103–121.

Super, Don. *The Psychology of Careers.* New York: Harper, 1957.

Sutton, Robert I. "Managing Organizational Death." *Human Resource Management,* Winter 1983, pp. 391–412.

Swigart, Richard P. *Managing Plant Closings and Occupational Readjustment: An Employer's Guidebook.* National Center on Occupational Readjustment, Washington, DC: 1984.

Szilagyi, Andrew D., Jr., & Wallace, Marc J., Jr. *Organizational Behavior and Practice.* Glenview, IL: Scott, Foresman, 1983.

Theorell, T., Lind, E., & Floderus, B. "The Relationship of Disturbing Life-Changes and Emotions to the Early Development of Myocardial Infarctions and Other Serious Illnesses." *International Journal of Epideminology, 4,* 1975, pp.281–293.

Tichy, Noel M. "Networks in Organizations " In Paul C. Nystrom & William H. Starbuck, eds., *Handbook of Organizational Design, Volume 2: Remodeling Organizations and Their Environments.* London: Oxford University Press, 1981, pp. 225–249.

Tichy, Noel, & Barnette, Carole. "Profiles in Change: Revitalizing the Automotive Industry." *Human Resource Management, 24,* Winter 1985.

Tichy, Noel, & Devanna, Mary Anne. *The Transformational Leader.* New York: Wiley, 1986.

Toffler, Alvin. *The Third Wave.* New York: Telecom Library, 1980.

——— . *Previews & Premises.* New York: William Morrow, 1983.

Tosi, H. L., & Carroll, S. J. *Management: Contingencies, Structure, and Process.* Chicago: St. Clair Press, 1976.

Veltrop, Bill, & Harrington, Karin. "Proven Technologies for Transformation." In Ralph H. Kilmann, Teresa Joyce Covin & Associates, *Corporate Transformation.* San Francisco: Jossey-Bass, 1988, pp. 330–349.

Walton, Mary. *The Deming Management Method.* New York: Dodd, Mead, 1986.

Walton, Richard E. "The Diffusion of New Work Structures: Explaining Why Success Didn't Take." *Organization Dynamics, 3* (3), 1975, pp. 3–22.

——— . "From Control to Commitment in the Workplace." *Harvard Business Review,* March–April 1985, pp. 77–84.

Wilcock, R. "Employment Effects of Plant Shutdown in a Depressed Area." *Monthly Labor Review, 80,* 1957, pp. 1047–1052.

Williams, Clifton J. *Human Behavior in Organizations*. Cincinnati: South-Western, 1978.

Yankelovich, Daniel. *New Rules*. New York: Random House, 1981.

Yates, B. *The Decline and Fall of the American Automobile Industry*. New York: Empire Books, 1983.

Yoder, D., & Staudohar, P. D. "Management and Public Policy in Plant Closure." *Sloan Management Review*, 26(4), Summer 1985.

Young, E. "A Case Study in Plant Shutdown." In G. Somers, E. Cushman & N. Weinberg, eds., *Adjusting to Technological Change*. New York: Harper & Row, 1963.

Zuboff, Shoshana. *In the Age of the Smart Machine*. New York: Basic Books, 1988.

INDEX

308

Credits and Permissions